Also by Barbara Yates Rothwell:

T0104457

1994: THE BOY FROM THE HULKS
Juvenile Australian historical fiction. Published by Longman Cheshire, Melbourne.

1998: DUTCH POINT
General Australian historical fiction. Published privately in London.

2004: COULTER VALLEY
Family saga. Published by Trafford Publishing in Canada.

2005: KLARA
Fact and fiction; the story of a Jewish refugee in England. Trafford Publishing.

2006: RIPPLE IN THE REEDS
Fiction: wartime traumas in Europe; a new life in Australia. Trafford Publishing.

2007: NO TIME FOR PITY
Short stories: a selection from 40 years of writing. Published by Trafford Publishing.

2009: STANDFAST
2nd collection of short stories. Trafford Publishing.

2011: THE BOY FROM THE HULKS
(2nd edition with sequel). Trafford Publishing.

2012: AN EMPTY BOTTLE
(3rd collection of short stories). Trafford Publishing.

BARBARA YATES ROTHWELL

A FRAGMENT OF LIFE

AN AUTOBIOGRAPHY

Lived by
HEBE MORGAN

Order this book online at www.trafford.com
or email orders@trafford.com

Most Trafford titles are also available at major online book retailers.

Printed in the United States of America.

ISBN: 978-1-4907-3124-7 (hc)
ISBN: 978-1-4907-3122-3 (sc)
ISBN: 978-1-4907-3123-0 (e)

Library of Congress Control Number: 2014905276

Trafford rev. 03/24/2014

 www.trafford.com

North America & international
toll-free: 1 888 232 4444 (USA & Canada)
fax: 812 355 4082

Remembering past years spent with my husband,
Derek Moore Morgan, Mus. D.,
and the past, present and future with my family,
Cynthia, Patrick, Helen, Keith, Alison and Fiona,
grandchildren and great-grandchildren,
of whom I am so proud.

The problems . . .

There are certain problems to be solved before embarking on the writing of one's life story. The chief ones are—just how much of one's life will one reveal, and does it matter anyway?

I thought about this fairly deeply before starting. Did I want all my little secrets out in the open, available for discussion at coffee mornings and in the shopping centres? The quick answer was 'no'. Did this embargo invalidate the things that were to be laid out for public view? I didn't think so.

As this 'fragment' has been snipped and sewn into a pattern I feel comfortable with—and as it is, as any family-based memoir must be, created to enlarge the family's understanding of where they have come from, and so help them to understand where they may be going—I have come to believe that the kind of autobiography that 'tells all' and 'pulls no punches' has been written for the wrong reasons. There is no rule that says 'warts and all'!

There is in any case so much in any creative person's life that is worth recording! Just putting down the facts of what one hopes one has achieved—in my case, for eighty-five years (and counting)—has proved to use up a lot of pages! I hope this 'fragment of *my* life' will feel like a chat by the fireside, or perhaps a lazy day on the beach with a friend.

Whatever your feelings as readers, it has been the greatest fun to do.

FRAGMENT OF LIFE

*Started and finished
at the request of my family*

'*I live in a constant endeavour to fence against the infirmities
of ill-health, and other evils of life, by mirth; being firmly
persuaded that every time a man smiles—but much more so,
when he laughs, that it adds something to this Fragment of Life.*'

*Dedication in Tristram Shandy, by
Laurence Sterne (1713-1768)*

1

It seems to be traditional to ask someone recalling their long life if they can bring to mind their earliest memory. Mine goes back to when I was probably about two years old, sitting in my high chair in the kitchen, wedged behind the table in a corner. That's it, folks! I don't think I was screaming, or refusing my rice pudding, or in any way having a tantrum. I'm just there, and I have no recollection of anyone else. It may be deeply meaningful, but I doubt it.

My next memory is when I was just three. I am standing in front of my father, who is squatting on the floor and dressing me in my Chilprufe vest and knickers. He says I have a baby sister. This is quite surprising. She and Mummy are in the bedroom and I have to be quiet. My sister was called Rosemary, a name we somehow reduced to Rosebud until she became too old for that.

I started school at Chasely School, Ruislip, when I was four-and-a-half—the normal school age in England at that time. The first day—or at least part of it—is burnt into my memory. I was put at a small table in what I now remember as a bay window, and given a book to write in. It had numbers in it, and I had to copy them out. That was fine, no problems. But I was extremely daunted by the other children, whom I found very threatening, though in honesty I cannot recall that anyone ever did anything unpleasant to me. I was a very shy child, a fact that will surprise my many friends today.

In 1934 my brother Philip arrived on the scene. I was sent off to stay with my grandmother Rothwell while this event was happening; my cousin Pat, a few months older than I was, lived with Grandma, and in due course she and I came back to my home in north London. Grandma lived in Lancashire, and I have always had a real affection for that part of the world.

Home, for me, now contained a small baby and—horrors!—a nurse, as well as my parents and Rosemary. I took a strong dislike to the nurse, who seemed to come between me and my mother. At the far end of the garden, as yet uncleared of weeds, was a large patch of sorrel, and I gathered the seeds and made a cup of tea—well, I put some in my toy teapot and poured warm water on it—and offered it to Nurse, who really annoyed me by saying 'no thank you, dear'. I think I had hoped it would make her sick—or at least go away. I wonder if there are many five-year-old murderers about. And could this be a link with the crime stories I started writing half a century later?

Pat and I stood at the foot of my mother's bed. Somewhere, no doubt, the baby snuffled, but I don't remember it. We wondered why Mummy was in bed. Pat, always more outgoing than I in those days, said: 'What's the reason for the cause of the poorliness, Auntie Lily?'—a saying that has gone down in the annals of my family ever since, though Pat doesn't remember it, and was much amused when I told her about it a few years ago.

Pat's early history is worth recording. Her mother, Lottie, was my mother's sister, and she and her husband Norman went to live in Canada with their small sons, Norman and Brian, in the latter half of the 1920s.

Pat was born in Alberta in August 1928, seven months before I arrived in Lancashire. Her home was in a small town, Red Deer, and in the winter after her birth they were snowed in. At this difficult moment Lottie became ill with pneumonia, and they were unable to get her to hospital. She died when Pat was a few months old.

Grandma and Grandpa Rothwell undertook to raise the children, easing a situation that would have been very difficult for Norman, still trying to establish himself. The three little ones were brought home by ship in the care of a nurse. *'Babes of bulldog breed'* was the newspaper headline announcing their safe arrival.

In due course, Norman remarried; he and Marjorie had three more children: and Norman junior, Brian and Pat grew up in the heart of the Rothwell family—a busy household, with two young uncles, Tom and James, also living at home.

By the time Philip arrived I had had my tonsils removed, a horrendous operation more in keeping with 19th century medicine than 20th. I developed pyelitis, a condition that has left me vulnerable for the rest of my life to 'waterworks' problems. Worse than that, it left me with a phobia involving mild suffocation and the fear of soft things over my head, as a result of extremely poor management of the pre-op situation, combined with a fear of being thought naughty which meant that I never told anyone, including my parents, how awful it had been. It is ironic that my father, then and for the rest of his working life, was employed at the Ministry of Health!

By the time I was about six, of course, I began to pile up experiences, and the memories are too many to relate (though perhaps I should confess that Tudor Harper kissed me behind the classroom door. He was an older man, almost seven, and I told my mother when I got home. 'Oh, did he!' she said rather meaningfully—and probably smothering a laugh—and I had my first lesson in What One Should Not Tell One's Mother). But my big crush was on my teacher, Miss Norman. When she left I tore upstairs as soon as I got home, shut myself in the toilet and cried very hard. School was never quite the same again.

Ickenham High School, when I was eight, mercifully only lasted a year. I went to school on the underground train—which was above ground by the time it got to us—from Eastcote to Ickenham in the variable care of the 'big girls', who were all of twelve years old and ignored us kids completely. To use the train I had to have a season ticket, and I suppose it is quite surprising that in that whole year I never lost it. I developed a fear, not of trains, but of the gap between the train and the platform. If one is determined to spend one's life in various forms of fear there are always plenty of opportunities. I think this one arose from the story that a woman had fallen under the train a short while before, and both her legs had been cut off. Whether this was true or not I have no idea, but the 'big girls' made a meaty story out of it, and had us, or me at least, properly scared.

I was also terrified of the headmistress, who had a way of taking misbehaving children into her study and 'slippering' them. I don't know whose slipper she used. I only know that I lived with the knowledge that I was going to do something wrong, however hard I tried not to, and the slipper would be mine! The day we were playing netball and my friend gave me a lolly—which if course was absolutely forbidden (as nearly everything except breathing and eating was)—and *I was caught!* almost brought my life to a shuddering end. Fortunately, nothing and happened—but I knew it would, one day.

I have wondered why I was so timid in those days. With a good home and loving parents I should have had more confidence in myself. I don't recall ever being 'put down' at home. Mum and Dad were encouraging, expecting me to do my best, but not reacting negatively if I failed at something. Although my fearfulness slowly waned over the years I was still very sensitive even in my early teens, and very aware of that terrible thing, being laughed at. I'm thankful that marriage and a family gave me greater confidence. Fear is all right in its place, but not when it inhibits growth.

I remember the old king, George V, dying in 1936. A solemn voice on the wireless said, 'The King's life is drawing peacefully to its close,' which to me, at 7, was very poignant. We all wore black armbands, which would seem quite odd these days—except on the footy field. Then there was a new king, and the deep respect in which the royal family had been held began to erode. The new king, Edward VIII, had been much loved as a young prince, but it soon looked as if the grown-ups were not too happy about what was happening. It's amazing to think, in these days when the Internet has made it impossible to keep anything under wraps, that the British press—unlike the American—made little mention of Edward's 'goings-on'. He was a bit of a womaniser, with a penchant for married women, whose husbands apparently managed to cope with the royal blessings being bestowed on their wives.

Edward was never crowned. Mrs Wallis Simpson, American divorcée, got him first; and though she may well have seen herself as being the first American queen of Great Britain, there was no way she would get past the politicians of that era, who were unitedly against her. Edward abdicated—thank goodness!—and he and Mrs S, now a duchess since he had been given the title of Duke of Windsor, left for France and were never again of any importance in British history.

Schoolkids, of whom I was one, sang about this great turmoil:

Hark the herald angels sing, Mrs Simpson's pinched our king!
If she does not give him back We will give her the sack!

Decades later, in Australia, I discovered that on the other side of the planet the children sang the same ditty!

I say 'thank goodness!' in particular because the Windsors were quite smitten by Hitler and his activities in Germany. Many people, including me, believe that he would have been prepared to accept a role under Germany as a puppet king. That, of course, would have been disastrous. We would have become part of a German empire, and that was unthinkable. Fortunately, his brother who became (rather against his will) George VI, and Elizabeth who in our time was the much admired Queen Mother, were inspirational during the Second World War, and together with Winston Churchill dragged us through the horrors to eventual, if weary, victory.

Meanwhile, on the home front, Philip was proving to have health problems which at the age of 4 gave him pneumonia. He was asthmatic; pneumonia in those days was very frequently a killer, and I imagine that my parents were deeply afraid of what was going to be the outcome. This is in the pre-antibiotic days, and there was very little that could be done, except to wait for 'the crisis', a moment when the body finally decided whether the fever would break or the patient would die. Very often they did the latter. Thankfully, on this occasion the fever broke and Philip slowly began to mend. But he had to learn to walk again.

My memory tells me that Rosemary and I were also very ill that winter, but I don't know what it was—perhaps bronchitis, which I was very liable to suffer until I was in my 20s. At any rate, I suspect Mum had a dreadful winter; and when we were on the way to health again she said in despair to the doctor, 'What am I going to do with these children?' He said something which none of us could possibly have known would change the pattern of our lives for ever. 'Take them to live in the country for six months and run wild.' What a doctor!

At that time we lived in Eastcote, near to Harrow in NW London, in a new estate of houses built after World War I. I dimly recall Dad saying that our house cost £1250. We had moved there in 1931. It was a good house: 4 bedrooms, lounge and dining rooms, bathroom and toilet, good-sized kitchen and scullery. In 2008, when I was with Rosemary, we went to find the house, and the young woman who lived there very kindly let us go inside and have a look at it after Rosemary had told her that she was born there. It was what in England is called semi-detached, and all the houses in quite a long street were exactly the same design; fortunately quite a good one. Next door to us was the dentist.

Life in the country must have been quite an amazing concept for my parents, brought up as they were in the smoke of Lancashire. By the next April we were settled for six months in a rather eccentric bungalow, surrounded by young forest and seemingly endless areas of heather, on the lower slopes of the South Downs at Storrington in Sussex. From the top of my favourite tree (I was a dedicated tree climber) I could see the Downs. We were on an unmade lane, sandy, with homes scattered about out of sight of each other. It was idyllic, and as a family we were never quite the same again.

I was 9, Rosemary 6 and Philip 4. As a cure it was not entirely successful: a few years later Philip once again escaped with his life from another bout of pneumonia, Rosemary had asthma but got over it with treatment, and I usually had annual attacks of severe bronchitis until antibiotics came in and I grew out of it. There were times when I dared not lie down in bed because I would choke, and Mum must have got heartily sick of looking after us. I don't know where the chest problems came from, whether they were 'in the genes' or what. I just know that I lost an awful lot of school time as a result.

But what joy Storrington was! How did Mum and Dad get it past the authorities? We had no schooling from April to October 1938, and we did no lessons at home! I heartily recommend it.

One of the spin-offs from this super holiday—during which, of course, Dad had to go up by train to London from Pulborough every working day, but didn't seem to mind it in the least—was that when it was coming to an end they apparently agreed that they never wanted to live in the suburbs again. We had all been spoilt, I'm afraid. So they began to look for somewhere within a half-hour or so of London by train. And in due course they settled on Dorking, as being conveniently close to necessities—shops, church, cinema, doctors and so on—but with countryside all around.

So we moved to Dorking at the end of 1938. Rosemary and Philip started school at Stanway, just up the road from us, and I went to Charlton House School, which was not as grand as it sounds, at the other end of the town. Many interesting things were to happen to us as a result of this move.

2

M y parents were Lancashire-born. As far back as I know, both sides of the family, Rothwells and Blakes, were Salford or Manchester people. Very few people outside the English Midlands have heard of Salford, which has long been swallowed up by its larger neighbour, Manchester, and is presumably now a part of Greater Manchester. But it was once a separate entity, and Salford people were proud of their heritage, grimy and smoky though it might be. And Salford is in fact a city in its own right, even if it is a bit obscured by the Manchester twin.

Southerners have always seen that area as something to be avoided at all costs. It is the 'industrial north', with cotton mills and pitheads and, always, the smoke and grime. But I used to love to go there as a child. It was so very different from the green and pleasant land which was Dorking. I felt there was something a bit romantic about the fact that under my feet were coal and salt mines, that land occasionally subsided into sink holes, that the sky was seldom anything but a pale grey, and that all the city buildings were apparently created out of black stone. I know better now, of course. The great clean-up that has overtaken all the British cities has revealed clean, pale stone, and the skies are now quite blue.

When I was a teenager I used to go with Pat and her youth club mates down to a particular place in Sedgely Park, where my Grandpa Blake lived, and 'hang out' (yes, we used to) at the milk bar. There was a place there with a parapet over a wide, flat area where there were the great wheels of the pitheads, slowly turning to indicate that there were men underground. This area extended into a kind of mist after a considerable distance, a mist which I failed to realise was smog. Many years later, driving through during a holiday sometime after we had emigrated, I found myself at that same parapet. The wheels had stopped turning, but they were still there—just no mining. And in the distance, where that mist had been, was a distant view of hills, presumably the Pennines. They had been there all the time, but I had never seen them until the clean air act came into force.

Mum and Dad were both born in 1901. Dad had a fine school and university career, much of it, I was told by Mum, paid for by scholarships. He was a student, first, at Grecian Street School before going on to Manchester Grammar School, where he had success not only scholastically but on the soccer field, and was eventually school captain of soccer. In about 1919 he went up to Queen's College, Oxford and read Classics, emerging in 1922 with a BA degree. He was fortunate to be too young to get involved in the Great War—as it was always known until the 1939 conflict began—and too old for WWII. But he was in the OTC at MGS, (Officer Training Corps); so presumably he learnt how to hold a rifle and to march. He also played soccer at Oxford, though he was never a 'blue' (the university team). He and Mum were engaged in 1922 when they were both 21. Grandpa Blake wasn't too happy about this, thinking they were much too young. According to Mum, he thought 25 was the proper age to get engaged—because he was 25 when *he* was engaged! But Dad had fallen for Mum when they were teenagers. He said he saw her, wearing a red tam-o-shanter (a sort of beret), walking down the road when she was about 14. Mum snorted when I told her this and said, 'I never had a red tam-o-shanter!' That just leaves a mystery. Perhaps he saw someone else and thought it was Mum! I didn't like to suggest that to him. I don't believe he ever looked at another woman while Mum was alive.

She, meanwhile, had finished schooling (also at Grecian Street. I wonder if they met then when they were small. Probably not, because girls and boys were carefully segregated). She was 14, and had never enjoyed school much. At the beginning of the year

9

in which she was fourteen (1915) she told her father, Grandpa Rothwell, that she didn't want to go back to school. He said she had to finish the year, and I don't think he was open to argument. By the end of the year, however, she had begun to enjoy it, and said she wanted to stay on. But he said, 'No, you wanted to leave, and that's what you're going to do!'

It seems unnecessarily brutal. But in those days there was still considerable pressure against having girls educated beyond a certain level. And it's worth remembering that Grandpa had had to leave school early, possibly when he was 10, which would have been about 1880 or so, and had done extremely well without a proper education. So Mum went to work, and a dim memory tells me that it was the ribbon department in a large Manchester or Salford store. She was a highly intelligent woman, and I have sometimes wondered what her future would have been if she had been allowed to do, for instance, as Dad did, and had gone on to a good senior school and the university.

A performance skill in those days was reciting—poems, monologues and so on—and Mum studied elocution with a teacher in the city. Eventually this would become part of the leisure activities for her and Dad—Dad played the piano, Mum recited, and Uncle Tom, Uncle Jack Rothwell (Great-uncle John's son) and Auntie Win (Dad's younger sister) sang. As I understand it, they had a sort of concert party which went around performing, probably in local church halls. Tom had an excellent bass voice and a great sense of humour; Win's voice was a rather fluttery soprano; I think Jack sang tenor. Tom and Jack did a very nice line in *The Two Gendarmes*—I remember hearing them at a family party. Both Tom and Win (and possibly Jack) were in the Halle Chorus, Manchester's pride, which performed with the Halle Orchestra, one of Britain's major orchestras.

Mum's great moment was when she achieved the London College of Music diploma in elocution. In fact, she gained two diplomas from the LCM, and would probably have done well teaching. But her moment of glory was also a moment of real disappointment, one which she never quite got over, and would talk about to me many years later. She took her diploma to show her mother, Grandma Rothwell. Pass mark was 70%, and she just got over—about 72%. It doesn't matter with a diploma whether you pass excellently or just scrape by—you have the letters after your name! Unfortunately, Grandma Rothwell looked at the marks and said, 'You only just got it, then.' Poor Mum! I believe she must have been devastated for the hurt to remain so long. She really deserved praise, especially since she was the first person in the Rothwell family to get a diploma or anything like one.

There is an old north-country saying: 'clogs to clogs in three generations'. Grandpa Rothwell wore clogs as a boy, as did his brothers. His father was Tom Rothwell—when Grandpa was a young man he went down to the canal where his father had worked as a bargee or (the family hopes because it sounds better) a barge owner. But I think it was probably the former, because when Grandpa asked around to see if anyone remembered his father they said, 'Old drunken Tom—yes, we remember him!' It gives some reasonable idea why the entire Rothwell family was strictly teetotal. Who knows what they all had to put up with while he was 'in his cups'?

Not only was he a drinker, but he was living with a woman called Miss Prince to whom (let it be whispered) *he was not married.* He already had a wife somewhere in the city area, and he was Miss Prince's lodger. My cousin Ken Rothwell in Devon has done a fair amount of research into the family tree, and he has unearthed the census details for several years that cover the period Great-grandpa was 'lodging' with Miss Prince. Over those years, while she was listed as the owner and head of the household and Tom was her lodger, they had four sons. John was the eldest, then Tom, then George and Herbert. 'Old' Tom died in 1884, and in due course Miss Prince—my great-grandmother—went to live with my grandparents, Tom and Charlotte.

I know this because she was there when my mother was a young woman. Great-grandma had well-developed selective hearing, which meant she couldn't hear what you wanted her to, but could always hear what you didn't want her to. And, according to Mum, she drank whisky out of a tea-cup! It must have been a real trial to my grandparents, who, like all Methodists at that time, were teetotal. She died in 1924, when my mother would have been 23.

To be illegitimate at that time in history would not have been advisable. My mother told me that Grandpa didn't know his parents were not married until he went to the local labour exchange and was called out under the name 'Tom Prince'. All these stories are anecdotal, having gone through several generations before they arrived at me; but there is clearly much truth in them. Poor young Tom must have been fairly devastated to know the reality behind his parents' relationship.

John and Tom were young men with energy and ambition. George and Herbert, it seems, went along in the jet stream. It's said that the two older boys worked for a local grocer or corner shop as delivery boys. Before long they were becoming business men in their own right. Grandpa Tom married Charlotte Shearman in the late 1890s, and they set up house with a brother; I don't know if he was hers or his.

But I cannot leave those early, struggling days without recounting the story of Great-grandpa's funeral. This was another of the stories my mother told me, and it does ring true when one realises that Mary Prince must have been a very strong-willed woman, unconcerned about what people thought.

Uncle John, in 1884, would have been about 13, I believe. When his father died and they were waiting for the cortège to arrive, a coach (probably a horse-drawn cab) drew up across the road. You can visualise, perhaps, a street of terrace houses with plenty of net curtains to twitch. In the coach were the legal Mrs Rothwell and her completely legal daughter. One assumes that they were waiting to take their rightful places as chief mourners.

Great-grandma Prince, my mother said, told 'the boy' (who would presumably be the oldest, therefore John) to go down to the undertakers and tell them not to come just yet. Anyone who tried that today would miss the whole ceremony! So off John went, and Mrs Rothwell sat—and sat—and at last gave up and drove away.

I like to think that the call of nature became too much. And Miss Prince sent 'the boy' off to tell the undertakers, 'You can come now!' Game, set and match, I would say.

John and Tom forged ahead. They developed an impressively large wholesale grocery company, J&T Rothwell, which, by the time we children came along, was established in Salford, Altrincham and Northwich. I don't remember ever going to the latter two warehouses, but it was always exciting to go the Salford one. It was the smell as much as anything that I can remember, a mixture of smoked bacon, cheese, coffee, tea and other delights that hit you as soon as you entered. I was told that in pre-war days they were the largest importers of sugar in the north of England.

As children we were rather proud of Grandpa's Special Sticky Butter! Our name for it, not the one on the packet. At Christmas we were able to order things from the Rothwell catalogue, which was a great excitement. One year, when I was about 7, I was given a presentation box of sweets, and snuggling in the middle was a box camera—a real one! I used that camera for the next 12 years, and it took excellent pictures. It's an interesting comment on today's expectations that Dad told me not to waste the film because it cost 1/3d for a new one.

Dad then had the 1931 Humber, a car large enough for a family of five—and incidentally the car in which I learnt to drive several years later. It had originally been Grandpa Rothwell's. We would draw up outside the warehouse, which was situated in the Salford slums, and immediately a swarm of poorly dressed children would be there, ready to scramble all over the car if they could get away with it. It must have looked a most elegant vehicle to them.

Two stories come back to me about the area around the warehouse. When a local child died (which was a fairly common occurrence) the family would come to the warehouse and ask for a tea chest—to make a coffin to bury the child in. And there is a very anecdotal tale of one of the younger brothers being discovered at the back door of the warehouse, cracking eggs— because they could be sold to the locals very cheap. Grandma

Rothwell, who spent much time nursing her younger son, James, through illnesses, asked her doctor why it was that her son, so carefully nurtured, was always being ill, while the children in the slums around the warehouse seemed able to run about ill-clad and barefoot without harm. The doctor said, 'When those children are ill, they die!'

There is perhaps a third story about the slums, though this was not to happen until many years later. Bombs on Salford during WWII blew these dreadful houses to pieces. One of the few things one could thank Hitler for. Later, when the remains of the slums were razed by demolition companies, rats in hundreds ran out of the ruins. Of course, when we visited the warehouse as children it all seemed perfectly normal that some children should swan around in a large Humber while others lived in squalor. I am thankful that our eyes have been opened, at least to the extent that we find such poverty unacceptable. Maybe one day we shall actually find the balance.

John and Tom, with what must have been a fairly basic education, seem to have been unstoppable. By the 1920s they were respected members of society, comfortably off, with growing families. Sons of the two families went almost automatically into the business, and they lived in good homes. What a tremendous boost to their egos when Uncle John became mayor of Salford in the early '20s! As a child, my mother told me, she had been ticked off for misbehaving by being told she would never go to the Mayor's Ball. Well—as a very attractive and well-dressed young woman, she did! For many years there was a large portrait on our lounge wall of Uncle John in his mayoral robes, looking austere and solemn. But behind that portraiture there must have been a small boy who was saying, 'I said I would—and I did!' Good on him!

When Mum and Dad moved back to the north in the '60s they discussed what to do with the picture. (I wondered why they had it in the first place—surely it should have gone to John's family?) Eventually they decided to give it to Salford City Council, so I hope it is still there somewhere on a wall, along with all the other celebrities. It's interesting to know that Uncle Tom, Grandpa's son, was a Salford City Councillor for some years until his death in 1963.

He was also the Liberal candidate for the High Peak of Derbyshire during several parliamentary elections. It was not a good time to be a Liberal candidate—the Party was something of a spent force. I was told that when he left school the headmaster said to him: 'Well, Rothwell, no doubt one day we shall see you sweeping the streets'. Hardly an encouraging send-off into adult life! But it does seem that Rothwells react well to other people's negativity.

I have two memories of Uncle John. One was when I was quite young, before the war. Pat and I were at the warehouse, and when we had poked and pried and thoroughly enjoyed ourselves we were taken to see Uncle, who was sitting behind his desk and looking fairly severe. 'I have a present for you,' he said. 'Something to keep your treasures in.' He pronounced it 'tres-suers'. I was quite excited. He took from his drawer a toffee tin, one of those with a picture of a kitten or a puppy on it, and handed it to me. When, later, I opened it, it was empty! Apparently I had to find my own treasures.

The other memory is of sitting at the tea table with him and Aunt Dorothy, Pat and Rosemary and Philip, during the later stages of the war in 1944. It was the first time I had had to choose between peanut butter and 'real' butter. If I chose the latter I could have jam. If the former, no jam. Or it may have been the other way round. Big decision!

In 1925 my mother was invited to go on what became a world tour with Uncle John, Aunt Annie (his first wife and mother of his children), and cousin Florence. The occasion was the marriage of Uncle's daughter Anne, who was a doctor and medical missionary in China. Mum and Florence were to be bridesmaids.

In those days when commercial flying was still in its infancy it was a journey by train and ship. They travelled across America, Uncle visiting canning factories on the way, making use of a unique opportunity. They also went to Canada, and in our childhood days we heard about Lake Louise and Banff and other exotic names. Mum wrote a diary, which Rosemary has computerised and which gives details of the trip.

We also heard about the young men who chatted them up. She told me once that if she hadn't been engaged to Dad she might well have fallen for one of these young men. I can remember saying, with a sense of shock, 'But what would have happened to me?' She said, 'Well, you'd have been someone different, wouldn't you?' It created a mystery in my mind which still causes me to think how haphazard this life is that we think is so firmly embedded in our own personal histories.

After North America they went on to China. But China at that time was somewhat unsafe for foreigners, and they were advised to go elsewhere for the ceremony. So the wedding eventually took place in Japan.

Anne was marrying the Rev Max Gratton, also a Methodist missionary. In due course they produced three children: Dorothy, Joyce and John. And, like so many others who had dedicated their lives to the 'foreign field', they had to remove themselves when the war began and the Japanese made their way down through China.

The girls went to a girls' school in England. John eventually became a pilot—and still is, in his seventies. Dorothy studied medicine, like her mother, and became a high-ranking gynaecologist in South Wales, where she still lives. Although I never knew her more than very slightly when we were young, she has now stayed with me several times and I have stayed with her in the lovely Welsh countryside. John I met only recently. He and his wife Sheila live in the delightfully-named Brandy-Hole Lane. So in my old age I am collecting relatives. Our mutual ancestor is Great-grandfather Tom, and we are second cousins.

By the time the world tour was over, Mum and Dad had been engaged for 3 years. It was to be another three before they were married. It was regarded as essential in those days for the man to be able to support his wife before they could wed, and I suspect that Dad, as a young articled solicitor, was not yet in a position to undertake this demanding role. By Christmas 1927 Mum had had enough and issued an ultimatum: either we get married at Easter or it's off! So they went to talk to Dad's parents, and Grandma Blake made a comment which Mum never forgot—or forgave. 'Is there some reason,' Grandma said, 'why you have to get married in such a hurry?' I think that is a classic.

So on March 31st 1928 they were married. They moved into a house in Salford and were there for about 18 months. On March 4th 1929 I was born, in a nursing home in Chorlton-cum-Hardy, another of those names much loved by the English, and caused quite a stir. I was the first grandchild on both sides of the family, and Dad had been very secretive about a name for this first-born. If he hadn't studied Classics, of course, I would probably have been called Mary or Daphne or something that people could cope with. But he had met the name Hebe in his studies, and decided that if his first child was a girl, she would be named after this Greek goddess of eternal youth, cupbearer to the gods! Mum went along with this—but when Dad rang his mother to say his daughter had been born, Grandma said, 'So what's this name you wouldn't tell us?' and he said, 'Hebe.'

Like many people in the years to come she said, 'What on earth is that?' and he explained about the Greek goddess. 'Why do you want to call her after a Greek goddess?' He was quick! He said, 'Why did you call your daughter Irene?'—another pagan name, but more respectable because her name had been in use for a long time. And there are many such names that have been used for Christian children—notably Diana, which would surprise no one.

So I don't know how the rest of the family took this oddity. I do know that the Methodist minister, who was asked to christen me, at first refused to do so. 'I cannot baptise a child with a pagan name'. But there was no way Mum and Dad were going to give in. They insisted. And when it came to the moment when I was handed over for baptism the minister glared at Mum and said, 'Is it still Hebe?' And Mum glared back and said, 'Yes!' I've often wondered if it 'took'!

I love the name. I have never met another Hebe, though Rosemary did once. There are a few Hebes scattered around, but I am more likely these days to see a notice at a garden display that says: 'Hebe's cheap, only $3.99'. (I sometimes feel like going in and protesting about the apostrophe). I have no idea why the plant veronica was re-named hebe, but most people who recognise my name think I was called after the plant, especially when they hear that my sister is Rosemary. I am always happy to set them right.

I have a rule. When I tell someone my 'real' name and they say 'How interesting! I've never met another Hebe,' I am happy for them to call me that, if they want to. If they say (as far too many do) 'Oh, heebie-jeebie!' I immediately say, 'But I prefer to be Barbara'. I am pleased to have an unusual name, but I don't see why anyone should be rude about it.

Becoming Barbara was a slow process that simply fitted the situation at the time. It started when I was 14 and used to attend a Saturday evening youth club in Dorking. Because I only saw the other young people there once a week they never seemed to be able to remember what I was called, which was embarrassing for someone who was still rather shy. One day, when I had been met by the 'er . . . er . . . er . . . what was your name again?' I got cross and said, 'Oh, call me Barbara!' And they did.

No one else, at school, for instance, or church, had any problems with the name, though I do remember a Sunday School prize with my name spelt 'Hébé,' which really annoyed my father. But when, many years down the track, I was thinking of having a pen-name and doing some serious writing, I decided on Barbara, as being easy to remember; and Yates and Rothwell, being the maiden names respectively of my Grandma Blake and my mother, seemed to make a good combination. And it has in fact served me well. In the UK, with friends who remember me from the school days at Dorking Grammar, I am always Hebe. In Australia, or when I am involved in something to do with writing, I am usually Barbara. This came about when I first visited 'down-under' in 1972, as a journalist. I was introduced as 'Barbara Yates Rothwell' wherever I went; and so, when 2 years later we came out to WA to live, the people that I had already met knew me as Barbara. And the name stuck. This suited me, because I had expected to settle into a writing career once we arrived.

Having two names can be quite challenging. While Derry was alive it posed the problem of 'who am I?' when it came to doing the Christmas cards. There were the UK friends and family, for whom we were 'Derry and Hebe'. For Australian friends it was usually 'Derry and Barbara'; but when Derry started writing for the paper as Derek Moore Morgan (and he had never used the name Derek before we came here, having been Derry from birth) I sometimes had to sign as 'Derek and Barbara'. All very confusing!

The first time I used my pen-name was when I was trying to set up an interview with a radio celebrity. The phone rang, and Derry answered it. I realised what was happening when he said, 'No, there's no one of that name here. What was it? Barbara . . . ?' I snatched the phone from him mouthing, 'It's me!!' I must say he took the name change very well.

Philip, of course, had no less than three names! It seems that Grandpa Blake believed that a boy should have at least two. So Philip was John Philip Humphrey. I've sometimes wondered where the 'Humphrey' came from—It's not the sort of name I would have expected our parents to choose—though having started with a Hebe, maybe Humphrey came easily! Philip, when asked what his name was, would say something which came out as 'Johnfli Pumfry'.

So this was the Blake family. With so many relatives in the two branches that came together to create us it sometimes seemed more like a clan: Rothwells as far as the eye could see, and enough Blakes—though rather less prolific than the Rothwells—to make the trips northwards worth the effort. I think we were all very family-conscious; and there was, at the top of the pile, the rather stern figure of Grandpa Rothwell to ensure that the family maintained the required standards.

I certainly found him daunting, though Pat, who was brought up by Grandma and Grandpa, did not find him so. He died when I was ten, at the beginning of the war in 1939, and I cannot remember him ever saying anything to me. When I mentioned this to my mother many years later she said that she thought he was quite fond of me, and that on the only occasion when he and Grandma stayed with us in Dorking and we all went shopping he followed me around Woolworth's to see if there was something I wanted. Apparently the thing that really caught my eye was a brooch with glass beads in a design of flowers—and he bought it for me. 'It was the only thing she seemed to want,' he said to Mum. I think it cost one and sixpence.

The Blakes and the Rothwells were a challenging lot—so many aunts and uncles that we saw rarely but were expected to remember at each visit. I was ten when we spent Christmas at Grandpa Blake's, and I had been learning the piano since I was six. Someone (I hope it wasn't my mother) suggested I should play something to the aunts, uncles, grandparents and so on sitting around the fire.

I was very nervous, but I played my 'party piece'. It was not well done, but kind rellies clapped me—all except one elderly aunt who said, 'Well, if I couldn't play better than that I wouldn't play at all!' She had a point!

Grandpa Blake was the younger brother of George, but I think he was probably older than his sisters, Amy and Florrie, who were always known as Auntie-Amy-and-Florrie, as though they were joined at the hip. They lived together in what seemed to me even as a youngster to be a totally stultified atmosphere. They had not emerged from the Edwardian era—or possibly the Victorian.

Amy was small and dumpy; Florrie was thin, with a red nose that argued either secret drinking (which I think is unlikely) or a poor digestion. I try to imagine them going out of the house, but they appeared to be totally reclusive. I believe that when their brother, Grandpa Blake, came to visit, they would speak to him through the chained door. But maybe they unlocked it once they were sure who he was.

The anecdote that makes one think of them with some sympathy goes back to when they were young women. A young man (or possibly two young men) escorted them back home from church one Sunday. They were met at the door by their father, who ordered the young gentlemen off the premises, saying that no young fellows were going to come sniffing round his daughters! And as far as I can tell, none ever did. By the time I knew them, Auntie-Amy-and-Florrie were eccentric and seemed to have lived lives without much meaning. So tragic!

But their eccentricity was not what bugged me about them as I was growing up. Every single time I saw them on our visits to the grandparents they would say the same thing, in a sort of thinly peevish Manchester accent: 'Hasn't she grown? Oh, hasn't she grown? Have to put a tuck in her, won't we? Have to put a brick on her head!' I did my best to smile, but it felt as if I was baring my teeth!

We called on them one day in 1944 when we were staying with Grandma Rothwell during the plague of war-time 'doodle-bugs' down south. We had been invited to tea, and we were conscious that with war-time rations they might find it difficult to provide enough. Mum was considerably taken aback when they opened the kitchen cupboard and showed her a great collection of tins: peaches, ham, you name it! 'What would you like, Lily?' I can't remember what she chose, but she was astonished enough to remember it for years.

The tragedy of Amy and Florrie was finally made very clear when Florrie died around 1950. Amy had died a couple of years before. Their sister-in-law, Auntie Meg, George's widow, had come to live in Dorking earlier (and that is a whole other story); and she had invited Florrie to come to stay with her. But Florrie never did, not until 1950, when she arrived with very little warning. My father met her in London and brought her home, and left her with me (we then lived in our flat above Mum and Dad) while he got the car out to take her to Auntie Meg's. She was very difficult to get a word out of, and I felt really sorry for her because she was wearing a shabby coat and lisle stockings cobbled together where they had been darned. Dad took her off to Auntie's, and we assumed she had come for a couple of weeks or so.

But it soon became clear that she was in the last stages of abdominal cancer. It seems she hadn't told anyone, and I have no idea if she had seen a doctor—quite possibly not. She was of the generation that would be very embarrassed by having a doctor probe her much swollen abdomen. So Auntie Meg was caught with a visitor who wasn't going away; and in fact I think Florrie only lasted about six weeks.

My father was her executor; he and Mum went north to open up the house and do an inventory. What they found was astounding, and truly appalling. It was one of those cases you read about in the papers, where someone has become a total recluse, living among piles of stuff that has accumulated and is never cleared or tidied. Under the kitchen table, Mum told me, were little packets of ashes wrapped in newspaper that had never been put out in a bin. In the larder were the mouldy remains of some shop-bought gateaux with only one piece cut out of each. One bedroom was almost impossible to enter because there were boxes stacked to the door. There were cupboards full of clothes: good winter coats, stockings never taken from their wrappings, all the 'bottom drawer' linen waiting for the day one or both would be married; and, saddest of all, clothes waiting for the babies they would never have.

Oddly enough, on the kitchen table was a piece of paper on which Amy had written that she was leaving me £25. It had been written two years before, at the time of my marriage, and was still lying on the kitchen table despite the fact that she had died a year or so before. As she hadn't had it witnessed, I never got my £25!

It was 5 years after the end of the war, and yet the blackout curtains were still at the windows, slowly rotting. Most bizarre— there were little heaps of money, some lying under hair combings (Victorian girls would keep them to make pads on which to 'put up' their hair when they were old enough), to the tune of over £2000! Who needs banks?

And we are talking about 1950.

Mum came home with a large pink teddy (Mr Pinky) for Paddy, who was a year old. 'I shouldn't have done it really,' she said. 'It should have been left for probate!' What was it doing there? Was it for some never-to-be-born child? Or perhaps a present for a small relative? I think perhaps the former.

Many years later—Mr Pinky having emigrated with the rest of us—he was living with Alison. She took him to a teddy bears' gathering in Sydney, and they went by train. Experts there were quite interested in him, and thought he might be French because of the colour; but no one could put a date or location on him. On the way out the lady selling teddy bear accessories, seeing that he was blind, said 'You can't take him home like that! Buy him some eyes.'

So Mr Pinky went back on the train with his new eyes in; and Alison said, 'He was so excited, now that he could see where we were going!' At least he had been rescued from a very dusty and totally eventless old age. I wish one could have said the same for Auntie Amy and Florrie. Their story seems to me a total tragedy. Why did no one ever realise what was happening? It's not enough to say that they resisted contact with the outside world. There were enough relatives around that someone, at some time, should have said 'This can't go on!' Unfortunately, once that aura of eccentricity has been established it's very difficult to find anyone to break through and make the rescue. And in the end, of course, perhaps we all have the right to live in whatever kind of turmoil we have chosen. RIP, Amy and Florrie!

3

Moments of family excitement came for us during the end of the '30s, when we were due to return from Storrington, though only briefly, to North London and normality. Auntie Rene, my father's sister, married—finally— Uncle Fred! I believe they were courting for about 19 years, so probably the older members of the family had a sense of relief that they had finally got to the altar. They went to live in a rather small house, and eventually had two sons, Alex and Brian. Alex now lives in Cornwall. Brian, sadly, died some years ago.

And Uncle James, my mother's younger brother, married Jean Chapman. Uncle was quite tall; Jean was very small. Although I was a bridesmaid I have no recollection of seeing her at any time during the marriage service—she was hidden by all the tall members of the party. James and Jean had two children: Frances, who lives in Canada (and with whom I spent some excellent days during my 2010 trip—and saw Niagara for the first time); and Ken, who is the family-tree expert, and has uncovered some very intriguing details of our forebears.

By this time, late 1938, no doubt the adults were all looking across the Channel to see if it could possibly happen again: another war. It would not have dawned on children that the previous war, which had left such emotional and physical scars, was only two decades behind us. I vaguely recall Mum talking about it, but I was secure in the knowledge that 1918 was a *very* long time ago, and not worth thinking about. After all, women still wore long dresses then! But for those who had been young in 1918, and were now approaching middle age, it must have been a very frightening thought. *Surely,* no one was mad enough to do it again?

The 'post-Storrington' period coincided with the Munich crisis in October 1938. For those who do not know about this— Prime Minister Neville Chamberlain, fearing the outbreak of war between Britain and Germany, flew to Munich to talk with Chancellor Adolf Hitler. There is a newspaper photograph of him getting off a plane, having returned from Germany. He is waving a piece of paper and saying 'Peace in our time!' This comes from the prayer book service, in the Te Deum: 'Give us peace in our time, O Lord'. Everyone took a deep breath and relaxed for a bit.

We were at that time in the Manchester area, for Auntie Rene's wedding. Rosemary and I were bridesmaids, and Philip was a page in blue velvet trousers which, I seem to recall, kept coming unpoppered. We girls wore ice blue dresses, very pretty, with little Juliet caps in blue with fabric flowers. We felt fairly gorgeous!

When we got home, everyone else had been fitted with gas masks, and we had missed out! This was only a minor worry, since there was a feeling that perhaps, after all the sabre-rattling, there wasn't going to be a war. Hitler couldn't be so stupid. When, less than a year later, war *was* declared, the rubber in many of the previously issued masks was found to have perished, making them useless. So I suppose we gained by not being there at the right time.

But in late 1938, back in Eastcote from Storrington, the moves were being made to shift us to Dorking. I recall that Mum said there were three houses that they had looked at: one was quite useless, one backed on to the recreation ground and the Pippbrook (which would have been quite pleasant), and the third was New Hatch, a much more up-market house, 5 bedrooms, 2 bathrooms, 3 toilets, 3 reception rooms, and a garden surrounding it, divided into 5 sections. One of these was almost, but not quite, big enough to be a tennis court, but had never been developed. One was a kitchen garden, where we met globe artichokes for the first time. Then there were the back garden, the side garden and the front garden. All well planted, and all needing quite a lot of time and energy to keep up to scratch.

The house was only available as a rental; London Road, outside our gate, was due for widening, so we didn't expect to be there very long. As it happened, with the war starting the following year, we were there until it was finally demolished in 1963—twenty-five years of comfort, not only for my parents, but for us when we moved into the upstairs rooms after our marriage in late 1948. A few years ago, when grandson Ash was living in London, his weekly rent for almost nothing was £100; in 1938 my father was paying the same amount *per annum* for our very attractive and spacious house.

In 1936, when the old king died, Dad had given me a lilac bush. It was in memory of George V, and was about 2 feet high; when we left Eastcote he dug it up and transplanted it in the new garden in Dorking. In 1952, when we moved to the other end of Dorking, I found to my great pleasure that there were two well-grown lilacs in the back garden. I have therefore always had a lilac tree 'of my own', and one of the things that I wondered about when we emigrated so many years later was whether I could manage without lilac! In fact, once I had been introduced to the jacarandas that bloom around Perth in November, I knew that I could. I thought they were magnificent.

And so we moved to Dorking, and settled into the luxuries of New Hatch. It was a really lovely house, and seemed very spacious after the Eastcote one, though that had not been small, even though it was a semi-detached. New Hatch was very conveniently placed. Dorking North station was just across the road, about a 4 minute walk. Stanway School was about 5 minutes up Chichester Road to the left, the Dorking County School (as it then was) was another 5 minutes up the Ashcombe Road to the right. 'Ashcombe' was named for Lord Ashcombe, the local 'big-wig'. He had a mansion on Ranmore, the hill to the west of us; it was palatial and dominated the scenery, and it was called Denbies. The original house was pulled down many years ago—I have no idea why. Today there would have been uproar about the destruction of a heritage building. There is now a rather choice restaurant, and they have a wide spread of vines which produce a very acceptable wine. When we moved there it was not a vineyard, it was the Bradley Farm, and we could walk in a great circle along the main road, onto the farm track, up so-called 'Little' Ranmore and then home. The area now covered with vines was known as 'the forty-acre', and it constituted most of the boys' cross-country from DCS, run every summer.

During the war a German plane came down in the area, and the pilot managed to get out more or less unscathed. He landed in the forty-acre, and someone still had a few pictures left in a camera (you couldn't easily get film during the war), and so we had a record of this remarkable event. The pilot was arrested by the local constabulary, and hopefully spent a more peaceful war than he had anticipated.

War preparations were everywhere. Houses with south-facing garden walls had slits made in them to take rifles (but looking exactly like the arrow slits in mediaeval castles). An Australian platoon turned up to cut down *our trees* where they hid the road. We all decided to hate Australians! Heavy machinery dug a huge ditch across farm land to the north of us, towards London. We were a line of defence for London if it came to an invasion. The ditch was a tank trap, and the theory was that a tank could go down into it, but would find it almost impossible to get up the other side. Fortunately, this theory was never put to the test. Scattered around the hills were 'pill-boxes', concrete emplacements overlooking the expected approach roads of the enemy. Many of them are still there. The reinforced concrete is simply too tough to tear down. Presumably they have provided some nice little desirable residences for the native fauna.

Our house, New Hatch, faced London Road, the main highway from the south coast to the city. If the Germans came, always supposing they landed on the south coast, they would travel up the London Road, past our house, and this was something that was in the minds of those of us who could work it out. At ten I was conscious enough of the problems to be a little scared, but

I think Rosemary and Philip would have been too young, at 7 and 5. I imagine Philip would have gone up his favourite tree and 'machine-gunned' them! He had a very nice line in machine-gun noises, and liked to 'fire' at the neighbours as they went past. He could also do a good impression of a diving bomber. But that, of course, was once the war had got going, and he knew what they sounded like.

It was in November 1938 that the infamous Krystallnacht took place in Germany—a government inspired pogrom. It must have been shortly after that a request went out, perhaps through the churches, for families who would take in a refugee from the Nazi regime. Mum and Dad decided this was something they could do, and so in due course Klara Leven came to us, a Jewess from Krefeld, near Cologne, whose family had already been deeply affected by the anti-Jewish laws. Klara became Clare when she was with us—at her request—and remained for many months, though I don't recall how long. Eventually she went on to become a waitress at the Stoneroof Café in South Street, Dorking; although we lost touch with her for quite a time after the war, she and I became good friends later, when she was in a fragile state of health and I was a young married woman with children. When she died in her late sixties I was chief mourner at her funeral. Her story, told in fictional terms, is in my novel KLARA.

The build-up to war during our first year in Dorking grew steadily more intense. Leaflets came through the letter box with regularity, instructing us in how to cope with everything from gas attacks to black-out. I remember the former particularly because for a while we children had a game where we would crawl along the floor, keeping our heads down, because the instructions told us that it was the best place to be if gas was used. We thought it was quite funny, but I can now imagine that our parents felt a bit distressed to think that we were 'enjoying' real war games.

New Hatch had a large front porch which, because there was a secondary front door, we seldom used. At some point the Air Raid Precaution people came and told Dad (you don't ask in wartime) that they wanted to store hurricane lamps and other gear in it.

The stuff was brought in, and I don't think anyone ever looked at it again for the whole duration of the war. I wonder if anyone ever came to claim it.

I well remember the Sunday on which war was declared. The solemn announcement came over the radio, and within a short while the air raid siren sounded for the first time. We all went to sit in the hall, where it was possibly a bit safer than anywhere else (the cupboard under the stairs was the shelter of choice), and as we sat about and waited for Hitler to do his worst I suddenly and desperately wanted to go to the loo. But I didn't go, because I thought the most awful thing I could imagine was if the house was blown up while I was in there, and *they found me sitting on it!* How embarrassing!

When Poland had been invaded, and following the declaration of war, everything changed. A day or so later the evacuees began to arrive from London, where it was expected there would immediately be heavy bombing. I remember going down to the station where children were arriving, each with a large label pinned on and a gasmask slung over the shoulder, everything from teens to toddlers, with a few mums and plenty of carers. There were buses waiting for them, and the huge task began of getting the children into new homes before nightfall. Mum had agreed to have two children—it was largely regarded as a duty rather than a friendly impulse, and over the next few weeks the good-heartedness of Dorking people (and no doubt people all over the country areas of England) was tested to the full.

Our two arrived a day or two later: John and Mary. I imagine they were about 10 or 11 years old, brother and sister, and they had not settled well into their first foster home. Mum was not best pleased when they were sitting in the lounge, looking around them like potential buyers, and one said to the other, 'I reckon this'll do,' or something equally promising. What I recall best about that evening is the awful smell that came from the bathroom while they were having a 'compulsory' bath—I gathered they really didn't think they needed it. The odour said something else. Of course, it may have said that they didn't have a bathroom at home—these were, if not slum kids, at least children from very poor areas.

Their mother came to see them once, a week or two later, and my mind blanks out the rest. Except that Mum said she couldn't manage them and they were taken elsewhere. Instead, Grandma Rothwell and Pat came as our private evacuees, Manchester being presumably on the list for bombing. Eventually, after many weeks, a considerable number of evacuees, including Grandma and Pat, decided to go home again; the bombing war for some strange reason never happened until later.

We had chickens during the early days of the war. This meant cleaning out the hen house, feeding the birds, collecting any eggs they might have inadvertently produced in a forgetful moment (once you have chooks they all decide to take it easy and forget about laying). As one was able to take on 'customers' for surplus eggs, it all seemed a good idea: except that I think the system was that if you registered with a private person (or private chooks, perhaps) and the chooks forgot to lay, you couldn't get the eggs from a normal egg supplier. So it was quite embarrassing to have to tell people that there were no eggs at present.

Of course, like all children who are not controlled with a heavy hand, we only did the cleaning/feeding/collecting thing for a while, and then found other, more exciting pastimes. So (does this sound familiar?) Mum did it. This was a real sacrifice. She was not an animal lover, and chooks are not always easy to control. But she did it, a bit grimly, and now and then we actually had quite a good production line. Then, of course, they all went broody!

The idea behind this farming enterprise was that looking after the birds would be our contribution to the war effort. We three children, that is. We were allowed to charge Mum for the eggs, because our not very large savings had gone into purchasing hens and a chicken coop. I'm afraid Mum lost all round.

At that time we had a small white dog with traces of West Highland terrier. Very lively; we had had him at Storrington, where he adored the countryside and would bounce over great bushes of heather so that one could see his head now and then as he bounded away into the distance. Bob had to be kept away from the chooks; he didn't realise they were an essential part of the war effort. But he got into the pen on one occasion, and chose as his victim the nicest hen in the hen-coop: Goldie. We liked Goldie because she would let us stroke her, squatting low as she felt our hands on her back. So to have her torn and bleeding body lying there, feathers flying, was deeply painful.

We would realise on the following Sunday just how painful it could be to lose a good friend. Goldie turned up, fresh out of the oven, for lunch. I was appalled, and had one of my least attractive tantrums. 'I'm not eating Goldie!' I shrieked. Mum was adamant. 'In war-time you eat what you're given!' Memory blanks out over whether I did actually eat the poor bird. I know I was very vocal until both Mum and Dad got cross with me. This shows that, even with fairly stringent rationing, we were by no means starving. On the other side of the English Channel there would no doubt have been plenty of people who would have regarded Goldie as a meal to remember.

Which of course I have done—but for the wrong reasons. I wonder at what point it was decided to have Bob put down. I don't think it was because of Goldie. When the time came I was having one of my bouts of chestiness, and Bob spent several hours on my bed. When he was called downstairs I thought nothing of it, but I did eventually wonder why he hadn't come back. He never did return. The vet had called for him, and that was that.

I was furious. Nobody had warned me. I hadn't been able to say goodbye to him. Why did he go? I don't know—except that, as I said before, Mum was not an animal-lover, but she was the one who was stuck with our pets while we were at school and Dad was at work, and it probably got too much for her. She had a mini-breakdown later, in 1943, and went away to stay with relatives for a few weeks; a dog, plus a war, had probably been a chore too great.

4

Pat and I started school at DCS (Dorking County School) in October. Normally the school year in the UK starts in September, but for us in the new intake there was not enough room in the air raid shelters for the entire school and we had to wait until the shelters were ready. I was one of 'Burton's babies'—year one. No one who was in Miss Burton's class would ever forget her. She kept perfect control in the kindest way, and steered us through the problems of starting at a new, BIG school under extreme difficulties. For example, because we also had the girls from Sydenham High School billeted on us we littlies didn't have a designated classroom. All our books and equipment were kept at the very top of the school in what was known as the modelling room—though I never found out what they modelled there! We had a tiny bit of shelf each, and were supposed to remember everything we would need—pens, pencils, geometry tools, exercise and text books and so on—for two whole lessons. It was a day's march to get to the modelling room if you forgot something, and we spent several weeks trying to get our little heads around the difficulties. We were, after all, only about 10 years old. But somehow we did it.

My first day at the school is very clear in my memory. Mum took Pat and me in through the front door of this totally enormous and daunting building and we went into the main hall where we were to be 'sorted'. Under normal conditions the staff would have had some idea of which class everyone belonged to; but these were not normal conditions. The place was overflowing with the expected intake for the year, plus assorted collections of evacuees, none of whom as far as we could see had been allocated classes. I, as a student whose name was actually on the lists, was sent to 1a. Pat, as a blow-in, went to 4b while they decided where she ought to be. As she was only 7 months older than me she should probably have been put in 2a or b, so she was well out of her depth. That would have finished me, but Pat was always made of tougher stuff.

We got through the morning, and then came lunch time. Eating school dinners was not at that time normal except for some who came from distances. It was later on that year, when rationing began to tighten, that mothers realised what a good idea it was to eke out the rations with a provided school lunch. After that, practically everyone stayed on through lunchtime.

But that first day we were to go home for lunch, so off I went to look for Pat, who was not to be found. I was so shy and acutely nervous in those days that I didn't know what to do and dared not ask anyone for help. I found myself in the front hall, where we had come in that morning, and Miss Burton arrived most fortuitously. What did I want? I couldn't find my cousin. What is her name? Pat Kirkham. Which class is she in? I didn't know. Just at that moment along came Mr Goffin, the senior master. I was much impressed by the fact that the staff wore their academic gowns, and Mr Goffin, as he walked, swung his out behind him in a most dramatic manner. He always looked as though he had a strong wind against him. He and Miss Burton conversed on the subject of my cousin, and then, bless him, he swept off to look for her. I stood there feeling totally lost and miserable until he returned, to tell Miss Burton that he had been unable to find Pat.

She kindly said to me that I should perhaps go home and see if she had gone on first. So I said thank you (well, I hope I did), and—walked out of the main front door! I didn't learn until later that only prefects and staff were allowed to do that, so that was the last time I went through it until I was a prefect. I've often wondered what Miss Burton's reaction was. Probably had a good laugh with Charlie Goffin.

And yes, of course, Pat had gone home. Well, that was just one of the horrors of that first term. The school seemed so big, and I was astonished that there were grown-up men who were apparently still schoolboys. These were the Sixth Formers, and I actually recall that one of them was Japanese; his name was Hashimoto; he must have been the first Asian I had ever seen. I sometimes wondered, as the war developed into the Pacific, what happened to him. I imagine he may have been the son of a Japanese diplomat or businessman living in England; and so he may well have been interned 'for the duration', if he didn't get out quickly enough.

There were other members of staff whom I dimly recall. 'Sally' Allsworth taught English, and was (to my very young eyes) an old lady. She wore her hair in a large 'bun' on top of her head, and the most dramatic event I can remember, involving her, was the time a child was sick into another girl's (fortunately empty) shoes during class, and we all had to go outside while some unlucky minion cleared up the mess.

Miss Willcocks (Wilcox?) taught—I think—geography. But the only episode I can bring to mind was the time we had to make up a sort of quiz, based on London, for the rest of the class; this meant thinking up a question, which then had to be read out to the others. I sweated over this! Eventually I came up with the question: How far is it from Trafalgar Square to Nelson's column? This was the limit of my knowledge of the London scene. Miss W came round to see what we had written, and she said 'A good question' to me, relieving my nerves a bit. I read it out, and some bright spark leapt up and said, 'Nelson's column is *in* Trafalgar Square'. I was just thankful that no one discovered *I* didn't know the answer. Presumably Miss W thought it was a trick question.

The only other thing about that particular class was that one boy said, 'My uncle took me to see a show in London, and some of the ladies in it were painted all over in gold'. Miss W was rather taken aback, and changed the subject quickly.

That winter was very cold, and one of the things that the school authorities were very concerned about was to avoid 'flu outbreaks. It was, after all, only a couple of decades since the previous war ended with the worst 'flu epidemic ever, when thousands of people died. So we had to have the windows open—not just an inch or two, but with the sashes well raised. As a result it was necessary to wear our winter coats, mittens (without fingers so that we could write), woolly stockings or socks, lined boots for those who had them; and some of us had balaclava helmets as well. I seem to recall knitting my own. It must have been quite a sight! And oh boy! Was it cold! At the end of each class we had to stand up and do exercises to keep warm. Outside, the snow was many inches deep, but my recollection is that we went out at morning break and lunch anyway—and probably got soaked playing with snow-balls. The end result was that there wasn't a 'flu epidemic, and looking back on it, it was quite an experience.

At some time in the first couple of years, once the war had really got going and we had spent some time in the shelters listening to distant guns firing, we were told that a film company was coming. Much excitement! By that time we had got 'going to the shelters' down to a fine art. Once the air raid sirens went off, the school could be cleared in 3 minutes—not bad going. So the film people wanted to see how the children of Britain were coping with wartime—we would show them!

The school fire bell rang. We took our normal routes to the shelters, running out through the girls' entry, and disappearing into our 'homes from home' in the ground. I clearly recall the cameraman standing on top of one of the shelters as I ran to my place. Our moment of glory was soon over, and it was back to work. But we all assumed that it would be on the cinema news the following week, and I think most of us probably went—just in case. But we never saw it, and it went into the realm of forgotten things.

Here, in Australia, many, many years later, I was watching the programme called, I believe, *The Finest Hour*. And there was something very familiar about the school building on the screen, and the doorway through which girls were running to go to the shelters—and there were Miss Burton and another teacher closing the doors after we had gone in! Of course, I wasn't visible in it. I have been told that the film was made for the American market, to show how the 'ordinary citizens' of Britain were managing to keep going. I was able to record it. How amazing, to see something quite accidentally that I remember so well—at least 60 years later!

My school years from 1939 to 1945 were obviously coloured by the war. There are outstanding moments that are worth recording, and among these must be the extraordinary retreat from Dunkirk, which in some amazing way became a matter of great pride throughout the country. Though, after all, a defeat is a defeat!

The details of the withdrawal from France, after that country's too quick capitulation to the German forces, are easily found. The fleet of little ships and boats that went to bring the men back from certain death or imprisonment will long be remembered with pride. Living through it was truly remarkable. But for us at the school the really memorable thing was that the trains that brought the men, weary and often wounded, back from Dover, one of the places where they had landed, came right past our playing fields. From the back windows of the building the railway line was not much more than the length of the tennis courts away; and as the retreat went on from day to day, and the special trains puffed their way past, no member of the staff would dare to try and stop us rushing to the windows and waving ourselves silly.

If the trains went by during morning break or lunchtime, of course, we were actually out by the wire fence. It was a very mixed sensation to see the soldiers, too tired to wave as energetically as we were doing, and often well bandaged with nurses standing by. I can still call up my image of one man, so wrapped in bandages that it was impossible to see anything of him. Behind him stood a nurse, holding his wheelchair. For me, that is the real memory of Dunkirk. Even now it can bring tears to my eyes. I wonder if he survived.

In the evenings of that early summer of 1940 the main activity for many Dorking people was to go down to the railway line and let the men know we cared about what they had done and suffered. It may have been a defeat, but it drew us all together, as disasters so often do.

Humankind being as aggressive as it is, we shall no doubt go on having wars; but as I grow older I wonder what it is about us that cannot be satisfied with what we have, either as individuals or as nations. The phenomenon that was Hitler, who had such charisma that he could lead a whole country into disaster, makes me wonder again what he might have done for Germany and Europe if he had been a good man. What a waste! But, since it seems inevitable that wars will happen, I am glad that I grew up in WWII. There is something about danger and deprivation that brings us face to face with what is valuable; and that is the lesson for me of that truly dreadful war and its aftermath. It brought into the world some things that we thought had gone out—in Europe at least—with mediaeval times: excessive cruelty, a lack of compassion, the lowering of ethical standards; and the desire not just to win, but to exterminate anyone who stands against you. The remnants of that are still, sadly, with us in too many parts of the world. Hitler opened a Pandora's box that should have been left shut.

I am writing this a few days after Osama Bin Laden was killed by coalition forces. I am not happy that we, as supposedly civilised nations, have descended to assassination, though I can understand the pressures to do so. I once asked my mother why no one had killed Hitler, and she said, rather wisely, that it might not make any difference, because someone else would take his place and it might even be worse. Time will show what will happen now that Bin Laden has gone.

Other memories of the war are sometimes much more personal. Uncle Norman, Pat's father, was in the Canadian army—a regimental sergeant-major, stocky, well-built, authoritative, in the Calgary tank regiment. When he could he would visit us, and would bring those things that delight war-time children: sweets! His wife Marjorie, back in Canada, sent them. I remember him asking my mother on one occasion if there was anything we were short of that he could get for us. Mum said, 'Yes, hair pins!' He stared. 'What—*bobby-pins*?' War-time had deprived us of the means to keep our hair out of our eyes! Presumably they were making them into tanks and Spitfires.

So, for a while, we were probably the best bobby-pinned family in the south of England. We children also discovered Chiclets, a type of (I think) chewing gum we hadn't met before. And we met his rather gorgeous young sergeants! My 11-year-old heart beat a little faster when he arrived with them. They all seemed to be about ten feet tall (which he certainly wasn't), and my no doubt faulty memory says there were about six of them. I can remember them standing in the hall at home, being introduced to my mother. One of them was called Earl, and Uncle said, 'You don't have to bow to him, Lily—it's his name!'

Top marks to anyone trying to feed a family in war-time for entertaining a bunch of doubtless hungry guys, though perhaps they brought food with them—I don't remember. They came more than once, and then the Calgary regiment was one of the army groups that were sent on the abortive and tragic raid on Dieppe. This was, I believe, a try-out for the later invasion. Whatever it was supposed to prove or test, it was a disaster. Uncle's tank carrier, which had taken them safely across the Channel, was damaged by bombing before they could get their tank ashore. But his young sergeants did land—and all were either killed or taken prisoner. Mum reckoned that this made a huge difference to Uncle Norman. He was no young blood looking for adventure. I suspect he joined up so that could see his first family in the UK at someone else's expense. But he was a real father-figure to his young NCOs, and he felt their loss acutely.

He went on to fight his way through Italy, picking up a serious wound on the way. We saw him before he went back to Canada and what I hope was a 'normal' life. I recall his description of war-time Italy—not at all what the travel posters would tell you. He reckoned there was only one road, south to north, which the invading Allies would be using in convoy to make their way towards Germany. Enemy planes could bomb the first trucks, then the last trucks in the line. Then they were free to machine gun the rest of the convoy, and I presume that that was when he was injured.

His son Norman was in Italy, too, and also warned us never to believe what the holiday brochures said. As far as he was concerned, Italy was knee-deep in mud. He had an injury, but I believe it was soccer damage—a broken leg!

Uncle visited us once, years later, with his wife and daughter; he had become very much the Canadian self-made man, and there wasn't much about him that reminded us of those war years.

But before I leave him to history I must mention the amazing day out that Pat and I had with him.

He took us to London. We were 13, and I have often wondered what would happen today, now that we have become suspicious of anyone adult accompanied by a young girl. Here he was, a middle-aged Canadian soldier in uniform, with *two* teenage girls. And what a day we had! It would have been 1942, rationing and shortages everywhere, including a real lack of money for 'treats', and we spent the day doing the most surprising things.

Lyons Corner House was the place that a 13-year-old would regard as the height of gracious living: the Viennese Room had gilt chairs and, even at that time in the war, a chamber music group at one end playing romantic tunes. Among other delicacies, we had sherry trifle. How grown-up!

We did quite a lot of walking, looking at some of the places of historic interest, such as Buckingham Palace. And in the afternoon (because he had seen it in that other war when he was in London) he took us to see *Chu Chin Chow*, a musical with a distinctly oriental flavour. We sat in the front row of the stalls, and—though he never knew—it changed my life.

At one point the soprano sings *Any time's kissing time*. When she finished, the audience clapped enthusiastically. And that was the moment when I knew I wanted to be a singer, and stand on a stage and have people clap me! These strange and unexpected moments in one's life are memorable. Because they come out of nowhere, one should always be prepared for them. That whole day had a magic about it that I don't think I have ever felt again in quite the same way. It was another year before I told anyone I wanted to sing, and six years before I had any singing lessons that counted. And it was three years before Derry appeared on my scene, and encouraged me to do what up till then had only seemed like a dream.

Isn't life strange?

Perhaps this is a good moment to recall another seminal moment in my musical life.

The Leith Hill Festival takes place yearly in Surrey. The town of Dorking lies in the North Downs, in the Dorking Gap. Around the Gap are several rather lovely hills: Box Hill, which stood right across from our house and is the dominating geological feature of the area; Leith Hill, about a 15-minute drive south, is the highest point in SE England (because the tower on the top of this hill raises it to 1000 feet, it calls itself a mountain); Ranmore Common, which dominates another viewpoint; and a number of smaller hills that create what is a really delightful scenic area. The view from the top of Box Hill shows the whole of the Weald, right down across this considerable valley to the South Downs. And beyond those hills is the English Channel.

London, to the north, is about 25 miles away.

The eminent musician Dr Ralph Vaughan Williams made his home in Dorking, about half a mile from where we eventually went to live, at the 'old' end of the town. He was the local Grand Old Man, and it was quite usual to see him making his rather ungainly way up the High Street. Many years before we arrived in the town he had started the Leith Hill Festival—I imagine it may be unique among music festivals, because it has produced a remarkable number of small choirs, based on the fact that Dorking is the hub, surrounded by a scattering of villages. I don't know how many, but some of those I recall are Abinger Hammer, Holmbury St Mary, Capel, Ockley, Mickleham, Westcott . . . and so on. Dorking itself had two choirs, the Madrigal and the Oriana. My father was the accompanist for the Oriana Choir for many years.

The festival is competitive, and each spring the town rings with music. I wish I knew how many choirs there were during that early period. I do know that some people would take their spring holidays at that time so that they could participate in this astonishing display of amateur musicianship.

Once the individual classes have done their best—or worst, I suppose—and everyone can relax a bit, there will be a major combined choral performance, and then, as a mighty finale, Bach's great *Passion according to St Matthew* is sung by the combined choirs.

VW brought together some of the best-known singers in the country for these final occasions, and they were splendid performances. Doing it every year meant that practically everyone knew the *Passion* inside out, and it was as a result a very joyous musical moment.

At some point, pre-war, the Dorking Halls were built. I imagine that they were built to accommodate the Leith Hill Music Festival. There are three halls: the large concert hall, the smaller Masonic Hall, and the Martineau Hall. These halls buzzed with activity during the festival. I have no idea how many hundreds of devoted choral singers would be there during the festival days.

Then the war came. And the War Office commandeered the Dorking Halls, which meant that the festival, if it was going to survive, had to find other venues. I don't remember where they did their competitive things, but the obvious place for the *Passion* was the parish church of St Martin, conveniently situated in the centre of the town.

And it was there, when I was eleven, that my father took me to hear Bach's wonderful oratorio.

Because we got there too late to find a seat in the main part of the church, we had to sit in the chancel; this placed us behind the cellos, the orchestra spilling out down the chancel steps, and the large choir completely invisible to me, hidden by a number of energetic cellists' backs. I could just see Vaughan Williams's arms waving as he conducted.

The music began. The cellos started their low, throbbing accompaniment to the lovely melodies soaring above them; and then the one repeated note on the cellos changed, they began the climb up the scale—and my heart leapt. I knew that I had to learn the cello!

I whispered to Dad: 'How do they know where to put their fingers?' My only experience of a stringed instrument had been the little ukulele my grandfather gave me when I was very small, and that had frets. I could see the finger-board of the nearest cello—and there was no indication of where the fingers went.

Dad whispered back: 'They have to learn where to put them.'

I have a recording, privately made for VW, of the 1958 performance. His widow kept it private for a long time, but then released it for commercial CDs. It is very idiosyncratic. His tempi would not suit everyone. But even now, hearing the sudden change in the cellos as they climb through the lower registers, I get that bump in the chest!

That recording has another interest for me. I am pretty certain that my father, and possibly Derry, sang in it. It may well have been the year that Derry was invited to conduct the Madrigal choir. (They didn't renew the invitation the following year. I wonder why?).

Very wisely, Mum and Dad didn't immediately buy me a cello. I had to nag them for a year or so before they found someone who would lend us one while I tried it out. And eventually they did buy one, through a member of the family. Just a short while ago I was visiting Jenny, my cousin on the Blake side of the family, and she asked me about the cello. It seems that one of *her* rellies had been wondering where the instrument had gone to. I told her that we had brought it out here in 1974, that I hadn't played it for years, and that in the end I sold it to a member of the UWA string quartet. He sent it to the UK to be taken apart and reassembled (without the wood-worm), so that he could use it for teaching purposes.

This seemed to me quite an operation if he wasn't going to use it in performance, and Jenny said the same. Perhaps it was worth more than I thought. Anyway, she took his name and will perhaps try to trace it. All I remember of its provenance is that it had the letters FB carved into the neck, which I think must be the initials of Florence Blake, my father's aunt, and Jenny's great-aunt. Watch this space!

My cello-playing career began when I was 12. I had lessons from a rather pleasant youngish teacher, and I would have done a lot better if I had practised more. All the same, in 18 months I passed my Grade 5, and I played in a piano trio—a great deal of Haydn, I seem to recall. I was in the school orchestra—not a very inspiring group, except for Biddy Fry, who was an excellent violinist. One of the players was Alan Griffiths, son of our French teacher. He was older than I was, and played violin and recorder. Many, many years later, in WA, he and his Swedish wife came to visit us, and we talked about the school orchestra. He disagreed with me that it wasn't much good. But because he left the school in 1943 I am able to recall that I would have been 14 at the time, and by the time I was 15 my interests were turning to art and singing.

Vaughan Williams was invited, as a Governor of the school, to come and listen to the orchestra. Poor man! Our teacher then was Miss Slack, and I have to say that her approach to music almost turned *me* off classical music during her tenure. I think we were probably a great disappointment to her—as she was to us. VW was given a chair in the middle of the school hall; anyone who has seen a famous photograph of the great man will know that he was large, heavy and tended to slump where he sat. We scratched our way through something—several somethings, in fact—and then awaited his analysis. He stood up slowly and advanced to the platform. He didn't say anything to comfort us, simply commented, 'You must get more people in. More instruments. Anything, doesn't matter what—guitars, saxophones, anything.' And he walked out of the hall. Miss Slack escorted him to the main front door and returned to us.

'Well, you heard what Dr Vaughan Williams said. We must get more people in. Though I don't think he could have been serious about the saxophones.'

That still makes me laugh. Anyone who could write a concerto for harmonica would certainly not turn his nose up at saxophones—and he does use them himself in at least one symphony.

5

M eanwhile, my own musical career was well into the future. I had been learning the piano since I was six, and had been amazingly aroused a year later when I first heard the second Hungarian Rhapsody by Liszt—the passionate outpouring astonished me. But around that time I became convinced that my future lay in missionary work, preferably in Africa. Looking back, I think I was easily persuaded that I was wrong—about anything!—and it only took one rebuff from our Religious Instruction teacher, the Rev James Clegg, who had himself been a missionary in China until the Japanese walked in, to change my mind. He stared at me as if I was mad, and made it clear that he didn't think I had a chance. So I let the dream go, and stayed with the music and art.

And the war dragged on. There are moments, both funny and scary, that stick in the memory. During the London blitz, in the early days, the air raid sirens would go off about 6.30 pm and the 'all clear' might not come until about 8 the next morning. Before long we would hear the thrumming of German bombers making their way to the city, and then, later, back again, mission accomplished; and it is amazing how soon one gets used to such an unusual situation. If the alarm didn't go off until about 7 pm, someone would say, 'They're late tonight', and we carried on with our normal evenings, homework, eating, playing games, as if nothing was happening. Now and then a plane would drop a bomb or even a stick of bombs—normally 6—and we would wait with a slight quickening of the pulse, until they had all dropped.

We were fortunate that none of them dropped nearer to us than a mile or so.

We didn't have a bomb shelter, as so many around us did. (In fact, at the age of 10 I 'helped' to dig the holes in two gardens nearby into which the Anderson shelters would go. One of them was still there when I last looked). But we did move downstairs to sleep. Mum and Dad slept in the lounge, with the couch as a bit of a barricade; we three children were in the dining room. If things got really tricky, we were sent into the cupboard under the stairs, which was reputed to be the safest place in the house. We were never able to test that theory.

Because of the chickens we eventually were hosts to a small plague of mice, after the food was stored in the garage. One night, when we had gone to bed, one of these came into the dining/bedroom, where we were still awake. We called for my father, who came with a flashlight to search for the intruder. There was no blackout at the window, so he was crawling around with the light, looking under the beds. Philip cried out for my mother: 'Come here, Mum. Dad's torchering a mouse!' Rosemary and I thought it was funny; Philip didn't.

Sometime in the middle of the war my father and I went shopping on a Saturday morning. The car was laid up 'for the duration', so it was walk or bus. We got off the bus with our purchases and walked the 150 yards or so home, which meant crossing the road. As we entered the house a German plane dived out of the clouds and machine-gunned right up the road, across a field and into the village of Westcott, about 3 miles from us. I said, 'What was that?' and Dad said, 'I think we've been machine-gunned!' Less than half a minute before, we had been on the road. It was sobering to hear that the incident had killed a Westcott doctor, who was about to get into his car.

We had days-long convoys of army vehicles along the road from time to time, the south of England being almost one big army base, and especially as it got round to 1944, before the invasion of Europe. Because we were at a three-way junction of Ashcombe, Chichester and London roads, they needed someone on point duty, so there would often be a couple of soldiers there outside our gate. And I remember one occasion when the mess lorry didn't turn up for at least one day, and Mum sent me to the gate to ask if they would like a cup of tea. Yes, they would! When she realised they had been dumped there without food or anywhere to rest (they were still there overnight) she and Dad put up a camp bed under the veranda at the back of the house, and fed them. I reckon that is amazing, when you consider that we were heavily rationed ourselves. But it was all part of the 'pulling together' that is one of the few good things about conflicts.

Early in the war we were coming home from a church meeting. Across from us, in a huge meadow at the bottom of Box Hill— perhaps half a mile from us in a direct line—they had put up a searchlight and an ack-ack (anti-aircraft) gun. This of course was a direct invitation to the German planes to put both out of action; but while it was there we were able to look up occasionally and see a plane caught in the searchlight's beams. On this particular night, however, a plane dropped a flare which lit up the whole countryside, just as we were going into the house. It was strikingly beautiful, but very dangerous. Half a mile is nothing to a bomber.

But that was not quite as close as the weapon that some enthusiastic soldiers put up in our garden. I looked through the window at the side of the house, and said to Mum, 'What are those men doing?' She came to look, and said something like, 'Oh, heavens, it's a gun!' They were positioning it to defend the vehicle convoy that had been going through for a while. But it was a very tempting target for any passing plane, and I imagine we were all rather thankful when it was dismantled.

At the height of the blitz on London, our parents got us up one night in May. Sleepily, we went to the open front door. Across from us stood Box Hill, dark against the sky. And as far as you could see it the sky was crimson. 'What is it?' I said. And Mum simply said, 'London's burning!'

I'm sure there must have been many times during those years when she was deeply worried about Dad being in London every weekday; in addition he did one night in ten as a second lieutenant in the Ministry of Health Home Guard, on guard at times—as we didn't discover until we read his memoirs—outside Winston Churchill's bunker. Whether it was blitzes or doodle-bugs or V2s, government had to continue unbroken, and I know Mum was sometimes very uneasy when he was home late. It could have been bombs in London or on the rail line, or simply a long delay while everyone sat in an almost totally dark train (only one blue globe overhead) until they had cleared rubble or whatever was the hold-up.

Throughout the war there was a ten-mile limit from the south coast, which meant that we could never go to the sea, which was about 30 miles away. You could only do that if you had a relative living there, or some equally good excuse. The whole of the southern region was a potential battle area. Just north of us, protecting London, there was that huge trench that went for miles—the tank trap.

Around, on the hills, there were army camps. The men would be brought down into Dorking for their time off, and the ones who were not content to drink all evening had to find something else to do. There were three cinemas at that time: the Embassy was a typical 1930s building, very modern. The interior décor was *art deco*, with enough glamour to satisfy us. Am I right in thinking that there was a cinema organ that rose out of the bowels of the building in garish colours and played during the interval? Or was that somewhere else? And there were not only the stalls, but an 'upstairs'—very swish if you could afford the money.

In the middle of the town there was the Regal. I suspect it had been converted from something else. It wasn't there for very long after the war started. Perhaps the clientele was seduced away from it by the glories of the Embassy. Up in South Street, right opposite the Methodist Church, was the third cinema, the Pavilion (Pav to the locals), which didn't have an upstairs and always seemed rather dusty, as if no one ever cleaned it. In time that too disappeared, but it was still there when we were married in 1948. I can remember being very impressed, at some point in the war, when Dad and Mum took us all to see something there—it cost ten shillings for five of us, because it was a Saturday afternoon, and so there were no cheap seats for kids. Ten shillings seemed an awful lot of money.

It's interesting to think, now that movies and all the technological developments are so much a part of our culture, that the first 'talkie' arrived about the time I was born, and colour later even than that. I think the first colour film I ever saw was *Snow White and the Seven Dwarfs;* later, *The Wizard of Oz.* And yet Mum and Dad had a projector, and someone, perhaps Uncle James, took some movies (black and white) of Pat and me at the seaside when we were probably only about 6 years old. We also had some reels of short commercial films: one of Charlie Chaplin, one of Felix the Cat, and another one I have now forgotten. So you can picture us, before the war, sitting in a darkened room with Dad turning the handle on the old projector (as with so much that is new, it seemed to break down quite a lot, and if the film got stuck and the projector light wasn't turned off quickly enough the film would begin to buckle), and laughing our heads off at Charlie's antics.

It's also interesting to realise that radio only came in when Derry was a small child, and that he built his own crystal set when he was quite young.

But the cinema didn't always help with the troops' pressing need for entertainment, and I fear quite a number of them simply drank the evening away. I can recall one night, after I had gone to bed, when I heard someone muttering and swearing across the road. I got up to see. It was a Canadian soldier, well over the limit, staggering home to his camp on Box Hill, having presumably missed the army lorry which would have taken him back without the effort. It's possible that, living in a teetotal family, this was the first drunken man I had seen.

The Methodist Church, after the evening service each Sunday, had a social session for any visiting troops who wanted church rather than pub—and there were a number of them who were missing what they had always had at home. Among them were two I remember: Ken Harris, who was later captured by the Italians and spent the rest of the war in a prison camp in Italy;

and Arnold Plummer, a Yorkshireman who later became a family friend when he married, and then settled in Dorking after the war.

When Dad went to lock the front door one evening at bedtime, he found two British soldiers curled up in the porch, fast asleep. He left them there and locked the inside door, and in the morning they had gone. Presumably they had missed the camp truck, too.

This makes an interesting point. In these days we are very wary of unknown people, starting with the 'stranger danger' learnt at school. This is such a pity. During the war the town was surrounded by strangers, all wearing battledress, all far from home, all at a loose end at the weekends. But I have no recollection that we were fearful. At fourteen and fifteen I used to walk through the town to the youth club without the least trepidation; and I don't remember anything more scary than a few wolf whistles or a couple of invitations to something unspecified. The nearest I ever came to having a problem with this huge influx of unattached men was being chased through Pippbrook Gardens, where the Council Offices were, by a soldier who was so drunk that I easily outran him. I could probably have knocked him over! It didn't strike any of us, even our parents, as being any kind of hazard.

One night, with everything closed up for the evening, there was a knock at the door. All day the trucks had been rolling past with troops going south. I opened the door, and standing on the doorstep, covered from head to foot in khaki, was my cousin Norman, Uncle Norman's eldest son, Pat's brother. He was on duty. What sort of coincidence would put him on duty right outside our door?

Mum brought him inside and he sat by the fire, took off his helmet, and immediately showed signs of going to sleep. I don't know how many hours he had been working, but he was exhausted. I imagine Mum gave him something to eat and drink, and after a while he got up and went back to his point duty. By the morning he had gone.

One reason why we had so many trucks, armoured cars, tanks and so on grinding past us was because one side of the bypass to the north of us, just over the railway bridge, had been taken over as a Canadian tank repair area. We were reduced to a one-lane road with a wide cycle track to one side. This hardly mattered, as during the war only specific drivers were allowed petrol. These were doctors, various kinds of officials and so on. Our friend Joan could have petrol because she was a government apiarist, and had to get round to the beehives regularly to collect the honey. Our car was laid up until after the war.

But the local boys got quite good at saying 'Got any gum, chum?' to the Canadians! And we got used to the rattle and roar of armoured vehicles, and to the mess they made of the kerbs. Tanks have a wide turning circle, and inevitably they would chew up the kerbstones. Opposite our house was a telephone box, rather close to the junction. This box was several times demolished by armoured cars; there is only a narrow slit for the drivers to see the road through, and they needed to know (which they didn't if they hadn't been before) that they had to make a wider turn than they were expecting.

On the last time it was knocked down (and not re-erected until much later) there was a young woman in the box, using the phone. The mess can be imagined. She was brought into our house by the soldiers, who used their emergency first aid packs to stop the bleeding from her legs, which was considerable. The ambulance came, and before long everything was back to normal—for us. We heard nothing about the casualty until about four months later, when the young lady arrived at the front door with a lovely bunch of bronze chrysanthemums for Mum. She was only just out of hospital, and wanted to thank us for helping her. She had had multiple lacerations to her legs from the breaking glass in the box.

We were not on any German list for bombing, so anything that fell in the area was accidental—either the plane was running out of time and needed to jettison its load, or it hadn't been able to get to its proper target.

I can remember the evening when we were sitting around after the air raid siren had gone, and in the distance we could hear the whistle of bombs falling. As I mentioned, a 'stick' of bombs was usually six, so we listened as they came nearer: one, two, three, four! It seemed likely that the next would be a bit too close for comfort. But when it fell, it was on the other side of us, and we breathed again. Unfortunately, the fourth one fell on a farm cottage garden about a mile from us towards London. We were told later that the father of the family had gone down into their shelter when the siren went, but his wife and family said they had had enough of it, and were staying in the house.

It was sheer bad luck that the bomb fell on the shelter and killed the man. I don't recall anyone else living that near to us being killed in a raid.

I had 'flu on one occasion when I would have been about 11 or 12. I was in my mother's bed during the day, feverish and not feeling good at all. As I lay there, staring at the wall, a plane swooped down and dropped a bomb on the railway line. This would have been about 250 yards from us, and it was an important position because two lines crossed there, one going north/south, and the other east/west. A bomb at the crossing would put two lines out of action at least for a while. As it happened, the bomb fell on the side of the line, and did very little damage. But I, in my fever, thought the sudden swaying of Mum's wardrobe was part of feeling a bit woozy (is that a word?), and I suppose I was lucky it didn't fall forward onto me.

These sporadic bomb incidents became a part of life, as did the warnings by the BBC from time to time of booby traps dropped by the German planes. We were told not to pick up something that looked like a fountain pen because it could explode, not to play with tinsel-like strips for the same reason. But 'show and tell'—known then as 'news'—could be quite intriguing. I recall the boy who brought the piece of shrapnel that had gone through his bedroom window and stuck in the wooden floor, and other similar souvenirs.

We were in the dining room one day, and I looked out of the window and said, 'What are those parachutes doing, Dad?' There were possibly three or four, and they were floating down well up the road from us, on what we called Little Ranmore, a small hilly area now overgrown with houses, but at that time a great place for children to play.

The police picked them up quickly—men from a shot down German plane. Sadly, one of them fell on the only bit of the hill that could kill him, where the kerbing for a road that had never got built was hidden by grass. His body was buried in the Dorking cemetery on Reigate Road.

We would occasionally see a low-loader lorry with the remains of a crashed plane being taken to some unspecified graveyard for planes; and sometimes they were German, with the big black cross on the side and wings. I think that, under the circumstances, we could be forgiven for wanting to cheer.

For a while I had a map on my bedroom wall to show me where the war was happening. It is probably a good thing, the Brits being island people with little concept of European distances, that we didn't realise how close everything was to us. The narrow strip of water—about 23 miles—between us and the continent was ludicrously small as a defence, and bombers starting off in French or other occupied territories were much too close for comfort. It was only long after the war, when I was looking at a map of Europe, that it dawned on me that we were no distance (especially in the age of flying) from Hitler's Germany. Coming to Australia confirmed me in that. It was particularly brought home to me many years later, while I was arranging my first visit to Australia, and was reminded that Perth was about 4000 kilometres from Sydney. 'As far as from London to Moscow', the QANTAS representative said.

I remember another map. It was fixed to the gate of the Dorking Council offices, and it showed Hitler's intentions for those parts of Europe he had not already vanquished; mainly us in the British Isles. Parts of the continent already overrun were in black, and the UK was shown with a date on it—the year he intended to overrun us, too. I think it was about 1943, so thank God it never happened. Though one might still wonder why a country that was so aggressively ready for war did not manage to invade a country that, as far as one can tell, was so unprepared. The British seem to believe whole-heartedly in the slogan: 'The English lose every battle but the last'! And, of course, we have always quoted history: 'England has never been invaded since William the Conqueror came in 1066'. And we intended to keep it that way.

Two blackout stories! The air raid warden came round one evening while Dad was out at church. He said there was a light showing from the front window. Mum rather doubted this—Dad had made blackout shields (not simply curtains) out of chipboard, so it was very unlikely that light could escape. She went outside to have a look, and there was a tiny chink of light at the top of the window. To see it one had to scramble through a bush that grew right up to the window and then peer upwards. Mum pointed out, rather scornfully, that any plane attracted by that light would have to fly below the window level. But the ARP man was adamant. There was a light showing, and that was a punishable offence. I expect Mum twiddled the blackout and he went away satisfied he had done his duty.

The other story was about the Evans family. Mr Evans was the Methodist minister, and his mother had come to stay with them. The family had gone to an evening meeting, and Mrs Evans senior was alone. There was a knock on the door and a 'very nice man', as she later described him, pointed out that there was light showing from one window. He went in with her and put it right, and stopped for a moment to chat.

When her family came home she told them. 'Such a nice man—a Mr Williams'. Her son said, 'Don't you know who that was? It was Dr Vaughan Williams, the composer. He's our air raid warden.'

VW was also, so I've heard, a member of the Heavy Rescue team, and delighted in sitting in the back of a truck, presumably going off to rescue something heavy! It's nice to think that during that same period he was still writing symphonies. What we would now call 'multi-tasking'.

6

One could go on for ages about wartime conditions. Those were the years when I was 10 to 16 years old, and one's approach to adult life is formed then. Much of what happened was tragic. But, as Shakespeare knew, tragedy and comedy are very close cousins, and there was laughter as well as grief. We learnt to 'make-do-and-mend'; we bought silk parachute panels, presumably salvaged from damaged goods, to make underclothes and nighties, we beat up milk and butter to make the fat go further; we bought strange fish, and sausages with minimal meat (and what was the rest of the filling? Probably not sawdust as was rumoured). We tried whale meat—too rich and oily and slightly fishy, we thought, and Mum didn't buy it again—though if the worst had happened and there was simply no other meat we might have had to—discovered odd vegetables like kohl rabi (though I don't know that I ever found out how that was spelt, and I've probably got it wrong now), and managed not to mourn the complete lack of bananas.

Inside the back door there was a sack for waste paper. On the street corners there were bins for waste food, which went for the pigs. Mustn't put kippers or onions in the pig-bin. They make the pork taste of—kippers and onions! We folded every piece of used wrapping paper, wound up every piece of string (and some of us still do it), and took our holidays 'at home'; this was not difficult, since there was nowhere we could go. On one occasion my father was deputed to buy new pyjamas for the three of us while he was in London. This meant the right number of coupons; but he managed to find the appropriate garments in the proper sizes, and came home with them on the train—three pairs of nice striped pyjamas, folded, and hanging without wrapping from his arm. No paper for wrapping goods, not even from quite a posh place like London!

And the war went on—and on. Because of the shortage of housing in towns like Dorking (every spare place would have been taken up by families who had moved out of London for safety, or perhaps had been in the blitz and lost everything) we had a succession of people living with us. Our house was, after all, fairly big, and by putting Rosemary and me into one bedroom we made space for others.

The first one was Dennis Phippen. Mum had never had someone living with us who would be paying for accommodation and food, and she was quite nervous until he arrived. Dennis was a very mature 19 from the Bristol area (actually his home town was Chew Magna, a name which I thought enormously funny); he was a competent church organist, as my father was, and he was friendly—I personally thought over-friendly—with Mabel, who was also an organist. An over-supply of organists, I suspect. They didn't actually fight to get to the manuals; probably had a roster to keep the peace. Dad did rather resent (I suspect) anyone else playing 'his' instrument, though I am sure he would have denied this. Mum once said (in a mildly spiteful moment) that she thought he only went to church for the organ! This, of course, was absolutely not the case; he was always to my knowledge an office bearer in the church hierarchy, and our family life was geared to run smoothly around church requirements.

At the age of eleven I was seriously smitten by Dennis—who, incidentally was always Mr Phippen to us until we all grew up: how things have changed. Unfortunately, he usually made me feel slightly stupid—he had a lordly manner that daunted me not a little. But I loved him from a distance, and when the war caught up with him and he went into the RAF, later becoming an instructor in Texas before being sent to Burma towards the end of the war, I wrote to him on the strange air letters that were available for the armed services. These were on special paper which was then photographed so that many could be sent in the space of one. At the receiving end they were then enlarged, and arrived by normal mail, having first been censored. If the writer had been ill-advised enough to write something which the authorities regarded as breaching security it would be 'blue-pencilled' out by the censor—and how infuriating not to know what the secret was!

So I awaited the letters from 'Mr Phippen', and meanwhile we struggled through our own branch of the war. It is interesting that I, as a young person, never received from the adult world any real idea that the end of the war might be defeat. It was clearly a possibility for several months after the collapse of France; but it wasn't something that was acceptable, so we didn't accept it. The blitzes on the major cities, which were intended to soften us up and strike terror into our hearts, seemed only to strengthen the intention to win at any cost. It's easy for me to say that, because I was in a relatively safe place; but there were many opportunities for city populations to collapse under the constant strain, and it simply didn't happen.

What it must have been like for those people, one can only imagine. Endless nights spent either in shelters or in the Underground stations, where there were stacks of metal bunks lined up each day ready to be put out at night for sleeping on; shop fronts in central London with boarded up windows, 'Open as Usual', or on one shop 'More open than usual': the sense of humour somehow kept going. An object lesson, I think, for anyone going through a traumatic time: keep smiling and see the funny side whenever possible.

After Dennis left for his war service, we made room for others. Among the ones I clearly remember are Wendy and her mother, who had lived in London. Mama was an officer in the Girls' Life Brigade, which I joined when I was about 12. Wendy was already a member when they arrived. Somehow the appropriate uniform was made, regardless of shortages, and I was rather proud of myself. Our branch was associated with our Methodist Church, and I remained a member until Mama and Wendy moved on elsewhere.

So many lives disrupted! So many people making the best of it.

Meanwhile, school went on. 62 staff changes during the war, I was later told. It must have been very difficult for the administration to keep us all educated; and probably there were better educations available somewhere. But with staff, students and parents often on the move it was quite amazing that the school maintained an air of normal life. We certainly had some odd-bods as teachers, from women just out of college to elderly maths teachers emerging out of retirement 'for the duration'.

That phrase, 'for the duration', took over from that other wait-and-see phrase, 'when the boat comes in'. And there was: 'When shall we do such-and-such, Dad?' 'After the war.' That was the other delaying tactic! Quite useful for parents, but infuriating for children. Of course, once the war was over things would not immediately return to normal. But we didn't yet know that. We were waiting for the one great announcement: that the Continent had been invaded by Allied troops. It seemed a long time coming.

Dad and I were standing in the garden one day not long before Easter 1944 when a whole squadron of army troop-carrying planes went over, trailing troop-carrying gliders. I imagine they were going towards the coast to be ready for use on the Continent. We were about to go for an Easter holiday to Colwyn Bay—being well to the north there were currently no restrictions on visiting—and Dad wondered if it would be wiser not to go in case we couldn't get back again. In fact, we did go, and spent a happy time in new surroundings—but the consciousness of what was likely to happen soon on the 'Second Front' was always there.

I recall that Dennis was somewhere in the north at the time, and he said he would fly over the house we were staying in and waggle his wings at us. We kept a look-out, and sure enough a small plane flew over and waggled! We stood below and waved tea towels and anything else we could lay our hands on. A moment of real excitement, to think that we actually knew the person who was flying the plane. Usually a plane was a rather anonymous thing.

Back home then, and the next hazard was the V1s, otherwise known as doodle-bugs or buzz bombs. That's one of the secret weapons for the British: the ability to turn everything into a joke. V1s are nasty things, sneaky because they seem to have gone past you, but they can turn round when the engine cuts out, and the thing that you were safe from is a threat once more. Calling them doodle-bugs seems to make them less frightening. We did the same with Hitler, who was by any standards a frightening person. We sang silly songs about him: '*When the Fuehrer says we is the master race, then we heil, heil, right in the Fuehrer's face*', (accompanied by rude noises after each 'heil'). And '*Run rabbit, run,*' which was really about Hitler. Reducing him to a rabbit was good propaganda. I wonder if he knew. I bet no one would have been prepared to tell him! Then there was Noel Coward's satirical song, '*Don't let's be beastly to the Germans*', which had probably put him on a Nazi black list.

I think I must have been one of the first to hear a V1 go over. Early one summer morning I heard overhead what seemed to be a plane with engine trouble. This was a sound we had occasionally experienced as a machine—ours or theirs—made its crippled way back to base.

I ran into my parents' room just as I heard a big bang, distant but still unmistakeable. 'I've just heard a plane crash!' We all wondered where it had come down.

At school that morning there were rumours everywhere. It was a German plane; it was a pilotless plane (we thought this was far-fetched); it was a pilotless plane full of poison gas! And so on. (And the poison theory was soon proved wrong).

It had come down a few miles away, near the village of Newdigate, a rural area with sparse dwellings and plenty of open countrywide to explode in. Sadly, as these nasty creatures began to come over thicker and faster, it was the close-packed areas of suburban London that bore the brunt of this new form of warfare.

But it did seem at last as if maybe the war would be over within the foreseeable future. Many wars have gone on for much longer, but there was, I think, something about World War 2, including as it did almost everywhere one could find on a map, that made it seem all-pervading. There is about any overwhelming situation that feeling that it is endless; and it is difficult to see to the end, when that end is still obscure.

There were still the even nastier V2s to deal with. These approached super-sonically, and the result was that the explosion came before the dreaded warning sound that other bombs made. My father told me that these were truly frightening; an entire house could be blown up with no warning, and only then would one hear the bomb's arrival. Too late for whoever was in the house at the time; though, who knows, maybe it was better not to know.

When these beasts arrived, however, we three children were up in Salford with Grandma Rothwell. I had spent several hours one night leaning out of my window, watching the V1s fly over. At fifteen, I suppose, I was a bit more aware of the imminence of death and destruction than younger children. At any rate, that night really scared me, and in the morning I told my parents that I had spent much of the night under the bed.

The way they exchanged glances made me feel that they had already made 'contingency plans' for just such a situation; within no time they had us ready to go north to Grandma, having rung her to say we were on our way; and we were on the train to Waterloo Station before we could turn round or protest!

My father later contacted the headmaster and told him we would not be finishing the term. No great loss academically, because there were only about ten days left of the summer term anyway. But very odd to be going off on what would be more of a holiday than anything else while everyone else was still at school.

The trip north was memorable. We arrived at Waterloo Station and went into the Underground (the Tube) to get to Euston Station, from where we would go to Manchester and be met by Uncle Tom. But the air raid siren went off as we were going down, and when that happened the Tube was shut down for safety. So we started going up again, to get to the bus stop in York Street, next to Waterloo. At that point, a V1 dropped on the station roof above that same bus stop. The explosion was horrific. Plaster and choking dust started falling from the ceiling of the Underground, and there was a sudden panic among the crowd, as people began to fear that the ceiling would fall in on us.

We were stopped in our tracks, most fortunately, by two American soldiers, who took charge and ordered us to stand still and not push. They did a good job, because panic is a bigger killer than almost anything else; and anyone who knows the areas underground at Waterloo near the elevators would understand how dangerous it would be for people to push and shove in their panic. It would be all too easy to crush each other; and this did indeed happen on some occasions during a raid. A sad and very terrifying way to die.

However, all was well for us on this occasion, and we emerged, dusty but unharmed, to catch a bus at the front of the building and make our way to Euston. As we passed the end of York Street we could see the bodies being taken away in ambulances. That could so easily have been us; just a few minutes either way meaning life or death.

We were well trained in keeping our mouths shut in case the enemy should learn anything through our careless talk—which, as the posters told us, costs lives! But Philip was only ten years old, and he had just been through what probably seemed to him an exciting experience. When we got on the train for Manchester he was ready to talk to anyone, and we were in a carriage with two businessmen. To my suspicious mind—at 15—they could well have been spies. I was furious with Philip because he was telling them all about how we had been at Waterloo Station when a doodle-bug fell on it, and we were going to stay with our grandma in Manchester. No amount of glaring would stop him. In the end good sense told me that the details of where the bomb had fallen was common knowledge, and I relaxed. But I had noticed that he and Rosemary both had black sooty rings around their nostrils from the ancient dust in the station, and I was old enough to be self-conscious about my appearance, so for the rest of the journey I probably worried about that instead.

We were ten weeks with Grandma; for a short while Mum joined us there, but I think she really wanted to be with my father, who was still in London every working day, and still vulnerable to those dreadful V2s. Thankfully, the bombs stopped because, at last, the long-awaited Second Front—otherwise known as the invasion of Europe—had started in June.

June 6th, 1944! I don't suppose any of us old enough to remember that date will ever forget it. We eventually heard that all kinds of false information had been leaked to the Germans. It seems that they did not really expect us to attack on the Normandy coast.

The sense of excitement, of sheer relief, was enormous. We listened to every available news broadcast. We followed every map in the newspapers. And we fully expected it to be all over very soon. But it was a bit like a convalescence after a long and debilitating illness: it seemed to take forever. It was a final battle that contained within itself many secondary battles, which have gone down in history with their own stories to be told.

And as the Allies slowly and with determination pushed on into the heart of Europe we became aware of what we had really been fighting for. Names like Belsen and Dachau began to figure in the news, and pictures unlike any we had ever seen were shown on news films and in the papers. They were sickening! Just looking at them made one feel ashamed. That any government, and especially from a country such as Germany, which had once stood proud for its gifts to civilisation, could perpetrate evils of such monstrous cruelty, was unbelievable. But one had to believe it. The proofs were there.

For some reason that I don't recall I went alone to see the newsreel about the opening of one of the death camps. It may have been Dachau, I don't remember, and it hardly matters, because the picture was the same in each of them: Treblinka, Auschwitz, you name it, they were all scenes of ultimate horror. All around me at the Embassy cinema, where I had seen Astaire and Rogers dance, wept over Rebecca, loved Olivier—everywhere were people in shock, some crying openly, some having to leave because it was too much. Far too much! I remembered Clare. I learned later that her mother died in Auschwitz. How can you come to terms with that?

I stayed to the end, and it was one of those moments in life that will never be forgotten. Nor can it easily be forgiven. What it did to the young soldiers, well tried in war, who went into the camps and had to deal with what they saw, I cannot imagine. I do recall that an American officer, faced with what he had found, with piles of naked corpses lying rotting where they had been thrown, rounded up the people, especially the mayor and officials of the town nearby, and made them walk through the camp to see what had been done while they lived no distance away. There were so many who said, 'we never knew it was happening'. But it's very hard to believe that. One can forgive the fact that everyone in the Nazi era lived in fear of retribution if they fell out of line; but some things are, I fear, unforgivable, and in any case it is not for us to forgive—it is for those against whom this crime was committed to do so if they can.

I find it interesting that the novel *The Mortal Storm* by Phyllis Bottome was written just a few years after Hitler came to power, and well before the beginning of WWII. The story concerns a German family in which the father is Jewish and the mother Aryan. It is clear, reading it, that the author—and, one presumes, others who had their eyes open to what was happening—was very well aware of the racial and political dangers at that time in Germany.

If she recognised the signs, how could people living in the shadow of the swastika not be aware? Having said that, I have to make the point that in Britain (and now in Australia) we have not in recent days known the kind of fear that makes good people shut their eyes to bad things.

And having written *that*—I am disturbed every time I see a Nazi news film with its wildly enthusiastic crowds, or a shop front with the dreaded 'J' painted on it while its proprietor is being insulted and abused in full view of people who managed not to see what was being done in their name.

Probably there will always be the differences that turn some of us off other nationalities—just as one cannot expect to like everyone one meets in life. But racial abuses and hatred engendered by governments as a policy must never be tolerated. Somehow we have to find the courage to speak out when we see this happening.

It's worth remembering that Hitler, if he had wished, could have saved much of the ultimate devastation of German cities by acknowledging defeat. Tragically, he just went underground into his bunker and allowed the country he had led to destruction to suffer on his behalf. So the Allies hammered their way across from the west towards Berlin; and the Russians, equally determined to get their pound of flesh, battled into Germany from the east. I still find the politics of this situation depressing to think about. Europe was about to be carved up by the victors, and the end result of that would be decades of suffering for millions. Berlin was neatly divided into sectors among the conquering nations. And we tried to remember how it used to be, before All That!

But things were never going to be the same again. For years, it seemed, people who had been released from death camps, soldiers who had been devastatingly defeated and whose homes had been blown to glory, so-called 'stateless people' whose only fault might have been that all their documentation had been lost as a result of war, wandered around Europe looking desperately for a nation that would accept them. They became known as 'displaced persons'—or DPs. Personally, I found this aspect of peace very hard to adjust to. The Europe that one sees today, buildings beautifully restored, the sun shining on gleaming rivers, ancient monuments skilfully maintained—this is not the Europe that I recall from my mid-teens. But I take my hat off to those dedicated people of many nations who set about making the continent a place worth living in once more.

VE Day (Victory in Europe) was celebrated with great excitement all over the country; but London was the place to be on that day. On the day after—VE+1—my parents and we three children, plus my friend Ann, who lived on the slopes of Leith

Hill, made our way by train to be a part of the celebrations. I don't remember many details of it, but I do remember very clearly being part of the crowd outside Buckingham Palace, shouting for the King to come out on the balcony. And suddenly, there he was, with the Queen and the two Princesses, waving as we cheered and yelled and got rid of a lot of our wartime stresses. And then the door opened again, and out came Winston Churchill, black hat and cigar and V sign—and if he ever feared that we would not acknowledge him as hero of the decade, he knew then that he had won his place in history as far as we were concerned. What a day! Sadly, the only way one can fully appreciate something like that is to have first gone through the hell of war.

I also remember that the gardens outside the palace were full of tulips when we arrived. By the time we had expressed our emotions to the full, the poor old tulips were a trampled mess, the final victims of Hitler's war.

Living as British people do on the edge of the continent, we were more involved with the European theatre of war. (That is an odd phrase, I always think. As if the whole dreadful business of killing and being killed is some great piece of drama being acted out—for whose benefit? I can't imagine). But once peace was declared in Europe we were able to look to the far eastern struggle and watch with horror as Japan paid the full price for its own atrocities. There is always discussion, sometimes heated, about whether or not the atom bombs should have been dropped on Hiroshima and Nagasaki, just as there is about the fire-bombing of Dresden in Germany. Personally, although I hate the fact that so many apparently innocent people got caught up in these raids, I cannot get past the other fact that in Germany and Japan there were people who cared nothing at all for the countries they were overrunning. Both those nations carried out the most abominable practices on the folk they conquered, and it is hard to see that they had much room for argument when their own countries were subjected to the horrors of war. One can only hope it will never happen again.

But as one looks around the world today, in the first and second decades of the twenty-first century, one sees the same evil practices being carried out on innocent victims. The fact that they are being done on a smaller scale does not absolve the perpetrators of these dictatorships from the results of their savagery. As I am writing, Libya is apparently finally coming under new rule, though Gaddafi has not yet been located and removed. But I really have to wonder whether things will improve for the Libyans. How can they implement democracy when they have had no knowledge for many years, if ever, of how it works? We shall see.

Anyway—back in 1945 there was a brave new world waiting. And the first thing the good citizens of Britain did was to vote Churchill out of power! It may well have been the best thing to do—I don't know. Certainly he was a great war leader. But I wouldn't have wanted to be in his household on the night of the election when he knew for sure that, for all he had done in the past 6 years, he was no longer wanted at the helm. I bet Clementine—Mrs C—had to keep her lips zipped while the storm raged. And one can't help feeling sorry for a man who had given so much, and was all at once told he wasn't needed any more.

He returned as Prime Minister a few years later, but his time had been from 1939 to 1945. Cometh the hour, cometh the man! Thank God for him. I seriously doubt if we would have survived without him.

7

L ife went on. I met a boy, Ray, for whom I immediately fell! And I have to say, all these years later, that he was a delightful person, 18 to my 16, and we were, as it is possible to be at that age, in love. I don't doubt that this gave my mother some bad moments. But she need not have worried. Ray was the perfect gentleman, and I was very safe in his hands. Plenty of kissing, but nothing to upset a mother. He was a nice-looking lad, rather like Danny Kaye, which naturally helped. What was really bothering her was that he had just come out of hospital having been treated for tuberculosis; and as I was notorious for my almost annual attacks of bronchitis, some of which were very serious in those pre-antibiotic days, she was clearly disturbed in case I caught the disease. As far as he or I or anyone knew, he was cured, but it would obviously be a concern for her.

For eight months, from July 1945 (I met him at the school sports day, at which he was a visitor) to March 1946, we were almost inseparable. I probably spent more time with him than with my family. And—if you can believe it in these free-and-easy days—I was reported to my mother by a school teacher who saw us walking hand-in-hand down the street. I was warned about my unacceptable behaviour—but it didn't stop us going walking up Box Hill, along the River Mole, and planning a sort of fairy-tale future together (which I knew in my heart was never going to happen).

Because only vital food was being brought in by the Merchant Navy ships, there had inevitably been shortages. One of these was bananas! These had to be brought from overseas, probably the West Indies, and during the war no one would want men to risk horrible deaths just so that we could have bananas. There are two things I recall about that time. One was the junior girl at school who had a group of other girls around her at break time. I went over to see what it was about. She was holding a small *blackened* banana on her hand, something that today one would immediately throw in the bin. The girls were staring at it with wonder: we hadn't seen any kind of bananas for several years. While we watched, she removed the skin and ate the fruit, bruised as it was. And we envied her! Her brother was in the navy.

The other story is from shortly after the war, when these fruits returned, in very limited numbers. They were only allowed for under-eighteens. Ray and I were with my mother and she had a very few of them. She gave me one and then asked Ray if he would like one (which was a really generous act under the circumstances). He said, 'No, thank you, Mrs Blake. I'm eighteen'. I wonder if I gave him some of mine? I don't remember.

Ray more or less moved out of my life (against his wishes) after my mother finally told me that it had to stop. I was devastated; but I could probably see some justice in it. I told him it was over, and that was that. But I came very near to a breakdown, and I have never forgotten that it is perfectly possible to be genuinely in love at that age. At the same time, I am thankful that our understanding of family, of parental control, and—if it's not a rude word today—obedience, was so strong. I knew I was too young, that it was not a relationship that would last, so ultimately there wasn't much future in it. And I knew that my parents were wiser than I was, not being blinded by love, and that I needed to listen to them. I wish more young people today felt the same.

Ray eventually married; sadly, he died at the age of 31. Whether it was TB or something else I don't know. I remember him with affection and my memories are happy ones.

Other things were beginning to stir in my life story, though at the time I wasn't aware of them. My parents were hospitable people, and this was how, one Sunday, I went through one of life's embarrassing moments: my mother invited the headmaster and his wife to afternoon tea. This is the sort of thing to be avoided when one is at the sensitive stage of knowing that you are not yet sophisticated, and not quite sure what to do about it. One tends to solve the problem by either being sullenly quiet (which means trouble afterwards from parents, who would have liked you to shine), or overly friendly, which would not be acceptable by the headmaster, and lead to those hot moments of alarm when remembered later that night in bed.

And of course that was not the end of it. They then had to invite us back! And that was even worse, because Philip was there, and an eleven-year-old boy cannot be trusted to say the right things—but you can bet he'll say the wrong ones!

So we went to the rather lovely house in Mickleham where Trefor Jones and his family lived. And as far as I know I didn't do anything outrageous. But this was to be a momentous day for me, even though it would be a long time before I realised it.

First, Mr Jones, being quite jolly (which in itself was a bit daunting) said that he hoped I had done well in my mock school certificate exams—the results were not yet out. This was April. I interpreted it as a threat with a smile—it meant I was expected to do well, and I was immediately certain that I had failed miserably. (In fact, I hadn't—except in maths!) Then he said, 'Well, Hebe, you'll be pleased to know that we are to have a full-time music teacher next year.' I can still hear his rich Welsh voice as he said it. He told us that this was a young man of 29, with a wife and baby, who was still in the Merchant Navy as a radio officer, but would be released for the September term (the beginning of the UK school year). Dr Vaughan Williams, who was a governor of the school, had interviewed him and said we should 'get him if you can'.

It's interesting that I remember that episode so well when others have disappeared from memory. But understandable when you realise that during the war period the teaching of music had been anything from scrappy to abysmal. For quite a while there was only a music teacher for half the week, and the school, being at that stage without any musical tradition, was for me, and for the few others who cared about classical music, something of a desert. I recall one elderly, and quite eminent, musician when I was about eleven. He had us singing songs such as 'The snowy-breasted pearl', a dangerous choice of words with 11-year old boys in the class, so there was much giggling; and my all-time favourite for having the whole class almost speechless with suppressed laughter—it was about the possible invasion of England by Napoleon.

'And should their flat bottoms in darkness come o'er . . .'

No one bothered to explain to us that the flat bottoms were barges, being used to carry troops.

By the time we had our tea with the head, I was in the interesting situation where, apparently being the only pianist— at least at senior level—capable of sight-reading, I was the accompanist for a couple of days a week at the daily morning assembly. I've been trying to recall how this came about, but I have no idea at this distance. Surely I didn't volunteer! Playing for about 600 people two or three times a week was quite challenging to begin with, but I got used to it. I would go to the head's office before assembly and he would tell me the hymn number; then I would go to open the piano, get ready and find the hymn—and in would come Mr Maunders, the caretaker, who would proceed to dust the piano all around me. I always wondered why he waited until it was almost time for assembly before doing this, but I never got round to asking him. He was elderly and rather morose, and certainly wasn't going to chat. I wonder if he hated kids!

So I was really pleased to know that we would have a full-time teacher; and probably quite glad that he would not be yet another old guy—there had been quite a number of those during the war, because all the younger men were out there fighting. But little did I know . . . !

Meanwhile, I had the last months of my Upper Vth schooling to complete, with School Certificate exams at the end of it. I was doing eight subjects: English, English Lit., French, History, Geography, Domestic Science, Art, Maths. By this time, Art was my main interest, though I went through the usual teenage confusion over my future. The only subject I felt really uncertain about was maths. I actually liked it, but it was always done too quickly for me—I no sooner learnt about an equation or how to divide a circle into bits than we were off into a new area of knowledge. As a result I never got to really *know* what I was supposed to be doing. I still maintain that if I had had two years to do one year's maths I would probably have done quite well.

I later—much later—discovered that Mr Woodman, the maths master, was brought in a year or two before to bring us up to standard for the exams. This meant that the bright young mathematicians were in their element, whizzing ahead, checking his work on the board (at his request: 'check me, check me!' he would say), and leaving those of us who were not quite so brainy in that department to wallow hopelessly in their wake. This, of course, was another effect of the wartime 'fillers-in' on the staff, who never quite got us to where we should be.

In the end, I passed in all my subjects, distinction in Art, credits in all but maths and—strange this, considering that three years later I was married and keeping house—domestic science. I think I was the first in my year group to have to put into practice the strange rituals we had learnt upstairs in the DomSci room.

And some of them were really strange. We had started on laundry and cleaning in our first year. No one was going to give us actual food to play with. So I learnt how to make starch (none of your bought rubbish for our teacher, whose name, oddly enough, was Mrs Mutton). Among other things, you have to grate into the starch mixture enough candle wax to cover a sixpence. Bet you didn't know that! It's to make the iron go smoothly over the material.

We were told that you should never wash woollen garments in boiling water. The girl who forgot this when the first exams came up, and had brought as her woollen garment a vest belonging to her baby brother, was totally humiliated when it emerged about the size of a very small doll, and felted beyond resuscitation.

Ironing was a skill we had to learn. No matter that we had done it at home for our mothers—there was a way to do it, and no other would do. I learnt to use a goffering iron. I asked why. Our new teacher, no longer Mrs Mutton, said we had to know how to iron the frills on a servant's apron and cap! The only use I ever saw for this gadget was doing the frills on choirboys' and girls' collars. But I feel privileged to know that at one time I actually knew what it was and how to use it.

I think we had two electric irons up in that room: plus a gas iron, and a whole line-up of flat irons. Only the pushiest girls ever got the electric irons. So I learnt another new skill: how to operate a flat iron. These have to be heated, and we had a metal heater with sloping ledges on two sides where the irons were stood while warming. Once they are hot enough—and you test them by spitting on them; if they sizzle they are ready to go—you take them to a sand tray and run them over it until the surface is smooth.

'Why can't we have electric irons?' someone asked.

'Because you may end up living in the country where there is no electricity.'

I don't think any of us accepted that. Anyway, there was a war on! The final answer to anything from 1939 to 1945.

Later in the war, the school having an allowance of rations for cookery classes, we started to learn the differences between baking and roasting and boiling, and we started on scone making. I will confess now that I have never made a batch of scones I was proud of. We had 80 minute sessions for cookery, and it took all of that to make the scones; this was partly because we had to take the mixture at every single step to show to the teacher. So there would be queues of girls waiting to have their scones validated, with the result that, once married, I was astonished that it doesn't take 80 minutes to make and bake scones.

The general idea was that we should take home the things we had made. This would help our mothers to provide the evening meal. They didn't unfortunately reckon with the mob of hungry wolves waiting at the bottom of the stairs—our male classmates. 'What have you made? Oh, good! I'll have some of that!' We were lucky to take anything home.

We came to our final School Certificate exams. We were about sixteen and reasonably competent when it came to creating simple meals. The previous week we had to make a timetable and menu for what we would produce at the exam, when there would be an external examiner prowling as we worked. Probably timetabling was the most valuable thing I learnt from those classes—the ability to work out when you must start to prepare food so that everything is ready at the same time. Not everyone can do it.

I decided I would make lentil soup. I don't remember what else was on my menu, because the making of that soup became not only fraught but ridiculous. The teacher said she would put the lentils into a bowl to soak in the larder, and I could come in first thing in the morning and prepare them. Why she didn't tell me to do it myself I cannot imagine. Surely it was a part of the exam to know what quantity of lentils was required? But I didn't argue.

So when I went to the larder on the exam morning and found a bowl almost overflowing with more lentils than I could possibly have required if I'd been preparing a meal for fifty people, I was a bit alarmed. On each table there was a bowl for each girl to put discarded items in: potato peelings, pea pods, anything. Nothing could be thrown away. And the examiner was wandering about and peering into every bowl suspiciously.

So what was I to do with my mass of lentils? If I put them in the bowl I would lose marks. If I told the examiner that I hadn't put them in the water myself I would lose marks. Over in the corner there was a large bin for other waste, and every few minutes I would take a couple of handfuls of lentils and drop them in—when the examiner was at the other side of the room. Eventually I got the wretched things down to a reasonable quantity; and as far as I recall I produced an adequate meal.

But it did occur to me that I only just passed in spite of doing everything else right. I have sometimes wondered if the examiner cottoned on to what I was doing, possibly because I was the only girl making lentil soup. What a giveaway! Guilty as charged!

A minor scandal at some time about then was about the DomSci teacher, who was using the cookery classes' allocations of food to make cakes for the male staff members. I seem to remember dimly that she disappeared soon after. I also remember that she had false curls, which we dearly hoped would fall into the soup.

Entering the VIth Form was a different thing altogether. My subjects were Art, English, French and 19th century European history. This was the first academic year after the war ended, and teachers, mainly male, were coming back from their wartime service. Mr Bradshaw, who was one of them, was our Form master; Mr Hayter, teaching Science, was another. I sometimes wondered, later, when I got to know them at a different level, just how weird it was coming straight out of the armed forces to the nitty-gritty and often pathetically silly atmosphere of the Staff rooms. And, of course, dealing with young people instead of the serving men and women they had been used to for four, five, even six years.

But I was too much taken up with my new syllabus to worry about them. Suddenly, instead of having information shoved into me, which I then had to regurgitate, I was expected to *think*. I still admire the way in which these teachers whom I had known in the middle school adapted their teaching methods to our woolly little brains! I can even recall two of the essays I had to write in those first weeks; one for Miss Macaulay (Mac: and what a good name for a history teacher) was a resumé of European history in the 19th century. It was enough to put you off history for ever. But for some reason it didn't, though I know I really struggled with it.

Miss Barter presented us with copies of Bernard Shaw's 'St Joan', which we read around the class. Then she gave us our homework: *Shaw uses St Joan as a stick with which to beat the church.* I didn't understand a word! I wonder if my father helped me with it. These were no one-page answers to given questions. These were *essays!* And after a couple of weeks of being bombarded with such things we all slowly came to terms with the fact that we were now Big People.

That was September 1945. In October the long-awaited music teacher appeared. We later discovered that when he came he was still technically in the Merchant Navy, and had been given leave to start the job that was waiting for him.

And so Derry arrived on the scene—and how much of a shock to the system would that be, after five years of dodging first U-boats in the North Atlantic convoys and then E-boats in the North Sea? Add to that that he had not been to a co-educational school, and had spent those five war years writing songs for Nancy, his wife, or occasionally managing to play a piano in, for instance, a South American port while the ship was loading. He would find a music shop and ask if he could use one of their instruments. And I imagine that when they heard him they agreed at once.

But when you take a dedicated pianist away from his piano there'll be trouble eventually. I think it would have been extremely hard for him. Doubly so because in general there was seldom anyone on the ships, officers or crew, who would have understood him.

There was much chatter, especially among the girls, as to what his name was. Notices began to go up on the notice boards, signed D. Moore Morgan (and later, when we knew him better, DMM). Morgan: must be Welsh. The only Welsh name we could come up with was Dai. So for the first weeks he was Dai Moore Morgan.

It was my day for playing the piano when he showed up. I went to get the hymn number from the Headmaster, and on the other side of the room, back to the window—which made it difficult to see his face—was our new music man. Trefor Jones introduced us, and said, 'Hebe plays for assembly two or three times during the week—and I think we could let her go on doing that, couldn't we?' All said in that lovely Welsh voice. Derry, with no opportunity of saying 'no', said 'yes'. I took the hymn number and went to open the piano.

That afternoon we had a class with him for the first time. I wonder if he was nervous. He walked into the room, wearing an academic gown such as no one else on the staff had, went to the ancient (must have been pre-war) radiogram, and stared at it. Then he said, 'Does anyone know how to make this thing work?'

One of the boys got up and showed him which knobs to turn, and we had a music appreciation class, about which I have no memory at all.

When I got home for tea, my mother said, 'Well, so what's this music man like?'

I laughed. 'Radio officer? He didn't even know how to use the radiogram!' So ended my first encounter with Derry. Not really memorable, except that for some reason I do remember it.

In the way in which it is possible to be friendly—if not exactly a friend—with a teacher, we were friends eventually. Because I was one of the few students who really cared about classical music, and the only one at that point who could play the piano adequately, we worked together a fair amount. And Derry was certainly a whirlwind. Whether we were gleaning the benefits of his years without active musicianship I don't know. It's not impossible. Anyway, he came in like a gust of wind, and carried us with him. Rosemary and I have discussed this a few times since he died, and neither of us can tell how he did it. He was faced with a school which had not been active musically within my memory (1939 onwards). There were girls who would be happy to join a choir, for example—not surprising, he was good-looking and vibrant with energy, and several had crushes on him.

But the boys were another kettle of fish entirely. So how he got a mixed, 4-part choir going so quickly I really don't know, even though I was there and saw him do it. One thing that helped considerably was that every class had a 40-minute music lesson every week, and so everyone, whether dedicated singers or not, got to know the music.

What it was like for the rest of the school, since the music room was not sound-proofed, can only be imagined, and particularly for the other teachers, who would be able not only to hear the music, but also his stentorian bass or tenor, according to need. His greatest supporters would not claim he had anything other than a 'useful' voice. It would drag us through anything!

The first major thing we did was a ballad by Stanford: *Phaudrig Crohoore*. This is an Irish story about love and loss, and those who sang it would remember the description of Phaudrig: *'for his arm was as stout as another man's thigh. 'Twas Phaudrig was great'*. I do recall that the main thing that struck me about this was that it took *14 minutes to perform*. We had never been trusted with anything longer than a part-song.

Within months we sang *Phaudrig*, and I have vague memories that at Speech Day that year (which could have been only months after he had joined the school) we sang *The heavens are telling* from Haydn's Creation (with the solos in the middle provided by members of the choir); at some point neither Rosemary nor I can remember, we performed *Zadok the priest* by Handel. These involved me as choir accompanist, and I can recall my sweaty hands as I began the long introduction in arpeggios in the latter work.

If this was not surprising enough for us at that time, the mind boggles at doing three nights of Handel's Messiah in March 1947, a bare 17 months after his arrival in Dorking. But that's what we did. I discovered the mysteries of continuo playing, and we had what you might call a 'scratch' orchestra—in some areas very scratchy! He even found someone locally to play double bass. Strings were some parents, some semi-professional players and some students: and I don't have any memory of brass and wind players, though I'm sure there were some.

By this time there were probably over a hundred students in the choir. No auditions; you came because you wanted to, and nobody checked on you if you weren't there. There would be lunch time recitals (I gave one, rather badly—some Chopin); and lunch time rehearsals when we got closer to a concert, as well as the regular Tuesday practice after school.

Before we knew it there was not only a Senior Choir, but a junior one as well. And at some point the Madrigal Society was born. It made a full load!

Following Messiah, a few months later, we sang several movements from Brahms' *German Requiem*. And my recollection of it is that it wasn't at all bad. I was again accompanist, and the Brahms' Requiem is not a simple thing to play. But I hammered through somehow, and we had added another triumph to our repertoire.

I was in my element! It's a wonder that I got any other work done. But in spite of all distractions, my Higher Certificate results were not too bad. At least I passed everything.

Looking back from this great distance, I am doubly astonished that he was able to put so much energy into his work. Those five years of war were not, for him, only a survival from death at sea; he was also deeply affected by the fact that Nancy, his wife, was suffering from tuberculosis, and spent some time in a sanatorium on the Northumberland moors. So when he came home on leave he couldn't be quite sure whether he would be able to see her or not. They were living with his parents 'for the duration', and like many other serving men he would always have in the back of his mind that his family was also at risk—from bombing and food shortages. Perhaps even from invasion.

All that was in 1942, two years after they were married. But the cure seemed to work, and within a year or so Nancy was very keen to have a child. His mother once told me that 'she was very bonny when she was expecting', and I'm sure they all felt that they had come safely through a very trying time. Cynthia was born in May, 1944; sadly, it was not long before the hopes of Nancy's recovery began to fade.

Nancy and Cynthia came from Newcastle to join Derry in Dorking when the baby was about 18 months old. They lived where they could, at one time in two rooms in someone's house—and try as I may, I cannot see Derry coping with that. He needed room to move! Eventually, through the good offices of the headmaster, they found a flat, one of four created in a small country house by the local Council; fortunately it was within walking distance of school, because he didn't drive and anyway they had no car. At that time there were still severe restrictions on petrol for private cars.

It was a fairly poky little place, but it was their first home together.

But that was later. My hospitable mother, feeling sorry for this nice young man whose family couldn't be with him, invited him home for an evening meal. More embarrassment for me! He was a great talker, and extremely knowledgeable about music; he and my father became good friends, their chief point of contact being that my father was a very fine church organist and didn't often have the opportunity of talking music on a rather higher plane than most at the Dorking Methodist Church were capable of.

I can remember us all sitting around the table. This, of course, was while we were still rationed quite heavily, so it was always a wonder to me that guests could be fed at all. We ate our way through the main course, and my mother put cheese and biscuits on the table. Anyone old enough to remember those days will know how meagre the butter and cheese rations were. Talking as he went, Dr Morgan laid into the cheese, and we watched in astonishment and some horror as he demolished most of our week's ration at one sitting.

It was some time before I discovered that when he was travelling up and down the east coast of England, there would be a share-out of food between the crew at the end of a voyage, such things as wouldn't survive until the next sailing. This meant that for their families there was a very welcome influx of cheese and butter etc., and Dr Morgan, with his large appetite, probably had little real idea of what rationing had meant in ordinary families.

My mother never forgot that meal. Neither did we.

Several of the VIth Form girls were invited for tea with the Morgans when his parents came to visit them in the summer of 1946. His father was at that time about 75 and his mother 71. They seemed to me extremely old; and even when I knew them better on a more personal level I still felt I was meeting a late Victorian couple. Now that I am older than his father was when he died in 1954 I find the difference between their generation and mine quite puzzling. Because they *were* old—old in a way I hope I shall never be, even if I go quite gaga! Things have changed quite radically over the decades, and I wonder why. What brought us out of our total acceptance that at a certain stage we had to start giving things up and becoming chair cases? It's not simply the way we dress. It's an entire attitude to what life is all about. Of course there were people, right through history, who avoided the worst problems of old age and kept active in mind and body for many years past the accepted norm; but far too many simply followed what appears in hindsight to have been a set pattern.

That summer Nancy was clearly very much affected by the TB that would kill her on New Year's Day the next year. When the term ended, Derry took his parents and Cynthia back to Newcastle for the holiday; Nancy stayed at the flat—as she said, 'To clean it up'. But I suspect that she needed a bit of time away from a very energetic husband and extremely lively two-year-old daughter, and parents-in-law who were not noticeably sympathetic towards her frailty.

She and my mother became good friends at this time; looking back, I have to assume that Nancy really didn't know anybody else in the Dorking area. Her state of health was against her making friends.

But my mother and I were both very worried about her. She was gaunt; and for a woman who was taller than Derry and fairly big-boned, this was very noticeable. My recollections of her then are of her sitting in a chair in our back garden while Cynthia played around her.

When the time came for Nancy to go back to Newcastle, my mother had what she probably called 'a good talk' with her, and told her that she must see her doctor as soon as she got there. A short while later there was a letter to say that she had done as she was told, that it was much as she had thought—one lung was completely gone and the other very badly affected. In fact, there was nothing to be done.

The new September term brought Derry back to school. Nancy's mother, Cynthia's Nana Smith, came with Nancy and Derry to run the home and look after the patient; and Cynthia stayed in the north with her other grandparents.

Nancy was a stoic. What this deprivation was like for her— she would probably never see her child again—I have no idea. On the rare occasions I saw her from then on she seemed reasonably cheerful. But it must have been a difficult, perhaps sometimes a bitter time for her. The Morgans were not very good at other people's illnesses!

Mrs Smith, the widow of a Scottish borders gamekeeper, was also a stoic. That's northerners for you. I went round occasionally to see if I could do shopping or other errands; she always seemed to be standing at the kitchen table making cakes and things. She was a meticulous housewife, which Nancy never claimed to be. I remember her saying, 'Oh, if that's the way she wants to go . . . !' and I suspect that the silent Mrs Smith, and the once lively and very intelligent Nancy, didn't see eye to eye over life in general and housework in particular.

I cannot imagine where Derry and his then mother-in-law could meet intellectually. Those 4½ months that led to Nancy's death must have been very difficult for him; the flat was not large enough to accommodate so much incipient tragedy. It was at this time that he began to 'drop in' for a cup of tea after school, before he went home. One should not read anything into this. They had both become friends of the family by now, and our house was on the way home to a place where his wife was dying in one room and his wife's mother was silently coping in another. It wasn't a good time. I think my mother was glad to be able to do something for them.

I remember that one day he didn't turn up to school in the morning and we all wondered what had happened. Apparently he had fainted just before leaving home. Knowing how sturdy he was, this still seems to me to be odd. My mother wondered if he was getting enough food; Mrs Smith rather seemed to focus on little cakes.

But he continued to make music. And there was the customary and now much-awaited Carol Service to be prepared. Work, of course, is a good way to get through a bad time.

One rather odd thing helped enormously to keep the choir provided with adequate quantities of music copies. He met my Grandpa Blake when Grandpa was visiting us. Grandpa was quite musically interested, too, and in a general discussion about the problems of finding enough vocal scores, he said, 'Well, I'm a member of the Manchester Central Music Library.' (I hope that's the proper title). 'You could get things on my ticket.'

From then on for a long time the school was a member of the library, and large boxes full of hard-backed vocal scores would arrive from Manchester months before the concert. This must have saved a fair amount of expenditure. Some members of the choir would always want their own copies to keep; but having dozens on loan was a great step forward.

It did seem as if our two families were becoming rather intertwined!

8

This is perhaps an appropriate place to look back at what had happened to Derry and Nancy before they became our house visitors. They were fellow students in the 'thirties at King's College, Newcastle, part of Durham University. Nancy's great friend at that time, and until she died, was Margot, who was chosen in due course as Cynthia's godmother.

In 1938, Derry had fallen for a German girl, Erika, who was working for a family the Morgans knew, as what we would now call 'au pair'. When she went back to Germany, Derry followed her, considering himself to be unofficially engaged to her. Many years later, his mother told me it was the worst day of her life when he left to go to this girl. Nevertheless, he went!

He soon found that the young Nazi element among her friends was not to his taste, and when he realised that she had Nazi sympathies too the whole thing was off. He also told me once that he discovered she had had an abortion, which at that time was a total 'no-no' in Britain, though apparently acceptable under Nazi rule. So he made his way back to England, coincidentally at the time of the Munich peace talks between Chamberlain and Hitler (October 1938), and saw trains full of soldiers being shipped to the western borders of Germany. I have wondered whether this may have been one reason why he joined the Merchant Navy so quickly after the outbreak of war. He saw how things were going; and he knew from meeting young Nazis that they believed Britain was too soft to fight. I can't imagine he would have taken that lying down.

Before he left, Erika had given him her father's violin, and there are two books of Haydn Sonatas for piano with her signature. I still have the books. Some years after we were married (we had moved to Howard Road by that time) he had, to my consternation, a letter from Erika asking for the violin back because she had a son who wanted to learn the instrument. She had been married and lost her husband during the war. We packed up the fiddle and sent it off to Germany. I wonder if it arrived.

I don't think Derry would be the sort of man to go through life on his own. So within a shortish time he and Nancy Smith were engaged. Her comment to my mother on one occasion that she got him 'on the rebound from a twit of a woman' indicates that she wasn't too worried about his former 'fling'. By this time he had his B. Mus degrees from Durham and Dublin, and was very keen to get his doctorate as quickly as possible. But Durham and Oxford, the universities he had approached, would have delayed him for 5 years between degrees, and he didn't want to wait that long. Again, I think he saw the way the war wind was blowing. Trinity College Dublin would let him take the D. Mus degree after 3 years, but first he had to take their B. Mus exams. So by the time he went to Germany he would probably have taken the latter and be on course for the former. And in due course he received his doctorate in June 1939. I believe he really appreciated the fact that his grandfather, Canon William Moore Morgan, at the Cathedral in Armagh, had been a top student (double gold medallist) at TCD in his day. Interestingly, at the same ceremony Vaughan Williams received an honorary doctorate—a fact which my father-in-law always mentioned with scorn as 'not being a proper degree'! Odd that both men ended up in the same Surrey town.

The juxtaposition of his success (he once told me he was the youngest doctor of music in the country at the time, at just 24) with the expectation that it was all going to be blown off course because of the political situation with Germany could not have been easy for a man with his burning desire to make music. By early 1940 he was in training as a junior radio officer in the Merchant Navy, employed by Marconi, a company under contract to the MN. But it was not enough for him to be a junior; eventually he went on to the advanced training which made it possible for him to be the boss and have juniors under him. I believe he could in fact have gone to sea after the war in the same job, because the rank was a permanent one, unlike the wartime qualifications. I once suggested the idea to him as a possible holiday 'escape' from family cares, but he rejected it out of hand.

Along with many thousands of other men who served in dangerous situations during the war, Derry had much to contend with emotionally. Once he was away from it all, with a peacetime position and work he loved, the stories of his war service slowly turned into anecdotes; it was all too easy to start to imagine that it had all been quite a lot of fun. But to take a very fine pianist, with many hopes for a future career, away from his piano for long stretches of time, to put him down among men who wouldn't have a clue what he was talking about on his own ground, to expose him to the dangers of U-boats, North Sea gales and the hours of what could only have been total frustration must have been tormenting at times, and not funny at all.

Add to that coming home to a wife who, within a couple of years, had developed TB, and —once that scare seemed to be over—wanted to have a child, it was quite a burden for a young man to carry for so long.

Once qualified, he was sent on the North Atlantic convoys, notorious for having been one of the most dangerous situations at that time in the war, with U-boats thick in the water. As 'Sparks' he would receive the information about the U-boats' whereabouts, but there was a radio silence for outgoing messages, so there must have been quite a lot of frustration attached to the job. Years later, when we were married, he told me that one of his great fears at that time was that, if the ship was torpedoed (bearing in mind that he was seeing others go down fairly regularly) and the 4-inch steel door of his cabin slammed shut, he would go down with the ship—but not drown! This fear led to a mild claustrophobia, especially in the early days after the war. He didn't like going in lifts, and once said he could never work in one of the newer office blocks, where he might have to sit next to a window, floor to ceiling, which looked down several stories to the ground.

In October 1940 he and Nancy were married. I don't know much about this, except that I have a fleeting memory that they may have honeymooned in Edinburgh—but I could be wrong. As happened to most service people, he had to join his ship soon after, and he assuaged his feelings by writing a number of songs for Nancy in the mezzo range. I never heard her sing, but I suspect she would have had a very pleasant voice—her speaking voice certainly was pleasant, low, with a slight accent which, thinking back, I believe had a touch of Scottish about it. But it could have been a very slight Geordie accent.

Nancy was teaching in the Stoke-on-Trent area, and when I was there in 2008 I enquired about the school she was at, Brown's; it's still there. When it was that Nancy went to live with them in Forest Hall I don't know. But I do know that when Derry came home, around 1942, he found that she was in a sanatorium on the Northumberland moors, having had tubercular glands removed from her neck. He went to see her, only to find that she had gone out for the day, and so he had to go back to Forest Hall—possibly even to the ship—without contacting her. Even years later, when we were married, this still hurt him. I think he may have been rather difficult to live with at that point, because Granny went to see Nancy at the sanatorium and told her she would have to come home because 'he couldn't manage without her'. I hope he wasn't party to this! It is a sad fact that the Morgans were simply not good at illness, apparently believing that if one tried a bit harder one would not be afflicted. Even as a schoolgirl I was quite upset by the lack of sympathy from Nancy's in-laws while she was clearly in declining health. I met the same attitude myself some years later.

It seemed that she had got over the TB scare quite well, and in 1943 she was very keen to have a baby. I don't know what Derry's feelings on the subject were. I suspect he might think he had enough on his plate with trying to win the war. But, as I was later to find out, he was quite obliging in this area. Meanwhile he had been transferred from deep-sea trips to the North Sea colliers, carrying coal *from* Newcastle! This was done by Marconi so that he would be home every couple of weeks or so, and I have always thought it was really thoughtful of them to see that he needed to be with his wife as much as possible. A bit surprising in the middle of a war. Though the North Sea was no sinecure — instead of U-boats they were faced with E-boats, which would race up the convoy, firing at them, and it was very dangerous to fire back in case one of their own ships was hit.

He was lucky, of course, in one way — he never lost his ship at sea, though the ship he was on in Belfast harbour went down during a massive air raid on the docks. Fortunately, he had gone ashore and came back to it when it was sitting on the bottom.

Knowing how vague he could be about the location of places it amazes me that he always seemed to get back to his ship, wherever it was docked. I remember Fiona saying to me once, when she was about five and we were on holiday: 'Mummy, where's Daddy?' 'Oh, he's back there somewhere.' She turned on me quite fiercely and said 'You shouldn't let him go on his own. You *know* he'll get lost!'

His war service up to that point had taken him to Canada and the US, and to Argentina and India. The Argentina trips had been with refrigerated meat, but I don't know what they carried on the North American ones. I know it was a very important time for the MN to get food through— later we were told that at one time there had only been enough food in the UK for two weeks. The India trip was, I believe, to take aircraft parts to be reassembled for the war over there. On his way back from India he went down with a serious bout of dysentery just off the west coast of Africa, but refused to be taken ashore. He said the ship's cook cured him with whisky! When he first came to the school in 1945 his eyeballs were quite yellow, so I suspect he had been quite seriously ill. (And possibly drunk).

While Nancy was pregnant she appeared to be in good health. In the fullness of time Cynthia arrived on the scene, rather inconveniently in the middle of an air raid, but fortunately while Derry was on leave from his ship. However, the timing was difficult for such great events in wartime, and he saw Nancy and the baby only for a very short time before he had to return to sea. I don't know who chose the name Cynthia, but I feel it was probably Nancy's choice. I don't think Derry's creativity ran to choosing babies' names—I always did it for ours! He did tell me once that Cynthia was very newly-born when he saw her so briefly, and that she was 'a bit like a radish, red-faced and with a spike of hair standing up on her head'. By the next time he saw her, she had apparently improved greatly. He had to go through the air raid to get back to his ship in time.

War has a lot to answer for in personal relationships, and he was not the only man who found it difficult to bond with his daughter at first, largely because when he came home to Forest Hall he and Nancy would want to spend some time together, and Granny and Ganga were there and more than ready to look after the baby. So for that first year I believe the true responsibilities of being a father didn't really register with him, and I can understand that. It must have been very hard for those young men coming out of perpetual danger to have to accommodate themselves to the requirements of everyday life. On top of that, not long after the baby arrived Nancy began the long decline in health that culminated in her death less than 3 years later.

With the end of the war in sight, Derry began to look around to see where he could revive his musical career. The MN was prepared to let him leave, although he was still not discharged officially. So in the spring of 1945 he applied for positions. I believe he was interviewed for a lecturer's post at Birmingham University, and a teaching post in Bristol, as well as the one he finally took at Dorking. He told me that Bristol was too hilly for Nancy in her state of health, and having a pram to push as well; and I think Birmingham turned him down. So he came to Dorking in April 1945 and was interviewed by Vaughan Williams, who, as we learned, was very impressed with him.

The first time I saw Cynthia and Nancy was when I was on the post office Christmas job that VIth formers were allowed to do. I was on the parcel run, and as we drove down the road in Deepdene I saw Nancy outside the front door, putting the baby in the pram. I must have guessed who it was, because I have no recollection of seeing her before that.

Eventually, the flat was found for the family Morgan in Riverdale; and although it was a fairly horrible little place it was a real improvement on sharing someone's house. During those months when they were fairly settled, and before Nancy's health became a real problem, I occasionally used to baby-sit for them. Cynthia was a very good baby at nights, and it gave Derry and Nancy a chance to get out and go to the pictures or whatever they did.

It was a mystery to us why, knowing what she did, Nancy was very careless about infecting the baby. She fed her off the spoon she was using herself, and drank from the same cup; and even I, young as I was, felt disturbed about it. Later, when Cynthia was five, and had pneumonia and was taken into hospital and X-rayed, they found that she had 'calcifications at the base of the lungs'. When I asked what that meant, the doctor said it indicated that she had been affected by the TB, but had fought it off. Nancy was a highly intelligent woman, so I have always wondered why she was so lacking in care over such a possibility.

Towards the end of the year Nancy was virtually bed-ridden. Such care as she was getting was provided by her mother, but I know she was developing bed-sores and must have felt very isolated in that flat, with few friends around, husband out all day, baby hundreds of miles away (and no phone at the Morgans so that she could keep in contact). When school broke up for Christmas, Nancy asked Derry to go to Newcastle to be with Cynthia. I suspect that Mum was visiting her fairly often by now, because on New Year's Eve she (and presumably my father, because he would have had to drive her there) saw Nancy's doctor at the flat, and he said, 'If Dr Morgan wants to see his wife again he'd better come home at once'. He commented on Nancy's courage in facing the inevitable end.

My father sent a telegram (neither phone *nor* electricity at Dunelm House) telling Derry to come immediately. He arranged for transport across London for him, and met him at Dorking North Station. They arrived late in the evening, so my mother was there when Nancy opened her eyes and recognised him. She died as they were with her, at about 1 am on New Year's Day, 1947. It has been bothering me for some time, thinking about this and wondering: 'Where was Nana?' And I can only think, because Mum never mentioned that she was there, that she must have gone to bed. This seems most unlikely, with Nancy's death hovering over them, but I think it must be what happened. When did they tell her it was over? I've no idea. It will remain another mystery.

In the early hours of that morning I woke up, and I could hear someone snoring. On the whole, we were not a snoring family, so I wondered what it was. In the morning I was fairly horrified to discover that Dr Morgan had spent the rest of the night on the settee cushions on the lounge floor. This seemed to me so embarrassing that I can't even remember what happened about breakfast. He would have gone straight to the flat, I imagine. Mum told me what had happened and I was suitably upset; but they arranged for me to go to stay with friends for a few days while Derry made all the arrangements for the funeral, including having to take Nancy back to Newcastle. So for those few days Derry slept in my bedroom.

I do wonder sometimes what would have happened to him and Nancy if my parents had not virtually taken them under their wing.

Derry came back for the start of the January term, and Granny and Ganga came with him, bringing Cynthia. At some point in all this they sold Dunelm House, but I don't recall anybody talking about it at home. Cynthia was very much 'their' child—it was almost as if Derry was her brother, rather than her father. They would get her to bed quite early, and when Derry came home they would say that he mustn't disturb her; as she slept in their room, not his, he seemed to have very little say in what was happening to her. It still seems to me quite a strange set-up, but it appeared to suit them. And I suppose he was so busy at school that it suited him too.

I imagine they often found it quite difficult to cope with a very lively nearly-three-year-old. I began to take Cynthia to Sunday School, where I was a teacher, partly to give them a break, partly to give the child one. And on one memorable night she came to stay with us and slept with me—and I was aroused in the middle of the night by a warm, wet sensation in the bed! My first introduction to the realities of child-minding.

Selling the home they had lived in for so many years must have been very hard for them. And it would have been difficult, too, to come to a place where they knew nobody but their son. Derry still kept in touch with two of his pre-war friends—Jack Rowell, who played the cello, and Cedric Armstrong, violinist, with whom he had spent Sundays in Forest Hall playing chamber music. Both had ended up in the London area, and I expect they came to see him and his family at Riverdale. But I do feel sympathy for Granny and Ganga, stuck in Riverdale without transport, without friends, in a flat at the top of a flight of stairs that were a real hazard for elderly people (Ganga later fell down them, but managed not to kill himself).

My mother had them over for tea sometimes. And, as by now Derry had apparently become a family friend, I did the odd errand for them—though probably not very often, as this would have been my final year at school, with all that entails: exams and too much homework and a general sense of dread that you can't remember a single thing you've been taught! I enjoyed the art course, and my place at Slade School of Fine Art was assured, so it wouldn't have mattered too much if I'd done really badly in the exam—except for my self-esteem.

So the academic year slid to an end, and I left school with a sigh and a tear! I have to say that on the whole I had enjoyed the eight years there, and have never been sorry that, in one way,

I never left. By that Christmas it was general knowledge which way things were going for me and Derry. Though when he told me that we were going to be married I was totally shocked—yes, he didn't actually *propose,* which implies that there is some choice for the person being proposed to. And I truly hadn't seen it coming. As far as I was concerned, he was a man I admired for his amazing abilities, respected for what he had achieved in a comparatively short time at the school, and who had become a friend of the family. He was still definitely Dr Morgan to me. One should always remember how one was proposed to, and in my case it was anything but romantic. He simply said, 'Well, Hebe, I always thought I was a sensible man, but . . .' I regret to say I can't remember how it went after that, but I think I was in deep shock for hours, if not days. In fact, I was quite appalled. Like several girls who had been at my level in school—and not a few of the female teachers, I may say—I probably thought he was a bit of a spunk (I can't remember what we called them in those days), but I had certainly stopped short of the idea of marriage. Anyway, I had a boyfriend—Derry told me to get rid of him. (Which I did—still in shock but always obedient to what I was told to do by a higher authority). Someone said to me during a recent UK holiday, 'But it must have been very romantic,' and I can quite categorically say that it wasn't, certainly not at first. It was quite scary!

Once I started thinking again, I realised what I might be taking on. Not only becoming a mother to Cynthia, but having a certain amount of possible responsibility for Granny and Ganga, since Derry was their only child, and they were getting steadily more frail. I was very torn for quite a while, though I suppose I was quite flattered that with the whole VIth form and a female staffroom to choose from, he had picked me. I asked him a few years ago, why? He didn't seem to know, but I think some of it may have been because I was a fairly cheerful character and he had missed a lot of that with, first, his parents, then the war, and then Nancy's long illness. But who knows?

We decided to get engaged at Easter 1948, on my birthday. He was determined that we should wait to be married until

2 years after Nancy's death, and I agreed. My parents offered us the top floor of New Hatch a few months later if we were to marry by Christmas—there was still a desperate shortage of accommodation in Dorking, and there was someone at church who could use the rooms if we didn't. Derry was reluctant, and felt he was being manipulated. But it seemed a good idea, and there was no way we could all live in the Riverdale flat (and I don't think I would have agreed to that anyway), so we accepted the offer, and were married just before Christmas, 1948.

We had Rosemary and Pat as bridesmaids, and of course 4-year-old Cynthia. I hope by now she has got over the humiliation of having to wear her baby shawl! I have always liked the picture of us outside the church, trying to indicate to her where the camera was, so that Derry and I both have slightly odd expressions while we are saying, 'Look, over there!' But I don't think she ever realised quite what was going on. She stole the day, anyway, for a lot of people.

She also walked up my veil in the aisle, and I came to a stop as I turned to meet my bridegroom, with a great tug on my head. My wedding dress belonged to Kate, wife of Derry's friend Cedric, who had offered to lend it to me in a mad moment some months earlier—an offer I accepted with pleasure because clothes were still rationed, and it was in any case much better than I could have afforded. It was insured for £50, which was big in 1948. Uncle Tom was best man, wearing—as he said with pride at the reception—the same tie he had worn at my parents' wedding 20 years before.

It was a very happy occasion, and we had a delightful honeymoon on the Isle of Wight. I decided to start my new motherhood role as I intended to go on, so I took some knitting and made a jersey for Cynthia. An elderly lady (all of 80!) became quite attached to me—probably thought I didn't know what I was letting myself in for—and asked me what I was knitting. I said it was a jersey for my daughter. She was so clearly shocked that I had to explain. It was yellow, and there's a nice picture of Cynthia wearing it.

We went home to our new flat—which I must say was really attractive; in my enthusiasm I had made new curtains—on New Year's day 1949, and my mother had invited Granny and Ganga to tea. Whether they thought that meant afternoon tea, or the invitation had not been precise enough I don't know, but Mum had done a cooked meal including smoked haddock. When I think about it now, it does seem a strange choice, but it was very 'north country' and I think my new in-laws should have enjoyed it. Anyway, our first meal back in Dorking as newly-weds was not a triumph—Granny said she couldn't possibly eat that, and my mother was, I think, justifiably annoyed. So the atmosphere on that occasion was—shall I say—slightly uneasy.

Cynthia was with us from then on, and was quite excited to be in her new room (the one at the end of the passage, next to ours, if anyone remembers it), and spent much of her time giggling at me. The next morning, at breakfast, Derry said to her, 'You can call Hebe Mummy now if you want to!' More giggling, hand over mouth. But by bedtime she was calling me Mummy as if she had always done so—and has done so ever since. I found it interesting that several people said to me, 'And will the little girl stay with Granny, or come to you?' as if there could be any different choice. It was high time for Derry to start being a proper Dad.

Her favourite game for those first few weeks was to have me lie on the floor so that she could sit on my tummy and bounce up and down. She was just small enough for it not to be too painful for me. But within a short time I knew I was pregnant, and I thought it might not be the best way to develop the baby by bouncing on it. So I told her we would have to stop playing that game for a while.

'Why?' 'Because I'm going to have a baby.' 'So?' 'Well, the baby's in my tummy and we don't want to hurt it.' (Disbelief!) 'It isn't!' 'Yes, it is.' 'It isn't!!' 'Yes, it is!' And this was why, when she was being taken to Granny's one Tuesday for tea—a normal Tuesday activity—she said to her small friend on the bus: 'My mummy's got a baby in her tummy. Has yours?' The friend's mother was so amused she told Granny—bad mistake! I got the lecture of a lifetime for having talked about my baby before either 'the bump' couldn't be explained away or was actually in the pram. She was really disgusted with me. She said 'Nobody ever knew it when I was pregnant until it couldn't be hidden anymore.' Which I think might explain why she and Ganga lost two still-born daughters before Derry was born. I suspect she may have corseted herself in.

It was an attitude that still prevailed among some older people even in the late 1940s—a sort of Victorian throwback which most of us had managed to get rid of by then. One of the other (male) tenants in Riverdale said (and it must have been transmitted to me by someone), 'No woman should ever go out in public after she's 6 months pregnant.' It's hard to believe now.

That summer was unusually hot, and I really suffered! By September I couldn't wait to get it over. Cynthia was very concerned in case we didn't know whether it was a girl or a boy. I told her that the doctors and nurses would tell me—it wasn't much use trying to explain the difference to a child who hadn't seen a little boy in the nude. 'You won't forget, will you?' I promised I wouldn't.

I can't possibly miss telling about the day before Patrick was born. I laughed so much that I think I brought it on—he was a week early. My maternal grandmother, Grandma Rothwell, decided that as this was the first great-grandchild she should be with us for the great occasion. So she came from Manchester by train (about 4 hours) having been driven to the station by Uncle Tom; was met in London and escorted by my father to the train that brought her to Dorking; walked for all of five minutes to our house (Dad carrying her bag); and spent the next day in bed. She must have been in her mid-seventies, an age which these days is regarded as quite a good time to jump out of planes and drive round Australia in a campervan. The mind-set has certainly changed!

But because she had to rest, I spent most of the day perched on the end of her bed. And she told me, in the most hilarious terms so that we were both crying with laughter, the awful tale of the day her first baby was born.

In brief, it went like this. When Grandpa Rothwell and the brother had gone off to work she knew that something was happening to her. But she decided not to tell them, because she knew that 'the first baby takes a long time to come'. Seized (as I never was) with a huge 'nesting' urge, she decided to wash the bedclothes and so on that would be needed when the nurse came for the delivery (This was in 1898, I believe, and it was Auntie Lottie, Pat's mother, who was about to emerge).

Once she had done the first washing she decided that the curtains needed doing, too; and then, with the curtains down, the windows obviously needed cleaning; and so it went on. At some point her sister arrived, and was horrified to see Grandma sitting on the upstairs window sill (a sash window, so she was half inside and half outside, and *very* pregnant).

Washing day then meant heating the water in a boiler, washing and rinsing the heavy sheets, possibly starching some, putting them through the huge hand-operated mangle, hanging them out in the backyard, taking them in more or less dry then, presumably, ironing them (I doubt if it was an electric one), and rehanging the curtains and making up the bed.

In the middle of all this, Grandpa and brother came home for their lunch, but she didn't tell them that her waters had broken and that she lost some every time she turned the mangle. And somehow they didn't notice that she was having regular contractions. Of course, she didn't tell them that, either. She knew that first babies take a long time etc . . . .

So they went back to work and she carried on spring cleaning so that the doctor would not be shocked by the state of the house, which was probably spotless anyway.

By teatime, when our heroes came home, exhausted from a day's work, she decided not to tell them, because she knew that first babies . . . And besides, they had a church meeting to go to.

So off they went (were they totally blind? Did they not see her as a person?), and what she did in the evening I have no idea, except that perhaps she allowed herself an occasional small groan.

In due course, day's work over and church business sorted, the two men came home. Did she then give them supper? I expect so. And, as Pepys's Diary so often concludes: so to bed! Well, she knew etc. etc . . .

A short while later she woke her husband up and said, 'Tom, you'd better get the midwife!' And so Lottie was born; mother and daughter lived to tell the tale. I hope the two men got their own breakfast the next day.

That evening, after a good, lung-exercising laugh together, we were all sitting around after tea. No hurry—the baby wasn't due until the following Sunday. But perhaps he didn't know that. Around 7 pm I was suddenly doubled up; within a couple of hours I was in the maternity home being prepared for the great moment. And (no doubt to everyone's relief) by lunchtime on September 25 I was the proud mother of a 6½ pound son. The one person who was not able to rejoice properly was Rosemary, who was in quarantine for some dread disease, and could only look at the baby through the window.

Some long time after, I recall saying to Derry, 'What did you do the night Patrick was being born?' Fathers, of course, were not welcome in labour wards at that time, for which I was quite grateful. He looked at me blankly. 'What do you mean—what did I do?' 'Well, did you sleep?' 'Of course.' 'Really?' 'What did you expect me to do?' 'I thought expectant daddies were supposed to pound up and down the carpet. Weren't you worried?' 'No. Why?' This was getting me nowhere. Of course, he'd been through the process before with Cynthia, but at least this time there wasn't an air raid to contend with or a ship to be caught. I felt a bit of anxiety would have been appropriate. Ah well, the ghost of Grandpa Rothwell, I suppose. And maybe I had a little of the toughness of Grandma Rothwell.

I was quite glad of a good rest in the nursing home. It had been a hectic nine months one way and another. While I was in there the local council realised that Derry wasn't living in Riverdale, though in fact he was paying the rent for his parents. They were given notice to quit. So when they came to see me they hardly looked at the baby because they were so upset over the insecurity of not knowing where they were going to live. I can sympathise now, but at the time I did wish they would appreciate the fact that I had given them a genuine Morgan grandson!

The flat situation went on for quite a long time, and I don't know whether Derry got an extension for them or not. Meanwhile, I now had two children, and on the first afternoon at home with Paddy (who was then Patrick) the time came to change his nappy and give him a feed. Derry very thoughtfully asked if he should keep Cynthia in the other room while I did all this in the bedroom, but I said we might as well get it over; so she watched in astonishment as Paddy's nappy came off, and stared down at the evidence of his gender with amazement. 'Oh, *that's* what he's got!' She was never worried again that I might forget if he was a girl or a boy.

But her total confusion when she saw me start to breast feed him was hilarious. 'Why is he biting you?' 'He's not biting. He's getting milk.' 'Where?' 'It's in there.' 'No, it's not!' 'Yes, it is. That's where mummies have milk for the baby.' 'No, it's not!' 'Yes, it is!' I had to show her that there really was milk before she would believe me. Not surprising, really. I sometimes wonder myself. Anyway, we had got over most of the hazards, and if she hadn't developed pneumonia a couple of months later it would have been a fairly successful year, one way and another.

Just as my mother was before me, I was haunted by family ailments. In those days—1950s onwards—it was mainly what we now regard as comparative rarities among diseases; such has been the impact of antibiotics and sophisticated medical research that the so-called 'children's ailments' are perhaps even on their way out. Chickenpox, measles, German measles, whooping cough, mumps—they took up so much time in our lives! I think we had at least one outbreak of everything that was available, and on one occasion, the older children having had chickenpox earlier on, I was not too pleased when we had a second outbreak some years later with the younger children.

My introduction to child nursing was not long after we were married, when Cynthia caught whooping cough. This is a particularly nasty disease, and thank goodness there is an effective vaccine which is making it less dangerous for our children. To watch one's child choking and vomiting, in Cynthia's case for several weeks, is distressing. I would say, after each bout of sickness, 'Never mind. Better out than in!'

She would chime in with this. It became a rather 'sick' joke, if I can be forgiven the pun. Towards the end of the time, when she was definitely over the worst and getting ready for her fifth birthday party, for which I had made her a rather pretty dress with embroidery down the front of the bodice, she put it on with some excitement. And I should have been prepared! It was about the last time she 'threw up', but she did it with style, all down the embroidery I had spent several hours finishing off. I said, 'Oh, Cynthia!' with some depth of feeling. She grinned at me and said, 'Never mind, Mummy. Better out than in!' It didn't wash very well.

And then pneumonia! I went to collect her from school one afternoon when Patrick was a couple of months old, and was met by Miss Gilbert (she had some years before been *my* teacher at Charlton House) who said, 'We haven't been ourself today.' I looked at Cynthia, and she was obviously ill. So I got her home, and Dr Brice came, and before I could turn round she was in hospital. She was over it very quickly, but it was quite a drama while it lasted.

So ended our first year of marriage.

9

I n spite of a constant and chronic shortage of money we still managed to get in some pleasant holidays. The first of these happened after Cynthia's bout with whooping cough; I was pregnant and tired, and my parents agreed to look after Cynthia, with Granny's help, while we took a few days off in the Easter school holiday.

So Derry and I (carless until several years later) went to Canterbury and fell in love with the place. I was fairly stunned by the sheer beauty and magnificence of the cathedral—and when, in 2008, I went back to the UK on my own, Canterbury was one of the places I had to visit. It's still an amazing city, and the combination of ancient and modern is intriguing and attractive. If I ever go again I think Canterbury will still be one of the places I cannot miss off the itinerary.

In 1950 (again exploiting the good nature of my parents as child minders—they were remarkably patient with us) we went to France for the first time. I have a feeling that that may have been the last time we went on holiday, just the two of us, until years later. We had 3 days in Paris (which I didn't like as much as I had expected) followed by 4 days in Rouen, which delighted me. Part of the trouble with Paris, I believe, was that it was only 5 years after the war, and the emotional atmosphere was a bit weirdly tense. Rouen, where Joan of Arc was martyred, was very old and perhaps almost immune to the stupidity of modern warfare. The connection with Joan was brought home when we were told that a certain stone tower was where she had supposedly been incarcerated before they took her to the stake.

I stood and stared at it—and then we were allowed to go in and look around. So small, with the solitary window very high up so that she could only have seen the sky, and it was all too possible to imagine her, very young and probably frightened despite her devotion to God and acceptance of her coming ordeal, lying there and hearing the town and market sounds of ordinary people outside, going about their daily business.

It was daunting to think that after 500 years of what we hoped was civilisation we had got no further than Nazi troops marching through this town, and behaving as badly as those who, so long ago, had pursued a teenage zealot to her death.

Light relief came with a bus drive to the coast, in a vehicle that bounced and shook us for an hour or so, depositing us at Fécamp, where the sea was grey and cold and there seemed to be nothing open for the lunch we had hoped to get. A notice at the front of the bus said '*Defense de fumer et de cracher*'. Well, everyone seemed to be *fumer-ing*, so I was a little alarmed in case they all began to *cracher*—which my French dictionary told me was spitting. But they didn't.

We found a barnlike hotel that would give us lunch, and it was a good one—very tasty soup in a large tureen with cream and chunks of bread floating in it, and probably an omelette to follow, that being about the limit of our vocabulary. Then I wanted a toilet before embarking on the bus ride back to Rouen. Nobody came for ages, so I went to the kitchen door and looked down into a cavernous and very dark basement. The woman who had served us came and asked what I wanted and I told her. She leaned into the kitchen and bellowed 'Jean!'

Out came a shambling giant, wearing a striped apron and a black beret. To say he looked like the village idiot is not perhaps very PC these days—but he did. He grinned at me and led me out into a courtyard, very French style, surrounded by balconies to about 3 storeys. He led me up stairs and along wooden floors, and finally came to a construction about the size of the average Aussie dunny—and built for the same purpose. He opened the door and bowed me inside with great dignity, and I entered and shut the door, wondering if I would have the courage to emerge.

But all was well. He had gone, and I found my way back to the dining room. When I told Derry my tale, he said, 'I must have some of that!' and went to the kitchen door. The woman called into the kitchen: 'Marie!' And out came a teenage girl, who proceeded to lead Derry to the same toilet. I think we laughed all the way back to Rouen.

When Patrick was a baby, still in nappies, we decided to take the two children to Cowes on the Isle of Wight for a week's holiday. The best we could afford at that time was two rooms in a small house, where the hosts were a young couple probably as short of cash as we were. No real facilities for coping with dirty nappies, only the kitchen sink, which I really didn't want to use for that purpose. But there was no choice. I had been very nervous of taking both children on holiday. Now, I can't quite remember why, but I suppose I felt it would be fairly arduous, not only keeping 6-year old Cynthia amused, but having the problems of bottles for the baby.

In fact, it was one of the most enjoyable holidays (problems apart) that we had in those early years. Cynthia and I spent much of the time looking into rock pools where small creatures lived, and I remember nothing difficult (except the nappy saga) with the baby. I recall deciding that the children would always come with us in future. And, as far as I can remember, they did.

In time, as the family grew in numbers and in size, we ventured further afield. Once we had a car we could explore our own country. The children were, on the whole, pretty good about trekking through cathedrals with us. We toured England and Wales, bed-and-breakfasting as we went; and later we 'did' Scotland. Probably the climax of our travels came when, with four children, the youngest being about five, we B&B-ed through France, along the Riviera coast into Italy, up the Grand St Bernard Pass into Switzerland, across to Dunkirk—and so home. We felt very intrepid. But there were many memorable moments, of which more later.

10

Meanwhile, back in 1952, we had no idea that our lives were about to change in various and not always welcome ways. We were still living upstairs at my parents' home, and while it was a very pleasant flat which we were very lucky to have it was getting a bit restricted for four of us. I was getting itchy feet, and searching through the newspapers for houses which I knew we couldn't afford.

Then Derry's mother, Granny, developed ventricular tachycardia, for which there seemed to be little medical help at the time. She was sufficiently ill for her to need nursing; I shall always wonder why it wasn't possible for her to be treated in hospital. The National Health Service had been active since about 1948—surely it should have been possible to have her properly looked after. I had been doing what I could while she was in bed in the flat at Riverdale by cycling over and getting their lunch ready for them before cycling home again to get Derry's.

Her condition became so worrying that Dr Brice said she should not be in their flat—which meant that, as we were the only family, she would have to come to us. My mother let us have Rosemary's bedroom (Rosemary was away in Cambridge) until the end of the university term, when she would be coming home. I hoped the situation would be solved by then and they could go back to Riverdale.

So, with strict instructions from the doctor that she must on no account get dressed, she was to be brought over by ambulance. Being Granny, of course, she was certainly not going to go out in her nightgown and be seen like that by the ambulance men! So she managed to dress herself, and the ambulance arrived with her and Ganga in it.

Strangely (because he kept popping up at various moments in my life) Arnold Plummer was one of the ambulance men. Two of them carried her up the stairs to our flat on a chair. She was scared they would drop her, and when her slipper fell off she became quite distraught. On the landing, she sat in the chair fussing about the slipper; my mother stood one side of her, and I stood on the other, holding her. And it was while we were standing there that Granny had a very severe stroke.

All at once she sagged, and her speech was incomprehensible. Her left side became paralysed. Mum and I stared at each other, and she whispered, 'My God, she's had a stroke!'

This changed everything. Suddenly, in this small flat, I had the two of us, our two children, a disabled old lady and an old man who was deaf and had poor eyesight. We had Rosemary's bed for Granny, but Ganga had to sleep for a few weeks on a camp bed, which at his age and with his physical limitations must not have been very desirable. I was 22, and this wasn't how I had seen my life developing.

And why, for heaven's sake, could they not find a hospital bed *anywhere* in the region for an old lady who was now bedbound? I often wondered how hard they tried. Dr Brice said there simply wasn't a bed available; and added that if she had collapsed outside the hospital they would have had to take her in! If I say that I was also pregnant, the mystery grows deeper. Looking back on it, I think that just about everyone washed their hands of the situation—at least, everyone seemed to think that I would be able to cope.

So I did! But those were not the happiest three months of my life; though it is often through these unexpected challenges that we grow. Over the 3 months that she lived in what must have been physical and mental misery—but I don't know how we could have done more than we did—I changed from the young, untried wife and mother into (as I could tell once it was all over) someone who did cope with just about all the things that life thereafter chucked at me. All the same, it would have been nice if it hadn't happened—for all of us, not least Granny.

Dementia is one of those diseases that hang in the backs of our minds once we reach what is tactfully and mysteriously known as 'a certain age'. Some of us will have it; it is not a new affliction, though it sometimes sounds like it, the way people talk. Most families in the past had a batty old aunt or uncle, or a dribbling granny, and it used to be almost expected, if one lived well past the three score and ten. Now that we think that we should all be immune from disease, we have forgotten how to deal with dementia in the old.

Wandering or serious aggression are very difficult to cope with; but many forms of dementia can be dealt with in the home, with love, and plenty of help from others and from the organisations that now exist to assist. It was not quite like that in 1952. The doctor came regularly, but there was little he could do. No talk of physiotherapy; no real help at all. Morning and evening the district nurse (Council equivalent in the UK of the Silver Chain in Australia—and it was free) came to change the bedding and keep Granny clean. And that was about all. She was on medication that kept her alive, but looking back one wonders if it wouldn't have been kinder to let her slip away.

Washing all those sheets was my responsibility.

Among all these other duties I had to go house-hunting. I have no very clear memory of all this (fortunately), but I do know that at that time there were only two houses in Dorking which were central —we didn't yet have a car— within our budget and suitable for our enlarged family. If Granny recovered (and even if she didn't, there was still Ganga to consider) they would need a bedroom and, possibly, a sitting room to themselves.

The first one I looked at was very attractive externally, one of an old-style duplex on a large scale ('semi-detached' in England), and I was very tempted. But once I got inside I could see it would be hopeless. Even if I had not been pregnant, I could not see how I could cope with what appeared to be endless stairs and a couple of rooms on each floor, and a paralysed old lady. It was either 3 or 4 storeys.

The second house I visited on a lovely sunny day. I was invited in, and the moment I entered the lounge room I was hooked. Because the couple living there didn't use that room much they had not curtained it, and the sun was pouring in. It was listed in the agent's leaflet as '30 feet long x 15 feet into the bay window', and it had, I was told, been two rooms knocked into one at some time in the past. The house was early Victorian (1852, though I didn't know that until we finally sold it), and there were four double bedrooms, dining room and small living room, kitchen and bathroom, the latter the size of another double bedroom. Down a flight of stairs was a huge cellar, including a wine cellar, coal store and room for practically anything one could imagine.

The décor was unusual. The current owners were commercial artists who claimed to have known Augustus John, a famous artist of the period. Some of the walls were papered, some simply paint-washed in a rather sickly salmon pink. The corridor leading to the kitchen had a Chinese red paper with snowflakes, hand-printed. I discovered what that meant some time later when I tried to wash off some grubby little hand marks, and the snowflakes came off too! But it was cheerful and very unusual and I really liked it.

The corridor above led to the bathroom, and it was an oddity because it had a lower ceiling than the rest of the house, and the wallpaper design—green climbing vines on curling wrought-iron trellises—was not only on the walls, but went right over the ceiling, so that one felt one was going through a garden arbour to get to the loo. I think we all appreciated it.

The main effect all this had on me was that I was never afraid of trying new décor; and slowly we got rid of most of the salmon pink and did our own thing. I'll draw a veil over the time Derry and I decided to paper the ceiling of the 30 foot long lounge room. I'm thankful to say that after it had fallen on our heads for the umpteenth time (the paper, not the ceiling) we were in hysterics.

And yes, we did manage it in the end; and yes, it did stay up for many years. There was no way we were going to do that again.

But I'm getting ahead of myself. It was time to find the money! This task looked insuperable until we worked out an agreement with Ganga that he would sell his few investments for a deposit, on condition that we would look after him for the rest of his life.

The house was £4350. Houses were just beginning to rise in price, but this was still bearable. Ganga's investment came to £1100, and I recall taking him to the bank in a taxi to complete the business. In early March we moved into Arundel Lodge in Howard Road, at the other end of Dorking from my parents' home. We were ten minutes' walk from most things we would want to get to on foot, and it was stunning to be in our own home and to have s-p-a-c-e! The long lounge room came into its own as storage: our furniture was coming, as well as Granny and Ganga's things that had been in store since they had come down from Newcastle, plus some wobbly rattan tables and chairs that I had not expected, presumably belonging to the long-deceased Uncle Arthur, who had lived in Ceylon in the '30s. Thank goodness my parents were there to help. It was a nightmare.

And don't forget the grand piano! That is another story altogether.

But above all we had to be ready to receive Granny when the ambulance brought her over from New Hatch. That was the priority. Not to mention that there were two children to be fed and bedded, and Ganga to be shown around so that he could get used to the place, and hopefully not fall down and complicate things that were already quite complicated enough.

I can remember being tired beyond anything I had ever felt before.

But somehow we did it; and slowly, slowly, the lounge room was emptied, and the awful rattan furniture accommodated in the small living room, which was a perfect place for Ganga to sit in his old chair that should really have been donated to Guy Fawkes' night years before—but he liked it. Granny and Ganga had one of the bedrooms with twin beds, and miraculously everyone fitted in and we began to live as householders.

Derry wasn't one to show great emotion about things like houses and wallpaper and so on, but I knew he was very pleased that we were now independent, even though it might be a struggle financially. I can remember standing in the hall a few days after the great removal; he grinned at me and said, 'How does it feel to have a house like this at twenty-three years old?' Well—it felt pretty good!

A washing-machine was a necessity with so much of Granny's washing to do. We bought a Goblin, a nice little thing that had to be filled from the tap and then, afterwards, drained into the sink. Patrick was very interested in all this, especially when I said that the Goblin man was coming.

When the man arrived and was shown into the kitchen, Patrick said, glaring at me with disgust, '*That's* not a goblin man!' What a sell for an excited small boy.

The next weeks were memorable but probably best forgotten. My sleep was haphazard at best, non-existent at worst. The theory was that Ganga would be responsible for Granny during the night; but it never quite worked out like that. She only needed to start moaning and he would be standing by our bed, saying, 'She's calling for you!' . . . meaning me. I seemed to be the one who could soothe her best; Derry found it very hard, and I could imagine that it was painful to see his mother reduced to such a state. Besides which, he had to go to work, and I could, if necessary, find a few snatched moments during the day to put my feet up and relax. But those two-o'clock-in-the-morning sessions were not pleasant. For one thing, Granny often did not know who I was, even though she had been calling for me; and we had a few bizarre situations in the half-dark.

'I don't want you,' she would manage to get out. 'I want the other one.'

Eventually it dawned on me that she must mean Nancy. 'Nancy's gone,' I said. 'Nancy died—don't you remember?'

'No—I want the other one.'

In desperation I finally said, 'Nancy died, and I'm married to Derry now.' She wouldn't accept this. 'You were at our wedding,' I said.

'No, I wasn't!'

'You and Ganga.' She wouldn't have it. So, in the middle of the night, I got out our wedding photos and thrust them under her nose so that she had to look at them. 'Who is that?'

'It's Derry.' *Very* unwillingly.

'And that?'

'That's Cynthia.'

'And who is that?'

'Gus . . .' Ganga's name.

'And that?'

Silence. Eventually—'That's me.'

'And who is this?'

But she couldn't bring herself to say that I was actually the bride!

'So there—you were at our wedding.' I doubt if it convinced her.

The other memorable crack-of-dawn conversation started with, 'I want to see the lady of the house!'

'Who do you mean?'

'The lady of the house! I want to see her.'

By this time my patience was wearing thin. I was longing for a night's sleep. '*I* am the lady of the house,' I retorted, very sharply.

She was quick. '*Yes, and you never let us forget it for a moment, do you?*' I hope it was to my credit that I started laughing. The whole thing was ridiculous. Here I was spending hours of my day looking after her, feeding her, trying to get water into her, giving her pills, looking after her husband, who spent a fair amount of time sitting by her bed, but once he'd done what he regarded as his stint was very unwilling to go back to her—and she clearly resented me.

So it was something of a breakthrough, and I suppose a comfort to me, on the night that I said to Derry, 'I'm sorry, I just can't do it tonight . . .' and he went in and said, 'Hebe can't come.

She's very tired and you know she's expecting a baby', that I heard her begin to cry and moan and say, 'Oh—oh—oh—I think Hebe's stopped being my mother . . . !' Poor Granny! We did our best as a family, but I still think we were badly let down by the health services.

She died at Easter. We accompanied Ganga to the crematorium on a very pleasant spring day, and I doubt if any of us remembered afterwards much of the service. Ganga had chosen to have her ashes scattered, and we picked a grassy slope beside a pathway and under a blossoming cherry tree—very beautiful and peaceful.

Nothing, I thought, could ever be more challenging than the situation we had just emerged from. I was now six months pregnant with Helen, and looking forward to a bit of peace and quiet for the final trimester. Kind friends kept telling me that I would have my reward for what I had done for Granny. I privately thought that a good sleep would be reward enough.

The following weekend was a Sunday School festival of some kind, and Cynthia, now aged 8, was a flower fairy, complete with a rather cute little flower hat. I was with my parents; and when the children came on stage and I saw Cynthia I started to cry—and I couldn't stop! I was very embarrassed, and I think my mother took me out. The next day she insisted I see the doctor, who said a few days away from responsibilities would probably do the trick.

So they over-rode any objections on the part of the men in my life, though hopefully there weren't any—objections, that is. My three men, Derry, Ganga and 3 year-old Patrick, and competent Cynthia, would have to get on without me for a while. My father booked me into the Methodist guest house at Eastbourne, and drove me down there straight away. I remember looking at the staircase that led to my bedroom and thinking that I would never be able to get up it. That was how exhausted I was. Then they left me to my depression and my tears and promised to come and get me on Friday.

On the first full day I undertook to walk down the hill to a café where I could get a cuppa and some cakes. When the cakes arrived I was almost in tears again because I didn't know how to choose—like most Mums I usually got the one that no one else wanted! Getting back up the hill took all my energy.

On the Friday, when my father arrived to collect me, I had left something in the bedroom at the top of that long flight that had so scared me when I arrived. It wasn't until I got into the car that I realised that I had actually *run* up them. The doctor had been quite right. Just a few days and I was ready to take on my duties again.

I've written about this episode quite fully because I think it is necessary for anyone who is undergoing something *avoidable* that is causing stress to realise that it is possible to break the cycle and get back to whatever is normal. There will always be 'things that must be done', whether it is looking after the children or keeping up with the housework or trying to balance work and home adequately. It is in our own hands to make that break, even if only for a short time; it gives us the possibility to take a more distant view of what our lives are becoming, and what can be done to improve the quality of those lives. The unavoidable things, like health problems—and floods, fires and cyclones, now that I am in Australia—simply have to be endured. The skill is in knowing which are which.

Helen was several days late in arriving. Dr Brice told me a week before that he was due to go on holiday—but would stay for a couple of days to see two of his 'matty' patients through their confinement. Doctors were like that then! The baby made her presence felt on the Saturday evening, and following instructions I turned up at the Rose Hill Nursing Home for my second session of baby production during the evening. They didn't like being disturbed in the middle of the night.

Early on the Sunday morning I woke up quite suddenly, knowing that something was wrong; I managed to ring the bell before I passed out. When I came to I found that the doctor and the matron were kneeling by my bed, one each side, as if I were a knight on a tombstone; they were watching what my blood pressure was doing. I realised that I must have been unconscious for quite a while for the doctor to be there, fully dressed, from the other side of town, when I surfaced.

It transpired that Helen, who had been well positioned for quite a while, all ready for making her great entrance, had decided to go for a swim! She was lying across me, and had to be manipulated back into the birth position. They gave me something to slow the contractions, and I lay there for the rest of the day. By evening everything started up again, and it was back on to the gas and air and trying not to groan too loudly. The doctor went off on his holiday, leaving me in his partner's capable hands.

Helen was born about 8.20 on the Monday morning. She had the cord around her neck, the result of her swim, but was otherwise in good shape. I rang Derry ten minutes later to let him know he had another daughter, and then rang my mother.

She was very pleased. She said, 'When was she born?' I said, 'At 8.20'. She sounded very put out. 'Last night, and no one told me?' 'No,' I said, 'Just now. 8.20 this morning.' I think that almost silenced her.

From then on things went reasonably well, except for the bit of afterbirth that the doctor failed to remove or notice, which gave me septicaemia. For a while I was quite ill, with a high temperature; but by the end of my time in Rose Hill I was feeling good, and ready to take home our newest member of the family.

It always pleased me that we never had any problems with the jealousy that many people seem to have when a new baby appears on the scene. Ours were welcomed, and very quickly taken for granted. Once they realised that this new sibling couldn't play or talk or do anything that made for entertainment or companionship, everything returned to whatever was normal before the newcomer arrived.

Helen was a remarkably good baby. I remember the few weeks after I took her home, when I had to work out how to deal with Ganga, Patrick *and* Helen, once the school contingent (Derry and Cynthia) had left in the morning. Once Ganga had had his breakfast and the baby had been fed, bathed and made ready for a quiet morning in the pram in the back garden, I was able to get on with other chores.

But first, when I had the baby wrapped in her shawl, I would give her to Ganga to hold. This was a nervy business, because I wasn't sure he wasn't going to drop her. All the same, I was determined that he should have some contact with her; Granny had told me a tale, with much laughter, that had quite horrified me.

When Derry was a small baby they had a maid—'the girl'—who looked after him much of the time. One day Granny went out to tea with a friend, leaving the girl to cope with Derry. Granny and friend returned to the house after tea: 'And when we went in,' she told me, as if it was the funniest thing she had ever seen, 'there was Gus—holding the baby! Oh, we did laugh! *He never did it again.*'

So much for paternal bonding! I was shocked. But it shows how narrow the Victorian conventions were when it came to babies. Fathers seem to have been kept available in order to inflict discipline in whatever shape they deemed necessary. Derry always remembered the time he was caned by his father for tripping up a boy in the playground.

Thank heaven that we have moved on from there. Anyway, I felt that perhaps letting Ganga hold *my* baby made up a bit for an inexcusable attitude. And he didn't drop her!

11

eanwhile, away from the pressing domestic life, there
was music! Whatever happened at home, Derry's life
was mostly centred on choir and performance, as well
as being responsible for music classes throughout the school—and
never forget the dreaded reports at the end of every term. Over
600 of them, and no assistant in the music department. Looking
back, I really don't know how he managed to fit it all in and still
be a husband and father.

In March, 1952, at the peak of the domestic upheaval, he was
producing a couple of nights of Handel's *Judas Maccabaeus*. As
what I described as 'resident comedian', I was singing the soprano
role. So, pregnant, totally involved with moving house and caring
for two old folks and the children, I spent much of my kitchen
time with a vocal score propped on the pan stand so that I could
learn the part while producing food for the multitude. I recall that
I was wearing a dark purple dress for the performances—it was
the only one that would accommodate my pregnant tum.

As always, performance lifted me out of the domestic scene,
and I thoroughly enjoyed doing it. If I had opted to 'go professional',
I would certainly have chosen to sing oratorio. The combination
of orchestra, choir, solo arias and ensemble numbers seems to me
to be just about perfect; and there is no doubt that some of the
finest music written has been in that genre. I was never a recitalist,
and opera would have been impossible because I don't have the
sort of reliable memory that carries one through a whole evening
sung without a copy. The occasions on which I have tried to sing
from memory have usually been mildly disastrous.

At some point, in the year after Helen's birth, I managed to get up to London to the Wigmore Studios for a lesson with Grace Vernon. She was the partner of Maggie Teyte, a famous soprano of that era. I didn't discover for many years that their partnership was also a very personal one—the kind one didn't talk about in those days. I wonder if I would have been sent to another teacher if my parents had known about this situation.

Grace was an excellent teacher, though, surprisingly, she was not herself a singer. Maggie taught the Jean de Rezske method, developed by the tenor who had been very influential in his day; she had taught Grace his system of voice production, and I was fortunate that I was introduced to her. She had the gift of indicating exactly what one should do with the voice by a simple movement of her hand.

This had all come about because Derry had put on Mendelssohn's oratorio *Elijah* in 1948, just after we became engaged. He had secured Robert Irwin, a notable baritone, for the Elijah role; and he gave the solo soprano and alto parts to me and my former classmate Valerie Pratt. We were both still in our teens, but I think we acquitted ourselves pretty well. When the concerts were over my father, knowing that I would not be going to Slade as planned, said I ought to have something behind me since I would soon be married: would I like to have singing lessons? This was an inspired thought on his part. Having a singing background not only gave me something of my own to nurture, but provided a small income for me once I was competent enough to teach.

I spent the next 9 months going up to the Wigmore Studios in London a couple of times a week. I think I was a bit of a puzzle to Grace: most of her pupils were older than I was, and they seemed to be aiming for the big London shows. I was only really interested in the kind of music Derry was producing. She said to me once, 'Your husband chooses very difficult things to sing'. Because she could never remember my name from lesson to lesson, she called me 'darling'—and once introduced me to another of her pupils as 'Phoebe—she comes up from the country!' I felt as if I wore muddy wellingtons!

Marriage interrupted this mini-career; but two babies helped to mature my voice. I was aware that it had strengthened. I had discovered two notes at the top of my voice, and two at the bottom, which extended my range considerably, and I have always said Helen was responsible for this! But perhaps it was the natural maturing in my mid-twenties.

I told Grace that I wanted to do two things: apply for a BBC audition for a broadcast recital, and try for the ARCM performance diploma in singing. She was considerably astonished. I think she had little experience of someone wanting to study more academically.

But for me it was ideal. While Derry was my piano teacher before we were married he had decided I could do the ARCM in piano; and I went along with this, sometimes in tears, because I really didn't think I had what it takes. But he kept me going, and in due course I went to the Royal College one day, ready to do my best, but not terribly hopeful. I was awed by the surroundings and by the number of students who were wandering around waiting for their turn.

I had also entered for the special theory exam, which Derry had prepared me for; and there were aural tests and music dictation.

When the results came I was not too surprised. I had failed by a very narrow margin on the practical piano playing; but I passed the theory and other tests. What I didn't know at that stage was that, having passed that part of the exam, I could retake the practical at any time during the next few years. And it didn't have to be the piano! This was something of a gift, because it meant that if and when I wanted to take the singing exam I wouldn't have to brush up on my theoretical knowledge.

So I put this to Grace, and she said, 'Well, let's see what you can do'. So we began on exercises (Vaccaj—excellent training and pleasant to do as a daily chore), and she turned to me, clearly surprised, and said, 'Well, what have *you* been up to?'

'I've had another baby.'

So, one day, Derry and I went back to the Royal College, he as my accompanist (one of the few times I have ever seen him nervous at the piano), and I, hoping I didn't look like a downtrodden mum, dressed to the nines in a rather striking dress, black lace over a lilac underskirt, plus a dinky little hat—we all wore them then on 'occasions'. On that particular occasion, for the only time in my career, I sang everything from memory without a hitch. I was very pleased to see that the three anonymous examiners, who had been sitting with their backs to me, turned round and watched me for the rest of my little recital. I felt I had made an impact.

A few days later Derry came leaping up the stairs, having collected the mail while I was still in bed; he was grinning from ear to ear.

'You've passed!' he yelled before he got to the bedroom. 'You've passed splendidly!' And this time I had. Pass was 100, I believe, and I was well above that. I was very pleased, and not least because I could now do something that I have hardly ever done since—put ARCM after my name. It didn't compare with all Derry's qualifications, but it was very heart-warming at that point in my life.

The musical calendar that ruled our lives had settled in the five years we had been married into a routine. Starting in September, when the academic year begins in the UK, we could look forward to the carol service in December, the oratorio in spring, and the speech day. Plus, for Derry, those never-ending reports.

He also taught piano after school, and some students came to the house in the evening. Then there were the Higher Certificate (later A Levels) studies for students who wished to take music at that level. He would decide by the summer what the next year's oratorio should be, and that would involve making sure that there were vocal scores ready for the beginning of the September term, and starting to create an orchestra from his lists of players, some professional, some good amateur, some borrowed from various student groups at the London colleges.

And then there was the search for suitable soloists for the big performances. These came from all kinds of places, and

117

were almost always professionals: the Guildhall School of Music produced for him one year a tenor, David Galliver, and a baritone, Richard Standen, who both sang with us on a number of occasions. David eventually became Professor of Music in Adelaide, and we maintained our friendship until he died many years later.

They came to sing Mozart's Requiem, and I will claim a small pat on the back for myself. I was sitting next to David at the rehearsal. He turned to me and said, 'I sang this with so-and-so last week', mentioning a well-known soprano who did a great deal of work for the BBC. 'But I prefer the way you do it.'

Derry was a whiz at choosing delightful Christmas carols. In the last few years, when John Rutter's charming compositions have become so popular with choirs, I have often wished he had been writing them when Derry was actively choosing choral music—he would have loved them.

Altogether he was for much of the time incredibly busy, and until, many years later, he gained an assistant teacher, he was the original one-man band. He organised everything—and swept all before him, like a sort of human bulldozer. Heaven help anyone who got in his way! This didn't always go down well with his colleagues on the staff. One was heard to say, 'He thinks it's an academy of music!', and there were indeed times when I had the feeling that he thought it was. It certainly sounded like it, with Handel or Brahms or Mendelssohn echoing around the school corridors—it was not purpose built for very penetrating music accompanied by a booming baritone and a crashing piano accompaniment.

In addition to this, from time to time Derry felt inspired to write something for the choir. Over the years he produced some excellent short choral pieces: *God is ascended* and *Behold a simple tender Babe,* to name only two. These were greatly appreciated by the choir and audience. His anthem, *Gloria*, was performed at a Carol Service in St Martin's church and probably shook the less musically adventurous members of the congregation. It has quite a savage side to it, in spite of singing of 'peace on earth'. It combines ethereal angelic voices, a high solo soprano part and several solo instruments played by students and a couple of teachers. It was particularly appreciated by Ruth Dyson, a Dorking resident who was a tutor at one of the London music colleges, a well-known harpsichordist and a governor of the school. A few days after the concert she saw Derry on a bus, and called down the aisle to him, 'I loved your Gloria!' He told me that attracted quite a lot of attention from the other passengers.

To keep all these musical balls in the air was a huge undertaking. His energy was apparently endless. I can remember, after one concert, when he came home wearing a wet rag of a collar from perspiring so much and wanting nothing more than to flop down and recover, that half an hour later he was up and full of beans. 'I could do that all over again!' he said. I was thankful he didn't have to.

Concert weekends were challenges for me. They involved a long rehearsal on the Saturday afternoon; making sure that my babysitter (usually my mother) was fully prepared; seeing that everyone got a good lunch; and having Derry's clothes ready— this involved the full evening dress including collar and white tie. Thank goodness he had a tie he could clip on—I don't think I could have coped with the drama of organising a 'proper' tie.

And, of course, I had to have my own clothes ready to slip into between rehearsal and performance, while making certain that the maestro got something to eat from the school dining room. I reckon I was able to get into my glad rags, plus makeup, in about 15 minutes. It took longer to get Derry ready.

With all this, his composing and the preparations for concerts did not, in retrospect, impinge inconveniently on normal family life. He was able to compose while the TV was on and children and dogs and cats were in the same room. If he needed to have a bit of peace and quiet he would disappear for a while. I can remember saying to one of the children, 'Where's Daddy?' 'He's in the other room, decomposing.' I have a photo of him during our 'courting' days, lying full length on my parents' lawn in his Merchant Navy summer 'whites' (just after the war you didn't waste good clothes), and writing something on manuscript paper. I wonder what it was.

So as our family grew they were used to pianos, concerts, instruments of various kinds, musicians coming to rehearse in our home, and later, a regular choir practice in our lounge room on a Monday evening. This was the Old Dorkinian Music Society, whose members participated in many of the concerts from the earliest days. Twenty or so people all singing their heads off created a bit of a 'fug' in the room, and Derry was perfectly capable of opening the windows wide in spite of the fact that we were surrounded by other people's houses. I was torn between feeling sorry for them and thinking how lucky they were to have Mozart and Handel wafting into the homes! Fortunately, no one ever complained.

When on one occasion Derry was practising daily for a recital he was going to give, I began to be a little worried by our neighbour (we lived next door to a pub, and he was the publican) who kept walking around the outside of the hedge between us and the footpath. I felt he might be summoning up courage to knock on the door and ask Derry to shut up. One evening I went outside as he came round the corner.

'I've been listening to your husband.'

'Oh—I hope it isn't annoying you. He's practising for a recital.'

'Oh, no! It's beautiful. I keep walking round so I can hear him. What is it?'

I said it was Chopin. And I hope they all felt the same way.

In these early days of his time at the school the choir was anything up to 150 or more students. One of the things that I have always found exceptional about this choir was that no one was ever auditioned for it. There was none of that 'No, you can't be in it. You can't hold the note'. So many people have been totally inhibited *for life* by teachers who have destroyed their possibility of enjoying what is the most natural approach to music that anyone can have.

Students joined because they wanted to. No one chased them if they missed a rehearsal. No register of names was kept. Derry's approach seemed to be, 'I am offering you something of great value. If you don't want to join me—keep out of my way!' He never appeared to have any problems over behaviour, either in class or at rehearsal. As far as I could ever tell, he ignored the few idiots at the back of the class who didn't want to be a part of it; there are usually a few of those in any group. And the fun of behaving like an idiot soon palls when no one takes any notice of you, especially if others in the class seem to be enjoying themselves.

I don't think I ever actually asked him if he had a policy about teaching music. If I had he would probably have said no. But over the years I formed my own opinions about what made him tick in musical terms. I have noticed recently that when a youth choir is formed the music they sing is frequently contemporary, and I was once asked why Derry always went for the classics. A music teacher told me that 'today, young people won't listen to classical music, so it's no use trying to teach it to them'.

I totally disagree with this theory. One reason why they 'won't' listen to it is because it is seldom presented to them. Too many teachers are in fact afraid of their students' reactions if they try classical music on them. Perhaps it is taught without the fire that inspires so many people to love the genre. If it is presented as 'something that is good for you', of course it will be rejected. Even with my own love for such music, the wartime teaching I received almost turned me off it. What happened when Derry began to inspire his students was that they saw a vibrant, youngish (30) man who had just spent five years of war dodging danger; and the sheer excitement of learning stuff that we thought was far beyond us gave us something that 'pop' music of the time never did. That appealed even to the boys, who might have been expected to stand outside and remain untouched.

By introducing students to the classics of choral music, the Handel, Mendelssohn, Bach, Mozart, Vivaldi works and so on that are the standards of choir singing, he established a level of achievement which would eventually prepare his young singers for whatever music they looked for once the school days were behind them. If he had started with contemporary music, they would have missed out on the solid background of knowledge that he believed was very important. The strong basis of classical choral works was what he believed in, and the outcome showed he had been correct in his beliefs.

To produce an *unauditioned* youth choir capable of performing, for example, the Brahms' Requiem *and* the Haydn Nelson Mass at the same concert, as he did one year, with full ad hoc orchestra in a large concert hall, certainly indicates that his theories and policies worked; and that his energy was still hugely in evidence.

He was approached one day by a girl who had read on her term report, 'She would probably do well in the choir'. She went to see him. 'But, sir, I can't sing.' He put a note down on the piano. 'Sing that.' She got somewhere near it. 'That's all right,' he said. 'We've got lots in the choir like that!' She told me many years later that she has always been in choirs ever since.

So the question arises: if anyone can come along, untested, what sort of standard can the choir achieve? We have a number of recordings taken at concerts, which answer that unequivocally. I would back the standard of Derry's choir, average age I suppose about 16/17, against that of many adult amateur choirs. Their training was excellent; their comprehension of what they were singing more than adequate. Moreover, the records span nearly two decades, early 1950s to late '60s; the standard is unfailingly high. With all student choirs, whether school or university, there is the same massive problem: every year the top students leave for life beyond school, and a new bunch of novices arrives. Despite this, year after year the choir produced wonderful concerts, and I know that for many of them the music they made was the most challenging and thrilling thing that happened to them in their school careers.

I had a letter from one former student that said that the evening of the concert, all of them in their place, the orchestra tuning up, and then Doc, as he was always called, and the soloists entering in evening dress, was tremendously exciting. It was for me, too. It was the culmination of many weeks of hard work, unseen by the other performers who had arrived on the night with their trumpets and oboes and violins, and hardly guessed at by the audience; and it made everything, all the hours spent learning a new part for me, all the days and nights spent by Derry as he made certain that nothing could go wrong when the big moment came, absolutely worthwhile—a proof that no time or energy had been wasted. I was very proud of him and his achievement.

One year we did 'Elijah' again. Derry was very particular about the trombones—the opening chords need to be well done, or they sound ridiculous. He had a reliable trio of army brass players booked for the occasion. Before the rehearsal began, a worried looking man came towards me. 'I'm afraid the trombonists can't come. They've been called on for an army performance.' I must have looked horrified. 'But I think it'll be all right,' he said. 'We've come in their place—we're from the BBC Symphony Orchestra!'

The chords were excellent!

12

B ack on the home front, life was still on the complicated side. Ganga spent his days sitting in the awful chair, and because I was very busy with children and music it was difficult to help him as much as perhaps we should have done. Cataract operations had left him with little sight for reading, though he did look at the newspapers. He was frail and very deaf, which made contact really hard. Try as we might, he would not have a hearing aid.

A visiting friend asked him once, 'Why don't you get a hearing aid, Mr Morgan?' This had to be said at high decibels! Ganga replied, 'I don't want people to know I'm deaf'. Considering that he never saw anyone but us, because he wouldn't go out, this was hardly an argument. I tried to leave him to Derry as much as possible, but the daytimes were all mine.

Eventually his frailty became a real problem; one morning he announced that he had decided he wouldn't get up any more. It was clearly time for the nurses to come and deal with him, and so we were back in the same system that Granny had needed. Somehow we managed.

Helen was now nearly 20 months old. Paddy was about 4½; Cynthia coming up to ten. I had singing students coming in the evenings; thankfully, not too many. And upstairs was Ganga, sitting in bed—what thoughts would be going through his head during those last weeks of his life? I have no idea. He never chatted to me, didn't talk about days gone by, except sometimes to Cynthia, and we maintained a rather distant relationship which I regretted then and still regret today. But, given the situation I was in, I don't know what more could have been done.

Like his wife, he had never really taken to the idea that I was now married to his son. This made it difficult for me. I would have liked to have been on easy, relaxed terms with both of them. On one unfortunately memorable occasion I found him threatening to hit Patrick, then three, with the coal shovel, because the child had refused to shut the sitting room door. I stormed in! What did he think he was doing?

On another occasion I heard him telling Cynthia that the family heirloom he was holding would 'one day be hers'. He explained that when he died it would come to her father, and then, one day, it would come to her, because she was her daddy's heir.

I had had enough. I said, 'Patrick is Derry's heir, if we're talking about family inheritance.' He stared at me. 'How d'you make that out?' 'Because he is Derry's son.' He clearly could not accept this. 'Ah,' he said triumphantly, 'but by a different mother!'

I said, 'It doesn't matter how many wives Derry has, the children are his.'

He was silent for a moment. Then, 'Good God, I must be his grandfather!'

I found this both funny and hurtful. How could he have lived with us for so long, and seen the children together for a couple of years before that, and never realised that he was Patrick's Ganga too?

It was about this time, when Helen started talking, that Patrick became Paddy. The reason was simple—it was the nearest she could come to saying his proper name. Anyway, he has been Paddy ever since. It was appropriate enough; the family on that side was Northern Irish, and Ganga had apparently been known as Paddy in his earlier life.

Retiring to his bed had its value as well as its difficulties. It meant I could deal with the school contingent and give Helen her breakfast before I had to do Ganga's. He ate corn flakes, so I took a tray up to him with his own bowl, cereal, tea pot and cup—not quite the Savoy, but it looked quite decent. He would serve himself and I would go in later and take the tray away before the nurse came. We fell into a routine.

One morning when I went in to collect the tray he gave me a huge smile, which rather surprised me. He spoke to me in the tones he reserved for visitors, very cordial. 'Are you the stewardess?' he said, and I, much taken aback, said, 'Well, I suppose I am.'

'Can you help me? I have to get on to that ship . . .' He pointed to the blank wall.

'I'll see what I can do,' I said, making my escape with the tray. When I went back he had quite forgotten about his trip, and I realised, not very willingly, that we had indeed embarked on a journey—he was showing clear signs of dementia.

He lasted nine weeks from the time he prescribed for himself complete bed rest. During that time he left us mentally to live in his own world, and I have to say he was usually happier during those two months than I had ever seen him.

One night, however, he was moaning and distressed. I went in to him. 'Oh, you'll have to tell them,' he kept saying. 'Who?' I asked. 'The RAF men.' 'Why? What do they want?' 'You'll have to tell them that I can't come tonight.' 'Where?' 'They take me out in their helicopter, but I can't come tonight. I'm an old man, and I'm too tired. You'll have to tell them.'

As fantasies go, this was quite a good one! I went to the top of the stairs and called down: 'Mr Morgan can't come tonight. He's too tired. You'll have to go away.'

Derry appeared downstairs. 'What on earth are you talking about?'

'It's your father . . .' I told him the tale. Meanwhile, Ganga settled down and went to sleep. Mission accomplished!

Easter, and it was clear that he hadn't long to go. He had been lying for a while without opening his eyes, and Derry and I were standing by his bed, watching. After a few minutes Ganga stirred, and tried to sit up. I was nearest, so I bent down to help. He put his hands on my arms and pulled himself up. Then he sort of *climbed* up me until his arms were round my neck.

'Shall I move him?' Derry said.

I shook my head. 'No, I'm all right.'

I stood like that for several minutes. I hadn't been so close to him for months. Then he put his head down on my chest, and gave a sigh. I wonder if he knew who I was. Perhaps his mother? Or perhaps he really wanted to have a moment of closeness with me. We'll never know. I cuddled him.

When I laid him down he sighed again, all without opening his eyes. We covered him up and tucked him in. At some point he slipped into a coma, and he died the next day, Easter Sunday.

Derry had the ashes scattered on the same grassy mound under the same blossoming tree where Granny's had been scattered two years earlier. Another part of our life had come to an end. From now on it was just the two of us and our three children. Normal life? I wouldn't have a clue!

A year later we embarked on another development in our family saga. I was very keen to have another baby—well, I had always wanted six!—and Derry was willing. So in December 1955 Keith Moore Morgan graced the world stage, around 8lbs of him, with legs that looked as if he might one day be a footballer; baby bootees looked quite odd on him.

The footballing didn't happen.

Well, it wasn't six children. But it was certainly all our budget would allow. Derry made that clear; and I could only agree. Keith was an obliging baby, even coping with an extremely cold winter (I put my fur cape over him to keep him warm in his crib), when the ice crept over the windows and made those wonderful patterns that are so hard to describe to anyone who hasn't endured a big freeze. Outside, the hedges by the front door were looped with cobwebs on which the water drops had frozen, and if I put the washing out to dry I could carry in Derry's shirts frozen so hard that they could stand up by themselves for a short while on the kitchen floor. It's amazing that the seemingly delicate flower bulbs in the garden don't freeze, too, and fail to emerge once the weather improves.

Before long it's difficult to believe that one was once so cold. Spring comes, babies can go outside in their prams, dogs can be taken for walks without their pads becoming solid with frozen snow. But meanwhile, perhaps the most trying time for someone like me with a pram and a toddler was when the snow ploughs had been through, and the snow was piled on the edges of the paths. Fine if we had a thaw; but often the piles would freeze hard during the night, and to try and push a pram through 30 centimetres (or one foot) of solid, rock hard snow would try the arm muscles to their full extent. All the same, it's amazing what we can do when we are young and vigorous.

I discovered over the next few years that having a baby born just before Christmas was very hard on the child as he grew. That final fortnight is when most of the preparations are done, and a small child can easily lose sight of his birthday while turkeys and Christmas puds are beginning to take all of his mother's concentration. When he was perhaps about four I decided that my final preparations for Christmas would have to wait until we had celebrated Keith's birthday. I dimly recall that this idea quite alarmed me at first; but over the years I found it to be refreshing. While all my friends appeared to be exhausted by mid-December I was just getting into my swing. And I found that I really enjoyed that mad gallop through the final two weeks. Only essentials were taken care of before his birthday: ordering the turkey, getting presents for mailing to distant rellies and so on. Then, on December 11th, birthday over, I made lists (and sometimes lists of lists, just in case), and it was all systems go for the 25th.

Some of the things I did just to help my own memory became a part of the family Christmas ritual. Notably the chart, made out like a table tennis competition and stuck up on the wall, with all the names of those who were to give presents along the top, and recipients down the side. As presents were bought, a tick was put where the two columns joined. As there were, eventually, eight of us, plus aunts, uncles, grandparents and possibly a friend or two, it would have been extremely complicated for me to keep a check on what had been bought or made.

The chart saved all that trauma. And one year, much later, when Helen came home from university, and rushing to the chart ticked off *all* her columns, calling triumphantly 'I'm first!', I realised that it had become more than an *aide-memoire* for me, but a real part of our celebration.

Those two weeks were also busy for Derry. The carol service, which was eventually established in the parish church of St Martin in the middle of Dorking, was always a delight and hugely successful in its ability to draw in people not only attached to the school but also town residents. If you were not in your seat well before the service started you would have to stand; and I have seen occasions when the whole of the back of the large church, behind the back pews, plus both the side aisles, were crammed with people.

In those earlier days my father was the organist, and thoroughly enjoyed having a chance to play the St Martin's organ and be involved in a real feast of lovely music. With the Christmas readings and the prayers this was a long service, perhaps at least 2½ hours, but I never heard any complaints about that.

It took place around our wedding anniversary on the 18th. Derry would fix the date for the main rehearsal, or even the service itself, without consulting me, so quite often it was on the same day as our anniversary. He would say, 'Will that be all right, then?' and I would agree, because it was the best way to celebrate I could imagine, and far more memorable than a candle-light dinner.

A few things stand out about those early Christmases. One year, when Alison and Fiona were probably about 6 and 4, we let them decorate the lounge room with garlands. These were the rather gorgeous things that opened out into complex layers and looked really good when hung. We left them to get on with it, not quite realising that they were not going to be able to raise them high enough for us larger mortals. When we went to see how they were managing there was a criss-cross of garlands at about head height—*their* head height! It seemed a pity to take them down after all their hard work, so we stood it for a few hours, then I suggested to Derry that this was going to give us both stiff necks before long, and we took them down and rehung them—as tactfully as possible.

In 1959, when Keith was four, I took him to the Carol Service for the first time. Standing on a hassock he could just see over the pew. For much of the service he slept on my knee; I woke him in time for the last hymn, 'O come all ye faithful', and he sang it with great energy. When we came to the chorus I realised he was singing 'O come let us adore me' which seemed quite reasonable—four-year-olds are pretty adorable!

Somehow, children have a gift for getting sick just in time for the festive season, in our family, anyway. Fiona went down with something vaguely lurgy-ish around the 23rd; I called the doctor, because we were going to stay in Lancashire with my parents. I doubt if the illness was anything very dreadful, but Fiona had a high temperature for a while, and the doctor said that *he personally* wouldn't take a child of her age on a journey like that in that condition, and thought we would be wise to cancel our trip.

That was all very well. I had bought nothing in the food line for the week we were to be away, on strict instructions from my mother, who made it clear that she would have everything necessary. I knew she would—she was a great caterer. So for a moment I had no idea what to do. She was expecting a family of seven (Cynthia was in the Navy by that time). I rang her and told her what had happened. I think she was as confused as I was. I said (very tentatively) 'Could you and Dad come down here instead?'

Deadly silence at the other end of the line. Then, 'But I've got everything here.' After some very quick thinking she said, 'I'll speak to your father'. Good move! He was excellent at planning. And so they agreed to travel down, bringing all the goodies with them, and I was *not to get anything!* Under pain of what, I wonder. I felt bad about it—but we had a good Christmas. Though I did get ticked off for buying in a few things—my own catering skills got in the way.

But generally our Christmases were excellent. The children behaved beautifully, they seldom squabbled over presents—and we usually managed to remember who had sent the gifts so that in the week ahead some letters of thanks could be written. Once the turkey had been removed from the oven and carved and we had remembered who liked Brussels sprouts and who didn't all was well. A very active holiday, but a very welcome change after the hustle and bustle of the term just finished.

All too soon it was school time again, woolly gloves and warm socks, and scuffing through the snow if it had been a white Christmas. I look back with considerable pleasure to those days. They were not always easy, but the rewards were there.

13

All the same, it would be silly to pretend that everything was serene. As early as the nine months of our engagement I had realised that I had taken on a challenge. Derry had a darker side that no one outside the family would have recognised. During those months, which I had thought would be idyllic as we got to know each other, he all too frequently lost his temper, sometimes quite alarmingly. It was interesting, when we returned from our honeymoon on the Isle of Wight, to learn from my mother that my newly acquired mother-in-law had said to her after the wedding reception that what she was really afraid of was Derry's temper. I was glad it wasn't just me!

Having said that, I am always truly happy to say that we had the most delightful honeymoon. Derry was relaxed and cheerful—why shouldn't he be? As we were there for the two weeks over Christmas (at Farringford, once the home of Alfred Lord Tennyson), the hotel soon filled up with families and couples and a few singles, and he was charming and friendly with everyone. We had taken some music with us 'just in case', and so we gave a very small recital one day in the hotel lounge, which went down well. And the weather, at that time of year when we might have expected anything, was perfect for every day except one, when it rained heavily. Apart from that one day, the sea sparkled on both sides of the island, and we met some very pleasant people.

On our first evening there, while we were signing the register with the magical '*Dr and Mrs D M Morgan*' (I was wondering if it was really true), the manager was standing next to us. (How odd that I can remember that his name was Pellisier). He saw what

Derry had written and said, 'Ah, we have a doctor in the house for Christmas. We shall know who to come to if someone is ill'.

I don't think Derry was particularly pleased, but he said, 'Sorry, wrong kind of doctor'.

The manager said, 'What kind?'

Derry said, 'Music', quite brusquely, but the manager was not going to be put off. 'Ah, then perhaps you'll be able to tell us what is wrong with our piano.'

Eventually Derry went to see the offending instrument. He stood across the room and regarded it for a moment, then said, 'Yes, I can see what's wrong. You've got it right up against the radiator'.

I think the manager thought he was a genius! But radiators and pianos don't mix—and any student could have told them that.

As the hotel filled up for Christmas, a young man shared our breakfast table. He was Jewish, and he was on his own. On Christmas morning there was a wrapped gift on our early morning tray: a perpetual calendar that I still have in my dining room—now well over 60 years old.

At breakfast we apologised for not having a gift for him, but he pointed out that Christmas is not celebrated by Jews. His name was Philip Cohen, and we got on so well with him that he came once to visit us in Dorking.

I think Derry was determined that I should be an educated reader; from time to time he would produce a book for me to read, which I obediently did—and I must say it was a useful addition to my future career as a writer. While we were on the Isle he decided to introduce me to Pepys Diary, which I had barely heard of. One day we went into the local village in search of a bookshop; when we found it, there was a very pleasant woman behind the counter who said with obvious regret that they did not have a copy of the Diary. Derry said we'd get one when we went home. Then she did a most extraordinary thing: she said, 'I have a copy by my bedside all the time. I'll lend it to you if you like.' We were astonished. She didn't know us—all she knew was that we were staying at

Farringford. She simply asked that we should return it before we went home, which of course we did.

As someone who had a burgeoning interest in history I was delighted with the Diary. What an amazing tale it reveals of the life of London around the time of the 1665 great plague and the Great Fire of London in 1666! I was both fascinated and appalled. But I have always been grateful to the bookshop lady for letting me read it while I had the time, before my newly acquired household duties washed over me.

One day, in an attempt to have some time to ourselves (for honeymooners we had been remarkably involved with the other guests), we asked the kitchen to let us have sandwiches and took off to walk the 14 miles from Farringford to Carisbroke Castle, up on the central point of the island. It was a beautiful day, and we took our time, getting to the castle sometime after we had eaten our picnic.

As all this burning of energy was at least partly to give us time away from the rest of the hotel residents, it was a bit daunting, on our arrival, to be hailed from the castle walls—and to find that a whole coach load of fellow guests had got there before us. But we made the best of it, and memory fails to tell me how we got home again. I wonder if they offered us a place on the coach.

With only three weeks' holiday for English schools at Christmas it was soon time for us to develop some kind of lifestyle and pattern for living. Derry was back to the music and staff rooms (I've often wondered if the other men pulled his leg about his child bride, but when I asked he wasn't forthcoming), and Cynthia had to be taken by bus to the other end of town for her school.

I think, from occasional remarks from the staff there, that her attendance may have been a bit irregular while she was with Granny and Ganga. One could hardly blame them. Getting the bus from where they lived would have been a trifle difficult, and timing things so that they could collect her at the other end of the day would not have been at all easy. Doing the double journey with a young and lively 'mum' was a very different matter, and we soon found a balance for it. We didn't possess a car for another six years, though in fact I was able to drive, as long as Dad would lend me the 1931 Humber.

But Cynthia was a very bright child, and I doubt if all the ups and downs did her much damage. It certainly didn't reduce her energy levels.

It was not long before I realised I was pregnant. We had discussed this possibility, and I felt that, with Cynthia being four already when we were married, it would be a pity to put off another child and lengthen the distance between her and the baby. Above all, I wanted us to have a united family, and not be conscious of the difference in parentage. Looking back on it, I believe I was right.

That March the school concert was *Israel in Egypt* (Handel), and it was one of the very few in which I didn't sing the soprano solos. I had been slightly sick in the mornings, but the main problem was that I was very occasionally slightly dizzy, and I was a bit scared at the thought that I might lose my balance on a platform—and fall off! So the soprano role was sung by Marjorie Avis, often heard on the BBC. I was able to sit in the audience and appreciate what this young choir was able to achieve.

And so we settled into married—and family—life. It was a steep learning curve for me, and there were a few dramatic moments over the creation of meals; but nobody got poisoned. One of my earliest meals was a beef stew. Derry always came home for lunch—school, after all, was only just up the road—and the stew was ready in the oven. As I took it out, my hands slipped, and the whole lot went on the floor. I regret to say that I let out a shriek and yelled for my mother, who was just downstairs. Clearly I hadn't yet quite grown up. I remember her running up the stairs (I probably sounded as if I had cut off my arm) and helping me to salvage what we could.

Whether we just put it back into the dish and said nothing about it, or whether I had to devise something else extremely quickly, I don't remember. Probably just as well. Whatever! I doubt if we went without lunch.

Derry gave me £4 a week for housekeeping. It is interesting, to me at least, to recall that we were still rationed; I had to learn how to make meals from rather sad and small pieces of meat, and there were limitations on other kinds of food. Clothes were rationed, too, right up to 1949, the year Paddy was born. I was delighted when I became pregnant to get additional clothing coupons for the baby; so it was a strange sort of blow when, during that summer, clothes rationing was abolished. On the one hand I was glad not to have to plan quite so carefully; on the other, I had never had so many coupons—and couldn't use them!

Meat was a real problem. Rabbit meat was usually available, but in those days it was not cut into neat portions that look nothing like a rabbit. I had been averse to rabbit as a food from the time, well pre-war, when I had found bits of lead shot in my dinner, and realised for the first time exactly what it was I was eating, and how it had died. But when food is scarce, you eat! And I set off for the butcher's shop to buy a rabbit for dinner.

The butcher, along with the grocer and anyone else who handled my green ration book, which one was given in pregnancy—presumably so that one could eat for two—was quite amused by my attempts to order a bunny. He had known me since I was a much younger schoolgirl, and took great delight in calling me 'Mrs Morgan' to make me blush.

'I've got one in the cool room,' he said, and disappeared out to the back. When he returned he was carrying a rabbit, skin on, on his hand. 'Will this do?'

I said yes, having no idea how one judged a dead rabbit.

He had a finger under its chin, and suddenly made the animal's head go up and down. 'Oh dear, I don't think this one's quite dead!'

I think I behaved with decorum. At least I didn't utter a small shriek. He took it away and skinned it and chopped it into pieces, and I took it home.

We were much more used to dealing with the reality of dead animals in those days, though less than the previous generation, whose cooks had to de-feather chickens (if they hadn't had to kill them first), draw everything out of the innards, and wash them through. Dealing with herrings was quite good fun, I found. Chop off the head, slit down the middle, pull out the insides, keeping the roes, clean and fry. Very soothing after a difficult weekend!

From an early age we were used to seeing sides of beef hanging up in the butcher's shop, turkeys, geese and hares slung on hooks from bars across the poulterers (now, there's a word you don't get much these days), the hares with their faces stuck in a sort of mug, presumably for 'jugged hare'. As I never had that delicacy, and didn't fancy it, I can't say what it tasted like.

We hadn't been married very long when Derry told me one day that he could only give me 30 shillings for housekeeping that week. We were obviously having a financial crisis. I was shattered. That was about one-third of what I normally had, which in itself was a bit tight with three of us to feed. I went downstairs to my mother after he and Cynthia had gone to school, and poured out my woes. I am pretty sure that I thought she would probably give me a pound or so to get me through.

Actually, she said, 'Well, you'll have to be a bit clever, won't you?' And she gave me recipes and information that would help us survive. At the end of the week, Derry said, 'We've never eaten so well. I think I'll give you the same amount next week!' Another very valuable learning curve.

I was certainly learning a lot in those first months, including how to look after a very sick child—Cynthia, suffering from whooping cough. She was well enough by May to have her birthday party. My father had an old army tent, quite large, and we put it up in the garden for the children to play in.

The guests began to arrive. Cynthia shot out of the tent, rushed up to the child, grabbed the present and disappeared into the tent again. We had to fish her out and teach her about the duties of a hostess.

That is something which every child learns from scratch. I would say to them when they went to someone's party, 'Now remember, you are the guests and you must do as your hostess wants, because it's her party'. When the party was at our place I would say, 'Now remember, they are your guests and you must let them choose what to do.' Eventually one of the children said, 'But when do we do what *we* want?'

Good question. No answer.

14

Memories tend to come thick and fast once the door is opened. Unfortunately, they don't always come in chronological order. Still, that is a bit like life—the chaos theory (which I don't in the least understand, but it sounds good) should be best seen in our daily lives. And I find that once an idea has begun to grow it gathers other thoughts to it that are pushing to be recorded—presumably in case I forget them.

These days, those of us who use computers to write our deathless prose are so incredibly fortunate. When I think back to the early days in my writing career I remember the awful moments when, having done a 'good' copy of a short story, right up to the last page, I would realise that I had omitted a whole sentence (or even a paragraph), and would have to retype the entire piece. As I create these memoirs I can carry on, errors and omissions ignored, because I can go back and fill them in as and when I please.

And that leads me to thinking about the much earlier generations of writers, who had to do everything in pen on paper. When I started, I used to wonder about Jane Austen: how she would have written every word of *Pride and Prejudice* or *Emma* by hand in a notebook; and then how it would have been set up for printing. When I sent my most recent novel *The Boy from the Hulks* (second edition with sequel added) to be published, it was done on a disk, and sent *by email* to America! I don't even like to think what publishing will be like in another hundred years; perhaps it will simply be flashed into our brains in the same way that, today, I can order books through my computer or Kindle e-reader, and in a few seconds there they are, on screen. I think my mind has been boggled so much in these past years by the speed of development that it is now boggleproof.

Of course, the same speed of change is happening to so many parts of our lives. When, in about 1949, Ganga had to have a cataract operation, it was a long and arduous endurance test for him. He had to lie in his hospital bed without moving his head once the operation was over, and when he came home he was virtually unable to read anything because he was never able to make the 'pebble' glasses they gave him work to his advantage. So in his final years he could only read the headlines.

Recently I was told that it would be advisable to have my cataracts removed. The optometrist said that I would be feeling OK after about 3 hours; and apart from having to be a bit careful, and put drops in my eyes for a while, I should have no problems. The added bonus was that I would no longer need distance spectacles! It makes me think that my father, who was virtually blind in one eye as a result of a detached retina from his twenties or so, would probably not have lost his sight in that eye, and possibly would even have been able to have laser treatment for his extreme short-sightedness. I feel very fortunate.

Even so, I was quite taken aback when the opthalmologist I was sent to, having finished shining bright lights into my eyes, said that it would not be necessary at this time to remove the cataracts. He had in fact found that I was suffering from macular degeneration, a slow progressive disease which in its final stages can sometimes lead to blindness; though I feel (and hope) that having been attacked by it late in life I may get away with simply having to cut down on the things one never wants lose: driving the car and reading—or in my case, writing.

Strangely, and quite coincidentally, I had been to see old friends from the concert-going days; the husband has macular degeneration, which means he can no longer drive the car (which his wife, thankfully, can still do) or read, except the largest print. He 'reads' audio books—and this reminds me that I must see if

I can find an Australian company that will turn my books into audio, the UK firm I had contacted some time ago having turned me down.

The lesson to be learnt from this, I think, is that if you are going to do something, once old age cracks in—go on a special holiday, write a novel, learn to play golf—*do it now!* I remember our doctor's wife in Dorking saying long ago when her husband died in his sixties: 'We were saving all sorts of thing to do when he retired, and now he's gone, and we shall never be able to do them'.

So I am as I write getting ready for my next trip, the 2012 Eastern States round journey to see the members of the family who have opted to live a very long way away from me. I shall also be seeing Hobart and Darwin for the first time, and returning to Adelaide by the Ghan, which promises all kinds of luxurious things as one travels through the Red Heart of this vast country. It is supposed to be one of the world's outstanding rail trips. We shall see! After the amount of talking I shall have been doing while visiting, I shall be glad of a couple of days in a train where I don't have to talk at all if I don't want to. So—*do it now!*

I seem to have taken a mighty leap forward from those long-ago days when I was a young wife and mother. But that, I find, is how memory works: ancient flashes of past days trigger off recollections of things that happened last week. Today we look at old, curling photographs or something from the thousands of pictures we can take with our digital cameras to remind us of what we did, where we went, whom we saw, what marvels we have witnessed around the world. I wonder what reminded folk *before* photography? Did they only have mental images and the mutual exchange of memories to be able to reminisce about the past? Was their memory of days gone by any more or less exact than ours? I have no doubt that one person would remember things one way, and another would be certain that hadn't been how it was at all.

When there is a tragedy, major flooding or extensive bush fires, many people want to save their family photos above anything else. And the ones who appear on TV amidst the wreckage of their lives so often mourn the loss of family memories.

I know I wouldn't want to lose my family video, which covers our lives from 1958 to the time we emigrated. I have been meaning to get it on DVD and send copies to my children. Yes, I know—*do it now!*

15

I n the late 1950s a very strange thing happened to us. Like many people who are short of money, I sometimes went in for competitions; and the Daily Express ran them regularly. This particularly memorable one asked for household goods to be arranged in some kind of order (that's all I can really recall about it); so I filled it in and sent it off.

Derry always said that I left it on the mantelpiece, and that if he hadn't posted it nothing would ever have happened. I don't agree! It was on the mantelpiece because I hadn't yet got round to posting it. Whatever! Off it went; and one Tuesday afternoon (I do remember it was a Tuesday) I had a call from the local editor of the Dorking Advertiser. Could he come and see me? (I know it was Tuesday, because it was my mother's afternoon for the Women's Meeting at church—and I wanted to ring her and tell her, but she wouldn't have been there).

I was very puzzled; but decided that it was probably something to do with Derry's concerts. It wasn't. He seemed very pleased about something; he said he had been contacted by the Daily Express, who wanted him to let me know that I had won the prize!

I don't recall being wildly excited. I was certainly very surprised. We all have that little bit of cynicism about prizes: they're rigged, or no one actually wins them, or if they do it won't be me! But this time it *was* me. He warned me that that there would be a few days' delay because they had to check that no one else was eligible to share the money. The prize was £5000.

It's difficult to work out what that would mean in today's money. But I did estimate it, a few years ago, as possibly around

$100,000. Our house, for example, cost £4350 a few years before. The nice second-hand car we bought to replace our old banger cost about £700. Derry's annual salary was probably less than half the prize money. It was going to make a big difference.

I recall being very calm about it; not so Derry. On the day we had been told to expect the confirmation in the newspaper, he was up early and off to the newsagent down the road; and he came back in a high state of excitement, waving the paper. 'You've won! You've won!'

I think I said something a bit dampening, like 'Oh, good!' I know he couldn't understand why I wasn't dancing around the bedroom. I have no idea myself.

What did we do with it? First, paid in the cheque. The bank clerk/teller sat and looked at it. 'That's really something,' he said (you can bet that everybody in town would have known about it). I divided it into two parts, current account and deposit account. For the first time I had a real bank account of my own—Derry had not been keen on the idea of letting me loose on his money! But I was going to enjoy using this windfall to the utmost, and being independent was the start.

We planned a holiday, the first without having to count every penny. We decided to tour England and Wales in our nice, reliable car (a maroon-coloured Vauxhall). I bought the movie camera that would record the family for years to come—a simple job with a wind-up handle, no technological mystery, but very effective. It was a lovely holiday, three weeks of seeing new places, travelling around the west of England, seeing Tintagel, Arthur's reputed castle, with a steep cliff down which a fragile-looking line of steps led across a chasm which I refused to attempt. Merlin's cave is down there.

At this point the age range of the children was from Keith at about 2½ up to Cynthia at 14, and we had decided not to book ahead but to chance the availability of bed-and-breakfasts. We gaily said that if necessary we could sleep in the car; but on the one or two occasions that we began to think that we wouldn't find beds for the night we were less keen on the idea of sleeping two adults and four children in a vehicle that was not exactly built for it.

We saw the charms of the west country; Wales delighted us, being very different from our home base in Dorking; the Lake District was beautiful—and it was there that Paddy and Helen both went down with severe sore throats. We were going to cross that narrow neck of England to get to Sunderland, on the east coast, where Nancy's long-time friend, Cynthia's godmother, Margot, lived with her husband—also named Paddy. This was to be a new introduction for me, because Margot and I had never met, and I had a feeling I might be under inspection as Nancy's replacement.

But we arrived with Paddy feeling extremely bad with what looked like a holiday-stopping throat. Margot found a local doctor who would come and see him, and he gave him a block-busting antibiotic. We had a nervous night, but in the morning Paddy was up and doing again, the pills having worked some kind of magic. We took a deep breath and relaxed.

Margot was very nice to me. When the children, including Cynthia, were all in bed, she turned to me as if there was something she must say. She said: 'When Cynthia came to stay with us after you were married I waited to hear that things were not easy for her. I thought she might pour out things to me that she had been hiding. After she went to bed I went up to see her, and she was sitting up, crying. I thought, "*Ah, now we'll see!*" I asked her what was the matter, and she said, "I want Mummy!" And I knew she meant you. So I knew that everything was fine.'

I was glad she took time to tell me. I hadn't been surprised or hurt that people would think I couldn't manage what I had taken on. As far as they were concerned, I was a girl straight out of school. How could I possibly cope?

All the same, by then we had four children and they were all nicely dressed and well behaved. And Derry wasn't complaining! There really wasn't any need to worry.

By the time we left there it was clear that Helen had Paddy's sore throat. In her case this was to be no quick cure job. It was many months before it became a real concern, with recurring attacks of something that was eventually diagnosed as rheumatic fever, sometimes fairly mild, occasionally severe. She was six, healthy, a lovely child who was doing well at school, in the classroom and on the sports field. I never knew when the next attack would come.

Over the following months into 1959 she began to show signs of serious health problems. She lost weight and I became increasingly worried. Today I would have bombarded the doctor with questions, but I was younger then and inexperienced, and I thought everyone knew better than I did. At last it was my mother who asked him the question: 'What's the matter with Hebe's daughter?'

He said, 'Yes, I shall have to go and tell her.' This seemed very odd, when my mother told me. I was by then certain that Helen had leukaemia, and at that time it was a certain killer. I had made up my mind that we were going to lose her.

The next day the doctor arrived. He seemed nervous, and for a man who was always so self-assured this was strange. We were in the dining room, and he kept walking around the table while I sat and watched him. He said, 'I want you to see a specialist in London. I think Helen has rheumatic heart disease.'

It sounds really weird, but *my* heart lifted. I was thinking, they can do something about hearts. It's not leukaemia! The doctor made an appointment for the next day, and Helen and I went up to the posh end of London town where the consultant had his rooms.

By that time, she was light enough for me to be able to lift her quite easily. She was not quite seven, and she should have been too heavy for me. I remember the doctor examining her, listening to her heart, stretching her across his knees for some reason and listening again. I felt very calm, because it all seemed to be under control. Then he said, 'I want her in hospital'.

'When?' I said.

'At once. Today.'

That's when I said a really silly thing. 'Oh, but she hasn't said goodbye to her father!'

I recall he stared at me; then he said, 'Well, all right, tomorrow then. But she mustn't walk. Wheel chair or carry her.' I realised we were talking about something very serious.

He said, 'Do you want her to go to Great Ormond Street or University College Hospital?' We had a friend, a young doctor, who was at UCH, so for that reason only I chose UCH, on the basis that if I couldn't get up to visit her, perhaps he could pop in on his rounds and she would have a visitor.

Then the doctor said, 'Don't expect to take her home, will you?' It took me about two days to understand what he was telling me. I don't think he really expected her to come through the treatment. And in fact they told me a few days later that her heart had been 'in failure'. They didn't tell me what they had had to do about it, and I didn't ask. The diagnosis was mitral stenosis, and the treatment involved huge doses of steroids. She was in UCH for three months, and then spent another two months at Queen Mary's Hospital at Carshalton for recuperation.

I visited her as often as I could, but it meant most of a day, getting to London and to the hospital then home again, and fitting it all in with the needs of the other children. Keith was about 3½, and I managed to get him into Stanway School, just up the road from my parents' house; it was where Rosemary and Philip had spent their primary years. Until he began there, Keith had to stay with Grandma each day, which was fine, but I had no idea what the future held and I felt it would be best if he had a settled day ahead of him instead of being constantly shifted around. Derry was preparing another concert, and there was no way he could visit except at the weekends. Our good and wonderfully eccentric friend Geoffrey Bowers very kindly stepped in occasionally to see Helen—I would like to have been a fly on the ward wall to see what he did. He was always great fun, and in fact in later years became a professional entertainer on cruise ships doing the world tour. I bet he was a riot!

Shakespeare knew all about the effect of using comedy to offset tragedy. At this time, when we were struggling to keep everyone going (and trying to avoid the traps of concentrating on one child to the detriment of the others), a moment of sheer joy came into our lives. The work in rehearsal this time was a concert version of *The Bartered Bride* by Smetana. We had seen it some while before at Sadlers Wells in London. Whether this was Derry's reason for choosing it I don't know; but it proved to be totally memorable and the best thing that could have happened to me, personally, at that really difficult time.

I was to sing the part of Marenka (pronounced *Majenka)* with David Galliver singing the tenor part of my boyfriend, Jenik, Richard Standen as the wily Kecal, marriage broker (about to be defeated by True Love), and David Price as Vasek, the poor old village idiot. This meant a rehearsal at home (how did we fit that in?) for soloists, and the luxury of *two* orchestral rehearsals, playing from what I dimly remember as impossibly difficult to read orchestral parts—and did Derry really have to send to somewhere behind the Iron Curtain for them? Surely not. But that sticks in my mind—that they were very difficult to find in the UK.

So, by the weekend of the first full rehearsal and performance, on a June Saturday, we all gathered in the school hall, and the orchestra tuned up—we were all ready to go! And the rehearsal followed by the first performance (the second on Monday evening) was off to a flying start.

It was such fun! I don't think I ever enjoyed doing anything as much as that, and I have no doubt that a part of my enjoyment was because for a few hours I was able to forget what real life was about, and sink myself into the love story of Jenik and Marenka—with all its false starts and stops, deceptions, misunderstandings and ultimately the happy couple winning through because Jenik was as devious as Kecal! Of course, he gave Marenka a few shocks on the way; but if he had explained to her what he was doing there wouldn't have been an opera.

There were some funny moments during the rehearsal. Galliver was standing at the back of the hall, watching what was happening on the tiny stage, as I was explaining that I didn't want to marry Vasek because '*I have a lover!*' My husband was on the podium; my daughter was in the choir; over 100 students really seemed to enjoy the idea that Mrs Morgan had a lover. And at the back of the hall, David was nodding madly and pointing to his chest, saying, 'It's me! It's me!'

Jenik had been given the push by his new step-mother a long time before the action of the opera. He explains to Marenka (again, this was at the rehearsal) why he had to leave home in a duet in which Marenka joins him—'*Though a mother is a blessing, yet a cruel stepmother is a curse!*' As we sang this I turned to the choir and waved to *my* step-daughter, and she waved back.

The music in this opera is tremendous, full of melody, drama, excitement. A duet for tenor and baritone in which Kecal tries to persuade Jenik to drop his courtship of Marenka in favour of another woman went with such a swing on one of the performance nights that Derry stopped the orchestra afterwards and turned to the audience. 'I think you'd like to hear that again,' he said, and they clapped heartily. I had the tapes of this performance put on to CDs a few years ago; I still get a huge kick out of playing them to myself. They are not perfect as far as the recording techniques are concerned. The tapes were done by senior boys who were not involved in the singing. The technical balance was not always top-notch; but nonetheless they are still well worth listening to.

We were very fortunate to have those three men as soloists. Standen had one of the best baritone voices I can recall, smooth and resonant; he seemed to enjoy coming to perform for us as much as the two Davids, who also did a number of concerts with us. As they came for a pittance, they must have found it worth their while musically. David Galliver, eventually becoming Elder Professor of Music in Adelaide, remained a good friend until his untimely death some years ago. Other musicians, brought together for those two performances and—if they had not played for us before—knowing only that they were booked to do a 'school concert', came with the world-weary expression that orchestral players sometimes bring in their instrument bags. A few minutes of hearing the choir sing often changed their minds about what they were listening to. I recall two young wind players, oboists, I think, settling down at a rehearsal for one of the great choral works and bringing out books to read when they were not actually playing.

I was sitting a short distance in front of them, watching the choir. After a few minutes the books went down and the young players, probably from one of the music colleges, watched what was happening 'on stage'. After a while they saw me watching *them*, and one of them said, 'These kids are *really good!*' It was always gratifying when newcomers appreciated what they were seeing.

So we had a great time with Smetana, after ten days of deep concern about Helen. I really believe that break gave me strength to carry on. It was June, and before long it would be the summer holidays, and we could try to organise ourselves so that the inevitable difficulties would be less destructive for our family life.

Helen seemed to cope with the changes in her lifestyle extraordinarily well for a six, then seven-year-old. Once the three months at UCH were up, I drove her to Queen Mary's at Carshalton for the two months they had advised might be best for her. I still don't know whether it was the right thing to do. But she was vulnerable to infection, and we had three other children at home who might well bring infection into the house. Anyway, we made the decision, right or wrong, and I took her to her new 'home', and left her in the hands of Sister Matthews, who had a ward full of children with varying health problems. It couldn't have been easy to look after them, ranging as they did from quite young to early teens. But I was not altogether happy with Sister Matthews, who was a bit too 'old school' for me. She wouldn't let me eat my lunch in the ward (which I had done every time at UCH) because, as she said, 'It wouldn't be very nice for the other children'. I pointed out that I was quite a polite eater (I was beginning to get a bit more confidence), but she was adamant.

That first day, I drove home wondering what I had done. The second time I went by train; I clearly remember sitting on a bench on the station platform waiting for my train home, and crying my eyes out, silently, of course. I had a great feeling of helplessness. There was a young man sitting on another bench, and he had a 'tranny', playing it very loud. It was Cliff Richard singing '*Living Doll*', and for a long time afterwards I would find myself in tears when I heard it on the radio.

But all things come to an end. Nothing is forever. And one day we took Helen home and started on a long period of convalescence. She had put on weight from the steroids (but thank God she was alive!), and she suffered at nights from very painful legs. I got to a point when I found it really difficult to get up at 2 am to massage her; but someone had to. We were together again, and it was time to get back to whatever 'normal' was.

As a result of my big win we had bought a small weatherboard cottage on the Thames at Walton, and had a 'custom-built' launch created for us in a local boatyard. We called it the '*Hebe One*', and it only occurred to me long after that if you said it out loud it sounded like '*Hebe Won*'! So people thought I had been very clever with words, when in fact I hadn't.

The cottage was called *Hullo*. My mother quite rightly thought it was an odd name, until she came to see it. Then she said it was exactly right; it was painted orange, and it clearly said 'hullo' to visitors, especially when you opened the door to them. With it came a couple of rowing boats; so with our little launch and its outboard motor and two other boats we were ready for nearly anything.

In the time we had *Hullo*, which was roughly four years, the children became water babies. I have a vivid memory of Keith, at four or five years old, solemnly rowing me up the river. I would tap his hands to show him which he should row hardest with, and sitting aft I was able to steer. We ran the launch up and down the river and got to know it pretty well. The front half was covered, so if the weather was inclement the passengers could keep dry. Derry, sitting at the back with the engine to look after, was not so lucky. But we had a wonderful time while it lasted, and it was only when I was heavily pregnant with Fiona that we decided we would have to sell the house, and ultimately the *Hebe One* as well. Our life directions simply changed, and we with them.

It had seemed logical to me, if not to Derry, that—because we had a little more money than usual—it would a good time to try for the fifth child. He was full of common sense ('how can we afford to put all these children through school and university?'); I was full of determination. I knew that if I didn't achieve my six I would always regret it.

So, in early 1960, I became pregnant with Alison. When I was about two months on I was in the back of Dad's car, with Rosemary in the middle and Mum next to her. I leaned towards Rosemary and said, 'Ask Mum if she'd like to knit me a matinee jacket for January'. Rosemary stared at me, then relayed the message. There was what I might truly call a pregnant pause. Then Mum said, very firmly, 'No, I wouldn't!' At least it was a different way of announcing my condition.

January 4th saw Alison's arrival. She was a nine-pounder, and she was so soaked in fluid that her hands looked as if she'd just done a week's washing. Back in Rose Hill Nursing Home once more—but now I was an 'older mother', and I made my own decisions about when nappies needed changing.

The nurse came in one day. 'You'll be bringing this one back,' she said. Why? Because Alison hardly stopped grizzling. She sounded really annoyed about something; but a 3-day old baby isn't going to tell you why. She was healthy, and that was the important thing. But, once home again, I found that my previous experience in doing without sleep came in very usefully! I'll say no more.

Once Fiona arrived on the scene in 1963, I had achieved my six children—and I never became broody again. She was a good baby, much admired by the others, who were usually prepared to give her the bottle or play with her. I should probably make the point that of all the babies (all of them intentional pregnancies) she was the most planned. Alison was five years younger than Keith, so there was quite a gap there; and eventually I had suggested to Derry that it would be a good idea to have another one so that Alison wouldn't be a 'tail-ender'.

He said it wouldn't. I thought it would. We didn't argue about it, but I suspect I wore him down in the end. I really wanted that final baby! Once he had given in, I said 'when'? It was an important decision. We wanted to avoid the Spring concert, the school long holiday and Christmas! (I thought my mother might kill me if I had another baby around December/January). Finally I said, 'Well, the first fortnight in July looks OK'. So we got down to it, and I was able to tell the doctor (who thought I was mad to be having another one) that it would arrive around July 10. In fact, she beat my estimate, and was born on the 3rd. *That* is family planning!

At the time I was choir mistress at St Paul's Church in Dorking. When I got to about four or five months into the pregnancy I thought enough was enough. After service one Sunday I spoke to the choristers, and said I would be leaving as I was having another baby. There was some joviality about this, all good natured. But one elderly spinster lady, an alto who always took the seat closest to the congregation and was therefore extremely visible, and who shone a torch on her hymn book to emphasise to the vicar that there was not enough lighting in the chancel, took me aside afterwards, and with a disapproving air said that after *this* one was born I should go to the women's clinic.

I stared at her, not understanding for a moment what she meant. When it came to me that she wanted me to get 'fixed up' so that there wouldn't be any more babies, I laughed.

I said, 'Oh, this one is planned. They were all planned.'

She said, 'Really?' in a tone of voice that, if I had been ready to be offended, would have led to fisticuffs in the graveyard. I said, 'Yes, really!' and left her. But I don't think she believed me.

If she had been a more friendly I might have confided in her.

Apart from the fact that I had really had enough of making up bottles for babies (which I do think is one of the worst motherhood chores), I thoroughly enjoyed those first weeks with

Fiona. At about 2 or 3 months we had the christening at St Paul's, and I recall being quite pleased with myself on that day, when we went home for tea. I looked around my family, and realised that all four girls were wearing dresses I had made for them (including a *broderie anglaise* christening dress for the baby) and on the table were cakes and even bread that I had made. (I didn't make my own jam. Somehow it never set for me). Not bad going, I thought, for a mother of six. I tried not to look proud!

But we were about to enter another session of ill-health. Helen, now 11, and in her first term at Dorking Grammar School, came home one day looking quite ill. She complained of pain in her back, and was clearly distressed. I took her to the doctor and he arranged for X-rays. A short time later he came to see me, with the X-rays; and he put them up against the lounge window so that I could see them clearly.

'Poor kid,' he said. 'She gets everything!'

I asked what it was, and he said he thought she might have tuberculosis of the spine. This was a real shock. Helen still needed a certain amount of care because of the rheumatic pains she had in her legs. Dr Brice sent us off to a specialist, who said it was not TB (that was a relief), but that she would have to wear a plaster jacket for several months. This would hold her spine upright and stop her getting a curvature.

Ages later I realised that Granny might well have had the same problem. Her back was definitely curved, and her head came forward at an uncomfortable angle. She once told me that when she was a girl she had had to wear a 'backboard' at times, which I suppose was meant to have the same effect as a plaster jacket.

Anyway, poor Helen was sealed up in her plaster, waist to armholes, and she wore it for about two months. I kept her home from school for that first term, and she and I went through the maths and English syllabus together; in the end, she did well, her back was straight, school work not unduly tough in spite of the gap, and we had survived another health drama. I sincerely hoped we had now finished with the worst problems.

When she was six, and the doctor was talking to me about her heart condition, he gave me some excellent advice. He told me about a patient of his who had spent her life as an invalid because, as a child, she had developed a heart murmur, and her parents had decided that she couldn't live a normal life. By the time he saw her she was in her fifties, her life wasted.

'Don't do that to Helen,' he said. 'Let her live as normal a life as possible.'

So that is what we did. Derry and I discussed it, and agreed that she should do anything she felt able to do. As we had been told that she would probably not live beyond about 13 we both felt that she should have as good a life as she felt well enough for. The only limit we put on her was that she was not to play team sports at school; these would have meant that she must keep going for the good of the side. I arranged this with the sports staff. If she said she was tired she must be allowed to sit out.

As a result, I believe she did pretty well what the other girls did. And at 13 she showed no sign of failing in health. So the doctors told me, after her regular check-up, that she would probably be so short of breath by the time she was 20 that she would find stairs difficult. After she was 20 we heard that she would almost certainly have to have heart surgery in her 40s. No doubt that was why she went to Jamaica in her mid-20s and eventually had two babies in comparatively primitive conditions! For whatever reason, she came through triumphantly. As I write, at 60 she still shows no sign of falling off her personal twig.

16

It was while I was in Rose Hill Nursing Home that I read in the Dorking Advertiser, our local paper, that a woman who had been writing a 'mother column' for a while had decided to give it up because she was expecting her second child. I had found it an irritating bit of writing, because she was talking about her toddler son, and she never seemed to have anything positive to say about him. I used to wonder what the effect would be on him if he ever came across her cuttings.

I can remember lying on the bed, the baby snuffling in her crib, and thinking 'I could do that!' It seemed obvious to me that I should take over from a second time mum when I had just become a sixth time mum. I had had this niggling wish to write for quite a while, but I could never quite decide how to go about it. I had started a novel a few years earlier, but it came to nothing.

Around this time, the mid-1960s, I embarked on a writing course for short stories. I found it enjoyable and instructive, and the tutors were—understandably, since I was paying them—very encouraging. When I came to the end of the course they suggested I might like to have a pen name. This was a new idea to me, but I found it intriguing. I was already known in some areas as Hebe Morgan, soprano, and I thought it might be quite a good idea to have another *persona* for writing. Simply because I had been known at the youth club during the war as Barbara I decided that I would hold on to that. But what would go with Barbara?

In the end I chose Yates, which was my grandmother's maiden name, and Rothwell, which was my mother's. I think they go well together, though people do tend to get them back to front: Barbara Rothwell Yates. I sometimes think it doesn't really matter, since it's made up; but it has had the long-term effect that I am probably known to more people now as Barbara than Hebe, certainly in Australia. That suits me quite well; you don't have to keep explaining 'Barbara', but people always want to know what 'Hebe' means!

My first bite at the apple of success was when my short story was chosen for the BBC's Morning Story programme. The stories had to be the correct length to fit into the slot available—15 or 20 minutes, I'm not sure which. I was paid £25, and I was delighted. It was called *The Wallflower*, and when, a while ago, I made a collection of 20 short stories that I had written over many years I pondered whether to include it. In the end, I did. It was, after all, the entry into whatever success I later achieved.

But I was very taken with the idea of doing a regular column. So I wrote to the editor, put my case—and nothing happened. I was to learn over the years that this is not uncommon in the newspaper world. You really learn patience. But one day I received a letter from the newly appointed features editor, saying he had been going through the accumulated mail and had found my request. Could I submit something for them to look at?

Oh, yes, I could! I had had something boiling in my mind ever since I had sent off my letter. I wrote it quite quickly, and posted it. I have always thought that it could only have bounced once on his desk before he was on the phone to me. Could I do another one? If so, they would like to have something regularly.

I was thrilled! I wrote another and sent it off, and then I sat and waited for the weekly paper to arrive. That was my second lesson in patience. Absolutely nothing happened for several weeks. I began to wonder if I had dreamt it. Then, one day, I had a message asking me if I could have a photograph taken to put with the article. The photographer arrived, posed me, took a few shots and left. I was now rather nervous. I didn't like having my photo taken, even for family interest, so to have it on the page with my article was daunting.

I was right to worry. The article appeared—very impressive, I thought, with my by-line . . . and a photograph. I had written a bit about myself, including the fact that I had six children. I looked with some dismay at the picture (fortunately only a small one) of this woman who seemed to be a dismal, weary, over-burdened creature; it was easy to believe that she had six offspring! A while later I asked if they could do another picture of me, and the sad creature was replaced by someone who looked as if she actually enjoyed motherhood.

I was paid a small amount—I think it was probably £5 a time—for my featured articles. I would have done it for nothing, but I wasn't going to tell the editor that. Anyway, I was now a published author, in both journalism and fiction, and that pleased me greatly. It also pleased me that I began to get very positive feed-back from readers, who are the ultimate arbiters. And to my surprise no one seemed to think it was odd of me to have taken another name.

I was asked to do a few local interviews, and I remember the lady who lived only a matter of minutes from me. She was a writer, and had achieved a small local fame from something she had published. She told me in no uncertain terms that I must make up my mind—was I going to write fiction or be a journalist? It had not occurred to me that I had to make the choice. I tried to argue the point, but she was adamant. When I got home I thought it out and decided that was rubbish. Plenty of famous writers managed to enter both genres.

The other woman I remember, this time with some pleasure, was again someone who lived quite close to me, in two rooms upstairs in someone's house. Her book, about her early years, very beautifully bringing to life the first world war period, with her father off to the wars and her mother left to cope as best she could, was truly memorable. She told me that she had shown the manuscript to her brother, who said that no one was going to want to read about their family. But I thought it was excellent, very straightforwardly done, and very readable. I wish I could recall her name: the title of her book was *Tapioca for Tea*. I have no idea if she ever wrote the sequel that she had mentioned to me. If she didn't, that was a pity. It was historically important and convincingly written, and that period, which she recalled with a child's perception, was worth putting on paper.

Journalism, which has an instant impact, and short stories, which (if you are a quick writer) take little time to write—most of the writing, I found, was done in my head before it went on the page—are ideal if you want to write and don't have much time available. Derry took to my new hobby quite calmly—I even think sometimes that he was proud of me, though he was not one to gush. He never questioned my ability in anything, and this is a great support for someone trying out new ways, whether it be singing or writing, or simply bringing up rather a large mob of children! I feel sorry for women who, when they try something new, are met with the rolled eyes and mild sarcasm of a husband who obviously doesn't yet appreciate that women, too, have brains. That was a hurdle I never had to leap over.

Children adapt quite quickly to situations. I suppose the whole of life is pretty difficult to comprehend when you are little and just starting out to understand the strange world of grown-ups. My disappearance into the bedroom, where the typewriter was, was simply another odd thing about their mother, along with practising singing and dressing up to perform from time to time. I do remember one occasion, when I was working on something that had attached to it that dread word 'deadline'; my youngest child was outside the room with Daddy, who was preventing her from coming in to stop me.

'You can't go in. Mummy's working.'

'No she isn't. She's only writing.'

This brings to mind the tale of a well-known soprano singer, whose small daughter said when a rehearsal session was over, 'Have you stopped screaming, Mummy?'

I was yet to discover what goodies could emerge for the regional journalist. Because of these first successes, I found that other doors opened—just a little. I did a couple of music reviews; as far as I can recall one was at the Dorking Halls and one a bit further afield—perhaps Epsom. I expected the people I knew in Dorking would tease me about it, but I was taken seriously—always a great boost to one's ego.

But the real progress was yet to come. One day (I was making the bed) the phone rang. It was the features editor for whom I had been writing; he told me that the newspaper was intending to appoint a Woman's Page Editor—the first in the 80 years of its existence. Would I be interested in the job?

I can remember hearing myself say, quite calmly, that it did sound very interesting. If so, he said, could I come to see him as soon as possible to talk about it. It would be part-time, probably three days a week, and the pay would not be as good as he would like, but . . . ?

I managed—again—not to say that I would do it for nothing! We arranged to meet the following day, and I put the receiver down. That was when I discovered that I was on my knees beside the bed, my legs having given way.

I doubt if it would be possible in these days to get into journalism by that door. University degrees and experience are generally required. I count myself more than fortunate that, for about three years, I had the amazing experience of creating a job for myself, and that it was successful.

That was 1969. I was 40, and had spent years having babies, pushing prams and filling the dreaded bottles. I moved with the slow action of someone who usually had a toddler in tow. I was (just a bit) overweight. (Though may I have a small moment of glory? The first time I was weighed in the maternity home after Fiona, my last baby, was born, I was exactly the same weight as the day I was married—and that after five pregnancies).

Nevertheless, I was more wife and mother than go-ahead journo, and it took a little while to get to the point where I could leap up stairs and run for buses. Some months after I started at Redhill, where the newspaper offices were (spread around the town while splendid new buildings were being erected; we were in a tatty little shop in the main street and my office was at least three flights up), the young chief reporter said, 'We were really sorry for the stairs when you first came.' What did he mean? 'You stumped up them—we could hear you. But now you run up.' I was not sure whether to be flattered or offended. Then he said: 'And we were sorry for the chair when you sat down'. Enough, I thought. But it was nice that they had noticed the improvement.

But the important thing for me was that I was learning a whole new way of life, and a new vocabulary. While I was being shown around the somewhat unprepossessing premises on that first appointment the editor said casually, 'You will have to sub your own copy'.

I nodded, as if I knew what he was talking about. I had no idea what 'subbing' was, and I could only guess that 'copy' meant whatever I had written. But I soon learnt, and it was a matter of real gratification to me, some weeks later, when the editor mentioned that the printers had asked him, 'Who have you got up there?' He told them who I was. 'Well, she's a bloody good sub, anyway!'

My first introduction to subbing, which I soon realised meant everything that happens between writing a piece and getting it into print, was with the chief sub-editor, a man in the next room, who I suppose could be described as 'of the old school'. He had a rigid idea of what could and could not be put into the paper, and would appear in my little office with what I had just written to tell me I couldn't do it. Notably, he said I couldn't start a sentence or a paragraph with 'and' or 'but'. I said yes, I could—on a women's page! He was on the point of retiring, and three weeks later had gone, leaving me to remember what I had been told. It was yet another real learning curve for me, and I am really quite grateful to him for having given me the knowledge—and then leaving, so that I could do it my way!

This was well before the days of computerisation. I was given an outline of what my job would entail, and then left to get on with it. At the bottom of those flights of stairs the editor sat in his own gloomy little bit of Dickensian Redhill, and was available to me if I got stuck. I was handed a piece of paper marked out in columns and inches, and told that what I wrote, plus any pictures I wanted to use, had to fit into it. This meant knowing how many words I had written, how they would divide up into columns, what headlines were needed—and *that* meant knowing about fonts and other mysteries that I had never heard of—and how big or small the 'pics' needed to be.

But the exciting part was that at the top *I had not only my picture, but my by-line.* I was Barbara Yates Rothwell, Woman's Page Editor, and what I wrote would go to 19 local issues, ranging from south London to north Sussex, and out east towards Kent. It was a big district with many possibilities, and covering that vague area known as the 'stockbroker belt'—which implied money and influence.

There were days when it went like a dream—and a few when I felt like giving up in despair. Fortunately, not many of those. One that I remember was on a Thursday afternoon (the paper appeared on Fridays, so the page must be 'ready to go' by then), when I struggled with setting up everything I wanted to get in, and time ticked mercilessly on.

I was getting more and more desperate, when a guardian angel in the form of a colleague with long experience appeared at my door, and said, 'What are you still here for? Having trouble?'

My gratitude was overwhelming. 'I can't get the bloody thing to work!'

Of course, all it needed was a few deft moves by someone who actually knew what he was doing, and all was well. I went home, exhausted. Was it on that occasion that I staggered (mentally, anyway) into the house to find my entire family sitting gazing at our black and white TV? And did someone really say, 'You're late. What's for tea?' And did I actually not kill anyone?

'Aren't any of you capable of getting something ready?' Well, any working mum will tell you that this is par for the job. In general it all worked very well, and I was usually home in time for the after-school rush. It made me understand much better that a man who has been working all day needs a little time to recover before the family weighs in with the day's disasters. My father always had his tea before we attacked him with all the news of the day. So sensible of my mother to realise that he needed that break after work and a train journey home from London.

17

Many things were to emerge from this amazing job. I could not possibly have imagined what the end product would be, simply because I enjoyed writing and seemed to be reasonably good at it. One of the best outcomes was that I began to meet so-called 'important people'—celebrities who usually would have been out of my circle of activity. It was up to me, usually, to pick and choose among the VIPs in my area, and I made the most of it. Interestingly, meeting these people (one would expect them to be very much in control of themselves) revealed that there was a high level of nervousness among them. Whether it was because they were being interviewed by a woman journalist (these strange creatures are supposed to be hard-hitting, hard-drinking ladies, and some men seemed to be a little wary of me when we first met), or whether they were fearful of revealing too much of themselves, I really don't know. Sometimes it was a struggle to get the conversation going.

My first celebrity interview was with the daunting Baroness Wootton of Abinger, a parliamentarian with a reputation for being tough and taking no prisoners. I arrived at work that day, to be told that the lady was expecting me. I think it would have been kind if someone had told me that she had just published her autobiography. As it was, I was sent into the lioness's den without even a kitchen chair for protection.

We settled in her lounge room. I made slightly nervous light conversation for a minute or two. I think I admired her home. Then I began to ask questions.

'That's all in the book,' she said sharply. I felt the floor shake, and asked another question. 'And *that's* in the book! Why ask me?' Then: 'You've read the book? My autobiography. Just published.'

I decided honesty was definitely the best policy in a case like this, especially as I could probably blame it on the editor. 'I'm sorry. I didn't know that. I wasn't told. I only heard I was to see you when I got to work this morning.'

'Then this is a complete waste of time!'

I gathered my courage up in both hands. 'Not necessarily,' I said boldly. 'There may be things that haven't been said.'

So we continued, and she warmed (ever so slightly) until we were actually having a conversation. I was intrigued to learn that she had married a taxi-driver called George—and that's about all I can remember of the interview, except the wonderful feeling when I got into my car that I had done it! I had bearded a lioness and got away with it. (They have beards?)

As I left, she said, 'You'll let me see the piece before it's published, won't you?'

This is not something that is normally done, but on this occasion I agreed, and duly sent it. I had a letter back from her agreeing to let it be printed without alteration; and a comment: 'I doubt if I am as daunting as you seemed to find me'. Dear Baroness—you were!

It wasn't only celebrities that I was to meet. I had been told I was to 'personalise' the page for family reading. One way to do this was for me to become recognised in the area, so for the first time I had to learn to enjoy being photographed. We were fortunate in our photographers; I did quite a lot of work with them, so we needed to get on well. And in general we produced between us some good illustrated articles which did indeed make the page a popular feature of the paper. Later, I had two and sometimes three pages to fill every week; broadsheet, not tabloids—that was still in the future.

Among the daft things I did were having my face made up by the resident clown at Chessington Zoo's circus. I even had one of those gadgets that make the hair on a particularly horrendous red wig go up and down, and a plastic flower that sprays when squeezed. All jolly good fun!

I also arranged with a local airfield to be flown around the area covered by the newspaper in a single-engine plane. I have a photograph of myself climbing into the plane over the wing to prove it. It was really interesting to see everything from 'up there'—my first ever flight—and especially so when the pilot did a spectacular sideways slip so that I could see my own house below.

As I was officially the woman's page editor it was only right that I should do some female things, too. I had a facial—imagine doing that and having a photographer registering it for posterity at every move. One doesn't really look at one's best at such a time. I also had a 'hair-style for the busy woman', and this at a time when the secrets of the salon were not normally on view to outsiders. It was all good for the paper's circulation, and raised a few smiles at the same time.

I found I was becoming involved in other aspects of the community. I was invited by the Women's Institute and similar organisations to speak about my job at several of their meetings around the countryside, and I remember the occasion on which I was faced by about sixty elderly ladies at a Townswomen's Guild meeting. When I got up to speak, several in the front row folded their arms, made themselves comfortable—and closed their eyes! I was blowed if I was going to speak through their combined snores; I started with a funny story and got them involved, and there was no more sleeping.

Perhaps the most extraordinary occasion for giving a talk was during a very snowy winter at a Women's Institute out in the countryside, when everything was frozen solid and even driving there was a bit hazardous. I arrived when there had been a power cut; the hall was dark and cold (winter evenings come very early in England), and it was barely possible to see to the back of the room.

They were very apologetic about everything, but it was hardly their fault. So we got on with the meeting, the secretary read out the notices, outside it got darker and darker, and inside it was igloo weather. I was announced, and stood up. By this time the only light was a few torches, and a candle on the table in front of me. I wondered what they were actually seeing of me, lit from below so dimly; certainly I wasn't seeing much of them, nothing beyond the first row. It was a very good thing I knew what I was going to say! Standing there without visible notes could have been a problem if I hadn't known my job inside out.

On another winter occasion we were subjected to rolling power cuts, which meant that each area lost power for about 4 hours. If you were lucky you were always in an area that wasn't at that moment being cut. It didn't work out that way this time. When we got up at about 7.30 am the power was off, and it was dark. Off to school where with any luck the power would be on. I drove to Redhill where, by the time I got there, the power cut was in force. No hot coffee for me! I had an appointment a little way out of the town in the early afternoon, and—you've probably guessed it—the power came on in Redhill and off where I was heading. No hot drinks.

Eventually I got home, where, amazingly, yes—the power was off. I should have been used to it by then. By about 7 o'clock we'd had enough. Derry said, 'Let's go to bed and get warm, and get up when the power comes on!' So off we all went, and eventually, glory be! there was power—and probably several hot cuppas, though I have to say I don't remember that.

But undoubtedly the most memorable moments in this strange career were the interviews. If the formidable baroness was the first, she was followed by others who, for all I knew, would be even tougher.

Among them were Francis Durbridge, at that time a well-known British writer of radio plays; Cliff Michelmore, a well-respected radio and TV interviewer and definitely A Name; his wife Jean Metcalfe, the voice of Woman's Hour (a programme for which I did a couple of broadcasts on BBC, writing my own scripts); Marjorie Thomas, a well-known singer; and Eleanor Summerfield, actress, whom I had the pleasure of seeing again more recently in an episode of Midsomer Murders— and an earlier pleasure when Derry and I met her for a quick sherry before a performance at the Thorndike Theatre in Leatherhead.

These were fascinating people to meet face to face; and the joy of being an interviewer is that one can ask all those questions that cannot be asked when simply meeting someone, for instance, at a dinner party. The job does involve one in getting down to what were just then becoming known as 'the nitty-gritty' questions; and this is probably the reason for much of the initial resistance mentioned earlier. It is up to the interviewer to create a situation and a mood that encourages relaxation, and I was pleased to find that I was able to do this. It always helps if one is interested in people—and I am!

I regard this period of my life as one of immense privilege. To be able to choose which celebrity one would like to interview, contact them, and be given the right to 'intrude', is huge. I know quite a lot about them—but they know nothing about me. I never minded that I sometimes had to dig deep to get results.

I met Bill Travers, by arrangement, in the lounge of The White Horse Hotel, an old coaching hostelry in the middle of Dorking. He and his wife, Virginia McKenna were the flavour of the moment, having made *Born Free,* the film about Elsa the lioness; they had come to live on the slopes of Leith Hill, one of our lovely mid-Surrey beauty spots. Bill was a good-looking man and a popular actor, and when some friends knew I was about to interview him there were plenty of offers from the females to 'carry my pen'. But this was my moment of triumph, not theirs, and I carried my own pen!

In fact, on this occasion I didn't make notes or use a tape recorder, which I normally did. We chatted for about two hours, and about halfway through Travers suddenly said, 'You haven't made a single note!' Daringly, I said, 'I have a very good memory', (which I did at that stage of my life). I hope he relaxed and didn't feel the whole operation was a waste of time.

When the interview appeared in the newspaper, I had a message from him: 'Yes, you do have a very good memory!' The message was actually in a letter from his wife, as he was away, presumably filming. She was probably the bigger star at that time; but I never managed to get her into the interviewees chair.

With my interest in music, I was very pleased to be asked by *The Lady*, a women's magazine with a decidedly old-fashioned flavour, if I would do a piece about the Menuhin School, which was situated a few miles from Dorking. This involved me in visiting the school, talking to staff and a few students, and eventually going to see Yehudi Menuhin himself in his apartment in London.

This was a very big undertaking. Because it was a part of the celebration of the school's tenth anniversary there was no problem in contacting the great man, but finding a moment when he was available was something else. Finally we managed to coincide, and having been to see the school, which lies in a beautiful part of the country, and knowing a bit more about what went on there, I made my way to London. The Menuhins lived in a very pleasant large flat, and I was welcomed—rather coolly—by Menuhin himself. The coolness, I decided, was partly the old nervousness of being interviewed by someone who might understand nothing about him or his life's work, and partly his natural demeanour.

He also seemed a bit bothered by the fact that, as this was the morning, there was someone outside the door of the room we were sitting in wielding a vacuum cleaner. Perhaps he felt it was a bit *infra dig* to have ordinary interruptions in his day. But he was eventually very gracious.

After all, I was asking about his 'baby', the school, and he talked at some length about what had been hoped for, and what was being achieved. He told me how he raised the money to get started (rang up several friends and asked them for it—and got it), and what his aims had been.

I was really intrigued that part of my 'job' on this occasion was to go to St James's Palace, where there was to be a tenth anniversary concert at which Menuhin would play. Guest of honour was the Queen Mother, and I remember watching her entering the recital room, chatting to Menuhin. We had some excellent performances from students, and then Menuhin was on stage, in a duet with a girl of sixteen, who played like a dream. By that time, I think Menuhin was past his best—but it occurred to me that he had left a wonderful legacy.

After the concert it was time for the reception. We lined up as the Queen Mother entered, as regally graceful as ever, and it is the only time I have curtsied to a member of the royal family. Seen close up, she was a really gracious personality; and something that happened at the reception has remained with me.

The room was full of many extremely famous musicians, friends of Menuhin, who made their bows to the royal lady and then found their wine glasses and gathered in small groups. I was fascinated by being at something which was a 'royal occasion', but at the same time very informal. The Queen Mother was seated at a round table in the middle of the room, and over by the fireplace was Jenny Lee, then Minister for the Arts, and wife of Labour 'great', Aneurin Bevan, one of the 'real' Labour men from the post-war period.

The Queen spoke to her lady-in-waiting, and indicated Ms Lee, presumably asking her to join them at the table. Then, with perhaps fifty able-bodied men and women around her, any one of whom would have willingly done anything for her, she stood, went to a nearby chair, and carried it to the table, ready for Jenny Lee. I found that both surprising and encouraging, a sign of a very genuine personality.

That was a peak in my journalistic life. There were others; and my interview with Dame Sybil Thorndike was certainly one. She was in every way the *Grande Dame* of the British stage, and to be allowed to visit her in her own flat in a less than prestigious area of London was wonderful.

I wonder why I thought her apartment would be full of little gilt chairs and perhaps oriental hangings? Anyway, it wasn't. This was a 'granny flat', with settees well bounced on by children, and our conversation became quite cosy. When I stood outside her front door I could hear her rehearsing '*Façade*', chanting over Walton's music. At the time she was in her eighties, so this seemed extraordinary. Now that I am myself in my eighties, of course, I can see that there is no valid reason to stop doing what you are good at simply because the calendar says so.

She was surprisingly difficult to interview about her own life, however; she wanted to know about me. I had to tell her my own potted history, which seemed to fascinate her; and when I said that my son-in-law was serving on HMS Eagle, she nearly took off. It seemed that her son had also served on *Eagle*, though that was during the war and—I think— a predecessor to Arthur's ship. It was apparently a bond between us.

With plenty to think about I asked if she had a photo of herself that I could use in the paper. She leapt up and started to go through the drawers of a large chest, calling in the voice so well-known to theatre-goers to her husband in the next room: 'Lewis! Lewis! Where are those photos?' There was a sort of grunt from him, a photo emerged from the drawer, and I thanked her and turned to leave. As I went to the door she suddenly said (in that same clear, carrying voice), 'Do you have lovely names for your children, dee-ar?'

What a question. If she didn't like them, what then? I said, 'Cynthia, Patrick, Helen, Keith, Alison and Fiona'. 'Oh, lovely, dee-ar! Lovely!'

I left, with memories that have never died. At one point she had said, 'When I perform in Israel they don't give a bunch of flowers. They plant a tree in your name. I must have quite a little forest there now!' I thought that was a beautiful idea. Many years later, in Australia, I was asked to speak to an audience of Jewish women in Perth; at the end their secretary came to me and handed me an envelope. I thought it might be a fee, though I hadn't asked for one. But when I opened it, what it contained was a certificate to say that a tree had been planted in Israel in my name. I was momentarily overwhelmed. And when I spoke to them again, a few months later, they upped my little forest to two trees! I am very proud of that.

I've mentioned that Vaughan Williams was a long-time resident in Dorking, and his inspirational development of the Leith

Hill Music Festival was a wonderful way of bringing the town and the many villages together for mutual pleasure in singing great music. His death in 1958 led eventually to a request to me from the Dorking Council to edit a commemorative publication for his centenary. This meant that I needed to hunt out the people who had been a part of his musical success; and the obvious person was Sir Adrian Boult, then one of the foremost conductors in the UK. I managed to arrange an interview with this great man, and saw him in his office in London.

He was another interviewee who proved difficult to reach, but he had been the conductor who had given the first performances of several of VW's symphonies. His insights were valuable; I remember the story about VW (always known by his initials) after the first rehearsal for one of these works. When asked what he thought he said, 'It's not as bad as I thought it was!'

Boult was nervous, tapping a wooden pen-holder on his desk all the time we were talking, so my record player picked up some extraneous noise.

Another leading musician I needed to see was André Previn. Rather more glamorous than Boult, but a very famous conductor—and by a lucky chance he lived only a few miles from me. But getting an appointment with him was extremely frustrating. I spent quite a time on the phone, trying to locate him and tie him down for the hour or so I needed, but without luck. One day, however, I was passing the White Horse Hotel in Dorking High Street just as he was coming down the steps with his small son.

I pounced! I explained quickly who I was and what I wanted; he was very forbearing, and gave me his home number to call, with a promise to see me. And it was indeed a delightful occasion. His home was in the country with a large garden surrounding it; and at the bottom of the garden was a gypsy caravan, which he had bought for his then wife—Mia Farrow. There was no sense of having to rush, and at one point the door opened and Mia Farrow came in—with a tea tray. She said, rather memorably: 'I hope you don't mind having honey in your tea. We're on a honey kick right now'.

Not long afterwards I saw a documentary film made by Previn in which he was explaining the power of using the right music in filming. Mia Farrow was filmed in a room, staring into a mirror, and the mood was created only by the music being played—spooky, romantic, whatever! It was an excellent insight into what music does for the film world.

Previn's contact with the music of VW was his successful attempt to bring the symphonies to the music-lovers of Russia. This was still a time when the barriers were up, politically if not in actual fact; but he said they loved it. When we finished the interview—and the tea—he said that if I was doubtful about anything and needed to ask him about it I could ring him. A few days later I did, to clear up a small point. He answered me very courteously, then said he would have to go now 'to get his wife to London, because she had just gone into labour'! A very nice person to talk to, and I felt very privileged once more at being allowed to enter someone's private life.

Many years later, when we were established in WA, I heard that the Australian-born pianist Eileen Joyce, then elderly but once so much a part of the international music scene, was to be in Perth at the dedication of a recital room in her name in the University of WA. I spoke to Woman's Day, for whom I had done a fair amount of work, mainly fiction, and asked if they would take a piece about her. They said yes, so I bought myself a new tape recorder for the occasion, and loaded it with tape.

I met her in her hotel room and set up the recorder. We talked for about half an hour—she was friendly and open, and we were going very well—when I realised I hadn't heard the click that indicates that the tape needs turning. I opened the recorder—and all the tape came spilling out onto the table. I looked at it with horror; she gave a cry and said, 'Oh, you haven't got *anything*!' I smiled bravely and said, 'Don't worry. I've got a good memory'.

I doubt if she believed me; in fact I had plenty for the length the magazine had allowed me. But I don't know which of us, for that moment, was the more alarmed.

We have to go back to 1971 to complete the list of notables. One of the best interviews I ever had was really difficult to set up, and when I arrived at the 'victim's' office I found that he was a very tough subject, withdrawn and monosyllabic. It was Barnes Wallis, the creator of the bouncing bomb that smashed the German dams during the war.

He was another 'local', and I really wanted him for my page. At the time, I recall, I was 41 and he was 82. He also seemed to resent the fact that I was there, and possibly, too, that I was a woman, who couldn't possibly be expected to understand about bombs and such. It was very heavy going.

So why he suddenly relaxed and became quite friendly I don't know. About 20 minutes into the interview he began to talk openly about his life: as the inventor of airships in those pre-war days, as the later inventor of the bomb that everyone said wouldn't work, even of his schooldays as a 'Blue-coat boy', a pupil at Christ's Hospital in Horsham, Sussex, founded in 1552.

Suddenly he said, 'Would you like to see the test film of the dam-busting bomb?' Well, would I? I couldn't believe my luck. He called to a man in the little theatrette next door to his office: 'Put up the bomb film, please.' So I sat next to this iconic inventor and watched the original film with him, as he explained to me (in spite of the fact that I was a mere woman) how it operated and above all how they had tested it. So much failure for so long, and then triumph: the thing worked.

We discussed the film made of it with Michael Redgrave playing the Wallis role—very convincingly, I thought, once I had met the man himself—and I asked him what he thought of it. 'Oh, a wonderful film—wonderful!' I said, 'Was it like that?' and he chuckled and said, 'No, nothing like that! But a great film!'

That was one of the very few times I didn't get home in time for my children coming out of school. This was an opportunity I could not waste, so I ignored my conscience and stayed until I had everything I wanted for the article. We got on to the subject of schooling; as a private school boy himself, he thought that everyone should pay for their education. By that time I was sufficiently comfortable with him to point out that with six children on a teacher's pay there was no way I could do that. He considered this, then nodded. 'Yes, I hadn't thought of that.' Amazing! He gave me a book about education to read and said he wanted it back—with my own comments. So for a few weeks I was actually corresponding with the great Barnes Wallis on a subject dear to both of us—and nothing to do with bombs.

This was before he was knighted. Sometime later I had to cover the annual Women's Institute meeting in the Dorking Halls, and Lady Wallis was one of the platform party. As we went to an adjoining hall for morning coffee I passed her and the ladies she was talking with. One was saying, 'So, Lady Wallis, what is it like living with Sir Barnes?' In her very stockbroker belt voice she said, 'Oh, it's like looking after an ancient monument!'

I loved it!

The final one on this list (for now, anyway) is Sir Harry Secombe, Goon extraordinary, and the owner of that very pleasant tenor voice. He was another one I found really hard to get through to. It took place at the Pinewood Studios, in weather I would rather forget—iced roads, snow blizzards, and very cold. When I got halfway I almost turned back, it was so bad. I didn't have chains on my wheels, and it was quite dangerous. Then I reasoned that this had been a really difficult interview to set up and as I was by then more than halfway there I decided that if necessary I would simply find somewhere to stay for the night, if I had to.

I was received into deceptive warmth by the Publicity Officer for the studios, a very charming young lady who steered me in the right direction; and I found myself on the set where they were making *Doctor at Sea*. I sat and watched, and decided then and there that I never wanted to be a film actor. For sheer boredom and waste of time, I was thinking, this has to take the cake. They did the same very brief scene over and over again, and I really couldn't see any difference between the takes. Hopefully the director could.

It was supposedly a fancy dress party on the rear deck of the ship; so when the interview was over—it was really tough to get him to say anything that I wanted to print—and I was escorted by 'publicity' to the dining room, it was quite funny to see knights and ladies, nuns and kings and queens and some who were difficult to pin down, all entering to eat from the cafeteria.

There was no way I could tell that this lunchtime was to create a complete revolution in my life, and the life of our family. When, later, I considered how I had almost turned back I truly thanked my guardian angel for pushing me on.

I found out that the nice young publicity lady had lived for a while in Sydney, in a harbour-front apartment, and would like to go back. I mentioned that my daughter Cynthia and her husband had emigrated to NSW a few years earlier; that they now had two children, and I would love to see them. She said, 'Well, you can'. I pointed out the lack of finance. She said, 'You are a regional journalist. QANTAS has realised that people like you have a clout with the public that Fleet Street journalists don't have. Your readers actually know you. Go and see QANTAS in London. I'll give you a number to ring'.

So she did, and I did, and it was true!

18

But that should be put on hold for a while. Although no one had realised it, Derry had not been as well as his unbounded energy suggested. He had grown quite subdued in everyday life, though his activities with the school music were as dynamic as ever. When I mentioned this change of attitude to Rosemary some time later she said, 'I just thought he was maturing!'

At this time—mid-July, 1967—I was very busy organising Cynthia's wedding to Arthur. It would be a naval wedding, complete with uniforms and swords, and we were all looking forward to it immensely. But because they were both based at Haverfordwest in South Wales I was doing much of the planning. The whole thing was complicated by a change of orders for Arthur, on HMS Eagle; the ship was to leave the UK earlier than expected, which would have meant complete chaos as far as the wedding was concerned. So all invitations had to be brought up to date, church and reception hall rebooked and youngest bridesmaids' dresses (Alison and Fiona), made in a hurry by me.

As usually happens at such a time when everyone pulls together, everything went quite smoothly in spite of all our forebodings. Derry ordered his Moss Bros suit, Cynthia's dress was lovely, the small bridesmaids were ready in time, and we all got together at the little church on Ranmore, which is ideal for a wedding, with seating for about 100. The young officers lined up at the door afterwards with their swords raised to see the happy couple leave, we all ended up at the Dorking Halls for the reception, and afterwards a remarkable number of people from both families and the naval contingent came to our house. The presents had been laid out in the dining room; and the bridegroom's family all seemed to end up in there. The bride's family gravitated to the lounge room, and it appeared that in spite of having brought their two young people together at the ceremony, the two factions were going to remain rigidly apart.

Eventually I went into the dining room and asked Arthur's people to come and get to know us, and they came. Arthur's Uncle Len led the way; my Uncle Fred Hodson was standing over by the fireplace; as Len came into the room they both stopped and stared—and Uncle Fred said, 'What are you doing here, Len?' It turned out they had once worked together for some time at Vickers, 'up north', and had never realised that they would one day be distantly related.

It was a lovely wedding, and I was happy that we had been able to bring all these nice people together. The only blot on the day for me was that Paddy was somewhere on the African coast. At that time his merchant navy duties meant that he missed out on a number of family occasions.

I didn't know that within weeks our lives would be upside-down.

The new school term began in September 1967. I had just been appointed to the staff of Mowbray School, the girls' comprehensive in Dorking, as a part-time music teacher: one and a half days a week. As I recall, there were no dramas on that first day; Derry went to his school and I to mine. But that night, when I went to put out the bedside light, he suddenly said, 'Don't put it out. I can't stand the dark!'

This was so out of character! I turned to look at him, and he was clearly distressed. Whether we slept that night or not I don't recall; but in the morning he was definitely not fit to go to work. I took him to the doctor, who asked him what the problem was. 'I'm just so tired,' he said.

The doctor regarded him thoughtfully. 'In my experience, Dr Morgan, when people are tired they go to bed and have a sleep.'

But he was taking it very seriously, and said Derry should have some time off.

We went home; and for the next week Derry was in bed most of the time (another first), and, what was most distressing, he cried. In fact, he cried for about a week, as if he was getting rid of all the tears he had never shed over his war service, which had probably been far more traumatic than we had ever realised (because men didn't talk about these things); and over the stresses of Nancy's development of TB in 1942, the arrival of their baby in 1944—which could also have been quite stressful during wartime when you never knew if you would come home again—and his wife's ultimate death. If only people wouldn't be so stoic!

Alison and Fiona spent quite a lot of time during those 7 days sitting on the bed 'looking after Daddy'. I think they quite enjoyed the drama! I don't recall what medication he was on, but he was less disturbed, though still weeping quite a bit, which I felt was probably a very good thing.

But at the end of that week the situation changed. One night I found him standing at the foot of the children's beds, just looking at them. I went in and stood beside him. 'Poor little things,' he said suddenly. 'They'd be better off dead.'

This totally shocked me. But I managed to speak cheerfully. 'Don't worry about them. They think it's been really exciting, looking after Daddy'. I took him out of the room; and the next morning I rang the doctor.

'That's a different situation,' he said at once. 'We can't risk it. I'll arrange for hospital.'

This development, in which a distressed person transfers his emotions to others, can happen with mental breakdown; and as a result I have always had some understanding for the men who, embroiled in marriage failures and the loss of their children, transfer their own agony to the children—and in too many cases they can see no other way out than to kill them to take away the pain, which the children are probably not feeling to any great extent. We were fortunate to realise the problem in time.

It was also fortunate that Cynthia was living with us again. With Arthur away, and having left her naval career when they were married, she was able to help me a great deal during a very challenging time. I was trying to balance home, Derry's condition, the family and my new job, and it would have been very difficult if I had not had Cynthia's support.

Paddy, a cadet in the Merchant Navy, was coming home, if we had known it, from Aden, where his ship had been diverted to on the way home from S Africa, and carrying a cargo of military explosives. I'm glad I didn't know that until later.

The hospital we were sent to was Belmont, in Surrey, and it was, as Derry said later, not a place to go to if you were ill. For a man like him, who had a natural reserve with strangers, to be put into a ward of about 20 men, some very far gone in mental breakdown, and with so little room between the beds that two neighbouring patients could not get out of bed at the same time, was in itself a trial of sanity! Derry was extremely confused and unable to cope adequately with what was happening to him. I was very upset when I had to leave him; but I couldn't see any other options.

I was not impressed with the demeanour of the psychiatrist who was asking me the questions that Derry would not have been able to answer. He was a dry little man, and he never looked at me, or smiled encouragingly; I wondered how he had ever got the job. His understanding of people seemed a bit lacking. He simply went down a list of questions about Derry—name, address, phone number, DOB, our doctor—and then, in the same dry voice without looking up, said 'Sex?'

I stared at him. Then he did look up. 'Sexually active?'

For a moment I was speechless; then I laughed and said, 'If you mean when he says, "well, at least I can still do that!" then yes. He's sexually active'. Not a smile from the shrink. I couldn't imagine how Derry would ever get on with him.

Then we had the really difficult question. 'We can treat this one of two ways—drugs or ECT. Which would you prefer us to use?'

I managed to keep my balance. 'What would be the effects?'

'They would both work. The drugs would take longer. The electric convulsive therapy, if it's successful, can cut a corner off that. Sometimes it works extremely quickly.'

I wouldn't wish that decision on anyone. I had heard of ECT, and it was generally seen as a kind of torture; and probably in the early days it was. The doctor assured me that it was done under sedation, that Derry wouldn't know anything about it, and there should be no after-effects. I suddenly felt that ECT was the way to go, because if it did indeed get him back on his feet quickly that would be better than the long haul of drug-taking. Though, of course, there would be drugs afterwards to back up what I hoped would be a quick result. I chose ECT—and all the way home wondered if I had done the right thing. Though perhaps there was no 'right thing'. This was all outside our experience. We had to go with instinct.

That evening I had a phone call from Derry. Somehow he had found a phone and managed to use it in spite of his really dreadful confusion. He was in great distress—he had been told to go to *somewhere* and see *someone* to get his pills. Where or who, he had no idea. He said, 'I don't know what to do.'

He had been diagnosed as manic-depressive, now known as bi-polar. Why was no one caring for him?

I comforted him as well as I could, told him to find a member of staff and ask for help. I left Cynthia in charge and ran down the road to the Vicarage, hoping to see our friend the Vicar. He wasn't there. But his wife said he would be back shortly, and asked after Derry. I told her what had happened, and as I was doing so her husband came in. I asked him if he could go and see Derry the next day—I had been asked not to visit until after the first treatment, but they would accept a clergy visit. Bless him, he said, 'I'll go now!' and he did. Later he rang to say he had seen Derry, who seemed calmer, and I could relax and try to get a good sleep.

This was early in the week. He was to have the first treatment on the Wednesday, one of my days at Mowbray. I had told Derry's school what had happened, and they were from first to last very good, arranging a deputy teacher to take over his classes, and I was 'not to worry about anything at school'.

But at Mowbray that morning I was presented with a double class of 60 girls to be taken for singing in the school hall. Most of them didn't want to be there. Neither did I. Derry's treatment was to be about 9.30 am; at about 9.20 a girl at the back of the group suddenly started screaming. All singing stopped. She was hysterical, and it took all my patience and energy to get her calm enough to take her to the school clinic so that she could lie down. She had come out in a very dramatic rash, which rather bothered me.

Half an hour later, when all was quiet again, I could assume that Derry's ordeal was over. I was quite grateful to the girl for having taken my mind off it. As some of the students helped me pack up the music books, I said, 'Why was she so upset?'

'Her boyfriend chucked her last night. She really loved him.'

In the staff room someone asked me the same question. I gave the same answer. I was quite surprised that there was not an ounce of sympathy for the girl from anyone on the staff. They were really quite cruel and scathing. I wondered if any of them had ever been in love at the age of fifteen. Perhaps not. On the other hand, perhaps the girl was a bit of a drama queen. I gave her the benefit of the doubt.

Friday came, and I was able to visit Derry. I had no idea what I was going to see, but I think I assumed that he would be lying in bed, pale and wan, and hopefully a little less confused. In the event, as I parked the car I saw him coming towards me—and he was *smiling*. This was something that hadn't happened for quite a while. I was hugely thankful that my choice of treatment had so far turned out well.

After the first week he was allowed home at the weekends. He brought with him the first time a form that he had been told to fill out. I read through it—nothing very difficult, but some of the questions struck me as a bit strange. We sat together while I filled in the obvious answers; then I looked up at him and read out the next one. *'Do you habitually visit brothels?'*

He said, '*What?*' I repeated it, keeping a very straight face. 'Why do they want to know that?'

I said, 'I assume it's in case you do a bunk and they don't know where to look for you.' He didn't answer, so I read it out again. 'Well—do you?'

I can't remember if he ever deigned to answer. I think he felt they were going a bit far. Anyway, I simply wrote down 'No'. I doubt if he ever had the time to explore that particular pleasure of male life.

Three weeks and several episodes of ECT later, and he came home again, I hoped for good. He was on a few drugs, and he seemed to be making good progress. I had been told by the psychiatrist that it was unlikely that Derry would work again, so to see him returning to normality, however slightly, and however long it was going to take, was encouraging. In the event, of course, the natural fighter in him emerged; and in the post-Christmas term, January, he returned to school, and took up a modified version of what he had been doing before. Four months we were happy to put behind us.

It was not without its hazards, however. He was still fighting deep depression at times; and he too often commented that he couldn't go on, or that he would have to 'finish it'! I was as sympathetic as possible, but one easily gets frustrated by the constant challenge to buttress someone's failing strength, whether it is mental or physical. One day he said again, 'I can't go on'. I decided a bit of shock treatment of my own might shake him out of it. I said, 'OK, but not this week. I haven't got time for a funeral.'

It was risky, and it sounds cruel, but it worked. I think (and perhaps this is common with some potential suicides) that he had not gone beyond the desire to stop the mental pain; he had not thought through to what he would be leaving behind him. Does a person in this condition ever fully realise that if this way out is taken it will literally be 'your own funeral'? It seemed to stop him in his tracks, anyway. He never said it again, and he began to make headway.

But it was a long business. He was deeply offended when Surrey Education Department said he had to be tested to make sure he was not dangerous to children. Necessary, I know, but quite hurtful. Anyway, he passed that test, and we pretended that we were almost back to normal.

So this turbulent year, 1967, passed. It had started with my own trip to hospital for a hysterectomy, and ended with Derry's breakdown. In the middle a very happy occasion: Cynthia and Arthur's wedding. A fairly standard bit of life's ups and downs; and we came through it stronger for the challenge.

It seems odd, under the circumstances, that I thought it would be a good idea to have a continental holiday the following year. This would involve me in planning it, getting everybody ready for the off, and doing the driving—on the wrong side of the road, of course. Four children—Helen, Keith, Alison and Fiona—a language none of us was really handy with, and finding bed and breakfast every night in a series of towns and villages we knew nothing about. And on top of that a husband who was still on medication and not by any means a 'well man'. Whose idea was it? Mine, I suppose. And, in the end, it was a good holiday, taking in the long drive from north to south of France—where friends had lent us their holiday flat for a week (you can't let that chance go).

I managed the driving quite well after a near accident when I found the roundabout system (going in the wrong direction) a bit puzzling, and nearly knocked the beret off a local man. He wasn't pleased, but the advantage of not really knowing colloquial French is that you don't know what they are shouting at you.

We had a scary time on the Grand St Bernard Pass in the north of Italy, when I suddenly realised that I had a sheer drop of a few thousand feet just outside my window; at the top we found ourselves in a blizzard so that we didn't even see the wonderful Swiss panorama we were expecting. We located accommodation where Fiona was a great success with our hostess, who allowed her to sleep in a beautiful carved wooden cot. At 5 years old she was just small enough for it.

We saw lakes and the bottoms of mountains (the tops were obscured for much of the time by heavy mist), and eventually drove on to Dunkirk, which meant more to us than to the children. By this time, Dunkirk, that WWII icon of turning defeat to success, was a holiday resort; but Derry and I saw the beaches, and remembered that heart-stopping episode in 1940.

The movies I took show Derry with a beard; but more particularly, they reveal a man who has been seriously ill. The thin face and body and a certain lack of energy come through quite clearly. It would be another 5 or 6 years before he really emerged from his long ordeal.

19

Life returned as near as possible to normal. I finished the job at Mowbray School and not long after started to work at East Surrey Newspapers; this was very rewarding, and it came with all the goodies that I was discovering.

The Pinewood Studios publicity officer would never know that my lunch with her was to have such an amazing effect. I don't suppose I ever told her. But I was determined to make this work if I could, and I took up her suggestion. The contact she gave me was an Australian man. I went to see him at the QANTAS office in London, and he seemed not at all surprised that I should want to fly to Australia at his company's expense.

Behind his desk was a very large map of the world, and I suddenly realised what I was asking for. I would be flying to the other side, to a large island continent about which I knew very little. But it was apparently not only possible, but probable. Before I left him it was all well in hand; all I needed on my side was to get it past the editor.

His face, when I broached the subject, was a picture. I asked for five weeks off without pay. I said I would leave five envelopes on my desk with everything in them he needed for the time I would be absent. I hoped by being so efficient and so thoughtful I would pull it off.

He stared at me. He was clearly going to say no. 'I don't know whether it has dawned on you,' he said with a certain amount of irony, 'but this is a local paper. Australia is hardly local.'

'If I can make it local can I go?'

He almost laughed. 'If you can!' he said, and as far as he was concerned that was it.

I spent much time in thought. There must be a way in which I could make this far distant country relevant to the newspaper. It was just a question of hitting on it.

When it came to me it was quite simple. What do newspapers want? Bigger circulation, more sales. How can I, by going to Australia, make this happen? After some days of the deepest cogitation I thought that if I could find people in my area whose families had emigrated there, I could then go and find those families and interview them. If local authorities would do some photography for me I could create several pages of articles on these distant rellies, and surely this would mean that local families would want more copies of the papers?

My editor looked stunned, then grudgingly agreed that it might be a good idea. The Australian Tourist Commission completely floored me by writing to say they would like to 'pick up my hotel bills'. Well, I would like that too. Slowly but surely it all came together.

I'm talking about 1971. More and more people were flying long distances to see family or friends, or simply for exotic holidays. I was rather astonished at my own ability to shift things to where I wanted them; but I was also completely amazed at another unexpected activity that had come my way. This was certainly turning out to be an extraordinary job.

Among the 'perks' of my situation were press lunches, usually to launch some new thing on the market. In this way I found myself in swish London hotels or something a little more local, listening to someone rhapsodising about their product: ceramic stove tops was one (and I wanted one! I thought they were definitely the most improving thing I could think of in a kitchen. I didn't manage to achieve this wish until years after we came to Australia). The Land Rover was another, but I never wanted one of those. I attended an upmarket fashion show of tweedy autumn suits—they were nice, too; and tasted my first caviar and champagne at a big push for a new aspect of perfume. The perfume was heady; caviar and champagne didn't appeal, to my surprise and annoyance. No point in living in the fast lane if you don't like the booze!

I also found myself compering a fashion show in Reigate. I dressed up for the occasion in an Egyptian cotton dress, full length and a bit frilly, that I was very fond of; and topped it with a full length silver kaftan—where did I get that, I wonder? I picked up my microphone and started: 'Melanie is wearing a blue evening dress by '*A Stitch at a Time*,' and her evening bag is by '*All that glitters . . .*' It was one of the oddest things I ever did.

But this had the result that I got to know some of the publicity people; and it was why, sometime later, the perfume lady (who by that time had moved on to something else, which happens a lot in that business) got in touch with me to ask if I would do something for her new employers, Shaw Saville, the cruise ship company.

It was a fairly simple request. They wanted to run a competition for women to win a cruise for their families (two adults and two children provided for) in the Mediterranean; they wanted me to put their question paper onto my page every Friday for the next few weeks. I would then collect the answers as they came in, and post them off to their company. They would eventually decide who had won, I would notify the winners, and there would be a lunch for four finalist families at which I would be hostess.

Well, that all seemed fairly straightforward. The four finalists would be 'on show', parents and children, to make sure that they were acceptable people to be going aboard for this very generous 3 week holiday. Presumably if one of the children (or even the father) had started throwing the bread about, they would be automatically disqualified.

It went very smoothly. I did my bit, and the lunch came and went, and ultimately the winning family was picked. I was asked to meet a representative of the company to tie up final details. We met in a pub after work (my life had definitely changed!), and over a quick sherry he brought me up to date. Then he said, 'Have you got your tickets yet?' I stared at him. I truly didn't know what he meant. I said I hadn't. He said, 'Well, get in touch with them.'

Then he must have realised I was, as people were beginning to say, gob-smacked. 'You're going with them,' he said. 'You know you're escorting them?'

'No,' I said, very calmly. 'I didn't know. Nobody told me.'

'Well, get in touch,' he said. And that was that.

I discovered that my 'reward' was *two* places on the *Northern Star*. Derry could go with me. I remember that he was quite thrilled when I told him. The first two weeks fell neatly into the school summer holiday, so there was no problem there. The third, unfortunately, was the first week of the September term. This was where our honesty let us down badly. I wonder sometimes what would have happened if he had simply told them he was unwell, or had broken his leg or something; because when he told the school authorities that he would like that week off, and why, Surrey Education Committee turned quite nasty. No way would they allow such a thing. When I think of the overtime Derry did without ever receiving or even expecting extra pay; running the department without a deputy; putting on great and highly regarded concerts—all done because that was the sort of person he was, and in spite of the fact that for many years they wouldn't acknowledge his doctorate in regard to his salary—I still get mad.

I'm pleased to say that for once he did battle with them. In the end they said, OK, he could go, but they wouldn't pay him for that week. Well, it would be worth it. But what a mean-spirited bunch they were.

So I now had two amazing things to look forward to. I did my work with even greater diligence (I didn't want the editor, who was decidedly nervous about this whole situation, to have any reason for politely asking me to leave before I could do the newspaper any more damage). *We* were getting ready to become part of the cruising set.

I have no memories of what we did during the early part of that summer school holiday, but Dorking is a lovely town in the middle of beautiful countryside, so I expect we drove down to the sea at Littlehampton and picnicked on a few Surrey hills. There were always dogs or cats or hamsters or pet mice or whatever to be cared for, so school hols were usually fairly busy anyway.

Meanwhile, Derry and I were getting ourselves ready for the great moment when we were to board the *Northern Star* and start escorting my prize-winners. That, however, was a bit of a laugh. The woman who had won this excellent holiday was married to a BEA pilot—and he was used to flying all over Europe. I wondered if the holiday would have any interest for him as a result; but he said that he had only come into cities from the air, and entering from the sea would be a novel experience.

They were, as you might imagine, much-travelled; so my responsibility for them began and ended at breakfast. It would probably have been more reasonable for them to escort us, since we were very new to this kind of shipboard life. Derry's time at sea during the war hardly compared with the luxury of holidaying on the ocean waves. I doubt if there were table tennis competitions and lovely luncheons on the after deck in the North Atlantic in 1942.

But he enjoyed it as much as I did. We made our way through the Bay of Biscay to Malaga on the southern tip of Spain. At each port there was a break of several hours, with tourist coaches waiting—easily the best way to see as much as possible of a city in a hurry, and learn something of its history. In Malaga there was a choice between visiting a cave or going to a seaside resort. Derry was slightly claustrophobic, and said he wouldn't go to a cave. I didn't want to see the resort. So we parted company for a while.

I don't know what the resort was like; but the cave was the first really large one I had ever been in, and I enjoyed it. All over the massive floor there were stalactites and stalagmites that had fallen, according to the man showing us around, about ten thousand years ago during 'a cataclyms' (sic). Presumably they had been knocked over by an earthquake. He explained how slowly they formed, from the dripping water from the roof. Forty years to make a few centimetres.

Ahead of me there was one of those mildly irritating young boys that one inevitably meets on this sort of occasion. His voice went on and on. I followed him and his family along the wooden boardwalk that prevented us from trying to leap onto a stalactite and swing about a bit. There was just one remaining growth, looking rather like an enormous tooth, right beside the walkway. I could see the overhead lights reflecting on the little pool of moisture that sat on its top. When Sonny Jim got to it he leaned over and with one swoop wiped the top clean, saying, 'Bang goes forty years!'

Mature thought on my part caused me to realise that if he had done it so would others have before him. Perhaps it was left there so that idiots could satisfy their needs without damaging the rest of these very beautiful natural growths. His mother didn't seem to mind.

Then on to Athens. This city was very interesting, even on such a short stay. I was amused by the sight of a huge *HOOVER* publicity sign on rooftops just across the road from an area with ancient columns (some collapsed on the ground, which made it possible to see how they were made). Such a strange mix of periods and building styles; but of course it was the Acropolis and the climb up to the Parthenon that everybody was looking forward to.

However often one sees pictures of these ancient buildings, it is never quite the same as seeing them there, in front of you. This iconic view of the city, with its ruined building overlooking everything, is truly extraordinary. In one way it is a pity that it was so brutally blown up by the enemy (the Venetians, it seems) in 1687. Venice being such a beautiful city itself, you'd think they might have spared this wonderful—and at that time whole— memory of the past. But, as they say, it was ever so! Mankind is unfortunately never happier than when blowing something up, literally or figuratively.

Yet in another way it was like visiting a very elderly relative, and seeing the lines of wisdom and experience in a face once recognised. The sheer age of so much of what one sees in that part of the world is particularly daunting when one is used to living in a 'new' country like Australia. The problem with our long Aboriginal history is its lack of visual relics that one can enthuse over, though these days there is much more interest in and appreciation of the very ancient rock paintings that can be seen in many places. And yet, for those of us brought up in a country with a considerable non-Aboriginal history stretching back into a dimly known past, the ruins and ancient buildings and the stories that go with them are so much a part of our lives that we no longer think about them. They are simply there!

For many years I lived in a town close to an old Roman road. A short way north of us was the Pilgrims' Way, which runs from Winchester to Canterbury, and is the background to Chaucer's *Canterbury Tales*. Chaucer lived from 1340 to 1400, and his stories are still valid. There are tiny chapels built for the pilgrims as they made their way along the hilltops (the valleys, I believe, were too swampy and full of animals one would prefer not to meet) to pray at the tomb of the murdered Thomas à Becket. One chapel, near Guildford, has been renovated, and was always good to visit, though it was quite a walk to get there, especially with a baby in a pusher—all the same, probably still easier than it was in those early centuries for the footsore walkers wondering how much further it was to Canterbury, and whether it had really been a good idea after all.

Closer to us were the ruins of another chapel; and in all the years I was there I only went to look at this 12th century building once. Familiarity breeds not only contempt but a lack of interest.

But back to Athens! We landed at the Piraeus, and had to walk along the quayside to our coaches. On one side was a row of small shop fronts, and in some were pictures of the delights that could be found behind these unappealing façades—presumably the local ladies of the night. What caught my sense of the ridiculous was that all these photos, grimy and curling, were of naked ladies. But in every case the 'naughty bits' had little pieces of blue paper fixed to them with drawing pins. Somehow this made them much more obscene than the nakedness would have been—and the placing of the thumb tacks looked remarkably painful. Whatever turns you on, I suppose.

Istanbul, modern Constantinople, was extraordinary. The hugely imposing edifice of St. Sophia, built by Justinian in 532 as a Christian church, was later (1453) turned into a mosque by the Turks. Now it is one of the 'must-see' places on one's itinerary, and I have to confess that I do not know its present status as a place of worship. It can be seen from just about anywhere in the city, and must have been truly astonishing for the early Christians, with its huge dome towering above everything else. Even in the cynical and world-weary 20th century it was still incredibly powerful.

We visited the Topkapi Museum, which didn't greatly impress, simply because everything seemed rather dusty and the lighting was not on a par with the kind of museum lighting we were used to. But what did impress was an amazing, gem-studded seat—shaped a bit like a dog basket, for sitting in cross-legged; and a great chunk of emerald, just lying on a shelf behind grimy glass.

Two silly things stick in my memory about that part of the holiday. I had been warned about the local men. They are apparently much given to pinching bottoms that look pinch-worthy. So I held on to Derry's hand, to indicate that I was an 'owned woman'. In spite of this, crossing the famous Galata bridge, *I was pinched!* I gave a small yelp. 'That man pinched me!' I said. Derry didn't even turn to look. He said, 'It's because you've painted your toe nails!' So much for gallantry—though I wouldn't have wanted him to start throwing his weight about with all those wiry, slightly sinister looking men around.

The second silly thing was that we, who had never been to a nightclub in England, nor even wanted to, decided to join with another couple to visit a nightclub in Istanbul! The Turkish man who had accompanied us on the coach trip during the day said he could arrange for a car for 6 people if anyone wanted to go that evening to what eventually turned out to be a sort of Smoky Joe's. Why we agreed—why *Derry* agreed—I have no idea. It was so out of his usual area of enjoyment.

We piled into the car and arrived in a smoke-filled den, where a few musicians were playing western style pop music (another 'first' for Derry). I had started out with a savage headache, and almost cried off; but when would I have another chance to become debauched in a smoke-choking Turkish cellar? The place was crowded, and I had my first sight of a genuine gigolo (yes, I was sweetly innocent in those days), a handsome young man sitting with his arm around a fat elderly woman. What a way to earn one's keep!

Some people were dancing. I can't remember if food was included, but I have no recollection of anything much except the steady beating of a Turkish drum, echoing the steady beating of my headache. At half-time the music changed and became raucously local, with strident wind instruments and far too much energy for me. That was when the belly dancer came on.

I was quite intrigued until she started going round the room and sitting on the men's knees. As she got closer I began to worry. If she sat on Derry's knee I wasn't quite sure what his reaction would be. And I still don't know; when she got within about three men of Derry the music stopped, and she disappeared into the smoke. I was relieved. I never got round to asking Derry what his overwhelming emotion had been. Was he thankful or disappointed? I decided a good wife wouldn't probe into that.

We emerged at last into the fresh air, and—glory be!—my headache had gone. The competition had been too much for it. Since then I have always recommended a Turkish nightclub as the cure for a migraine. As they say, it worked for me!

And there was one episode that wasn't at all silly, but rather moving. In Australia we use the name 'Gallipoli' with enormous respect. In the UK, where that aspect of the first world war seems very remote, and British eyes turn more easily to the French battlefields, the Gallipoli campaign was little spoken of.

As we approached the Dardanelles, I realised that there was something unusual happening on board. A line of elderly men was forming along the port side of the ship. And on shore one could see white buildings and the steep cliffs that had been so impossibly difficult to scale, all those years ago. As we came level with the beaches that have assumed such a prominent place in Australian history, the elderly men stood to attention, and the ship was quiet. I had to come to Australia myself and feel the emotion that the Gallipoli campaign evokes to realise what I had actually seen on that trip. For those men, this had not been simply a tourist jaunt; they had come to remember and to pay their respects to those who had come but never gone home.

We stopped at Rhodes. This is a fascinating island. The ship cannot go into the harbour because the depth of water is not sufficient, so we all went ashore in launches. In Rhodes I saw my first bougainvillea, a plant I have appreciated ever since. The town is charming, winding streets and shops one dives into, and in the tiny city centre there was a high wall completely covered with this huge bougainvillea. I had to come to Yanchep's National Park to find one as big, and every time I see it I am reminded of the town square in Rhodes.

But we were on our way to Naples.

There used to be a saying, possibly still is: 'See Naples and die!' I never really knew what it meant. Was it—once you have seen Naples, you will never see anything better? Or could you catch something rather nasty there, and die of it? Well, I still don't know what it means, because our impression of the city was not particularly enthusiastic. We started badly, waking up with delicate tummies that indicated that perhaps a coach trip might not be a good idea. So why did we decide instead to walk into the city? I very much doubt if there were any public conveniences, and we certainly didn't see any. Fortunately, the tummies recovered, and we made our way from the quayside through a depressingly shabby suburb where it would not have surprised us at all to have been faced with a machete and a demand for instant money. I think we were both fairly apprehensive.

But we made it to a more civilised area, with a broodingly black castle that we never quite reached. My chief recollection is that my well-used movie camera ran out of film at exactly the wrong moment—a black hearse with black horses and a general aura of gloom and doom came along the street, and everybody stopped out of respect; or possibly just interest, as we did. I got the new film in just in time to get a shot of it, and remember being thankful that in England we had managed to lighten up the last rites. It was not a happy sight. It had a Dickensian brooding quality about it. Oliver Twist would have fitted in very nicely in his role as paid child mourner.

One option was a trip to Herculaneum, sister city to the much better known Pompeii, but both victims of the devastating eruption of Vesuvius in 79AD. This place fascinated us. It had not at that time received as much attention in excavation as Pompeii, but the ruins that were emerging from the huge depth of volcanic material that had so swiftly descended on it 2000 years ago were totally intriguing. Wonderful mosaics and murals, and the layout of small shops and once-splendid houses somehow brought the tragedy back even more than the knowledge of how many people had died.

It is quite odd that my first thought when I arrived in Yanchep and visited the town centre at Two Rocks was that I had seen that little shopping area before. Of course I hadn't. But it dawned on me that the so-called Mediterranean architecture was highly reminiscent of our recollections of Herculaneum. The little shops on the lower level, the rectangular windows, the tiny balconies— they were all there in an ancient Italian city on the far side of the world!

Our final stop was at Ceuta, on the north African coast. It was a bakingly hot day. I watched as, below on the quayside, local sellers started to lay out their wares. I was amused by the tall, imposing gentleman who arrived in a car, wearing western clothes. He disappeared around a corner, and reappeared wearing a long white robe and an appropriate headdress. Every inch the north African until the selling was over, when he emerged in his western clothes again and drove off with his remaining articles, and hopefully a pocket full of money from the visiting cruise passengers.

Coach trips were organised, but we decided to stay on board for a change. Going into the desert and casting an eye over the nearest township there didn't seem to appeal to us. Perhaps we were tired.

My 'family', however, who always made their own arrangements and seemed to be having a great time without my escorting them, spent the day on camels in the nearest bit of desert, and were enthusiastic when they returned. I was pleased that they were having so much fun. There would be plenty to report to the sponsoring company when I got home.

And 'home' was the next stop! It had been a wonderful three weeks, and well worth Derry losing a week's pay. We had memories and plenty of film footage, and it had been good to be on our own and enjoying the change. Back to work on Monday for both of us, and absolutely no regrets.

20

I was full of my trip when I went into the office on Monday morning. My colleagues, all young men, were gratifyingly interested. The chief reporter said that a chap from QANTAS had been trying to get me for several days. I had probably almost forgotten by then that I was arranging an Antipodean journey.

I rang him. 'Yeah,' he said. 'We've got a trip going to Sydney next week. Can you do it?'

For a moment I couldn't think what to do. I hadn't prepared anything for the time I would be away, I didn't know who could look after the children in the daytime while Derry was at school . . . it just wasn't possible. But if I said 'no', would I ever get the chance again?

I said no. 'Thanks, but I've just got back from a cruise in the Med. I'd never get the time off.'

Well,' he said, 'if you can't, then there's nothing until next year.' I was relieved. At least it was still on. I said that would suit me fine, and we arranged to meet and talk about it later.

The lads in the reporters' room wanted to know what I was up to. 'A trip to Australia,' I said (I hope nonchalantly). And I suddenly realised that it was true. I was going to Australia—next year! What an amazing job this was.

But before that could happen there was a routine job to do. I was getting very good feed-back about my pages. The occasional third page was for household things, where I was supposed to write enthusiastic comments about the products being advertised on the page. This could be anything from beautiful table settings to cleansing agents; and on one occasion I was presented with a cleaner that would bring my sink to life so that I would be blinded by the glare.

I took it home and tried it out. It was no better than the stuff I was already using. That poses a problem. One doesn't want to lie, but the paper needs to show a bit of enthusiasm if it hopes to get the advertising next time. I'm not sure if it was my sense of ethics or a bit of laziness, but I wrote a very tame piece about it. The editor sent for me. What did I think I was doing? I said it wasn't particularly good. He seemed to think that was no reason for being truthful. But I got off without more than a nasty look.

The second time this happened (and I'm probably unique in journalism in that these two occasions were the only times I got pulled up short) was after I'd been sent one evening to sit in on a talk and discussion about drug use, which was just beginning to be a recognisable problem among the younger set. I sat through this rather sad event which didn't seem to me to be getting anywhere much, and at the end tried to interview a couple of teenagers who were prepared to say they were 'users' but then shut up. I thought I had managed to produce something readable in spite of this; but the next day the editor called me in and told me it was 'bloody boring'. I said I couldn't help that; the personal touch had been almost non-existent. That was when I discovered what his system for analysing my work was: his wife would read the pages and give me either the thumbs up or the thumbs down. I never met her, so I have no idea whether she was a reliable critic or not.

Apart from the celebrity interviews, I very much enjoyed a series on different kinds of therapies for varying physical or mental conditions. It was sometimes distressing to see what can happen to people through accident or disease, and how difficult it is for them to cope with everyday life; but it was always heart-warming to see the care and attention, even when there was very little that could be done for the sufferers. I particularly recall the young man of 21 who had been hit by a car on a zebra crossing. The oncoming car stopped quite properly; but the car behind zoomed past and hit the boy, who was then about 16. In that split second his life and the life of his family changed for ever.

On the day I met him the nurses were exuberant. 'He's doing so well! Today he dressed himself for the first time.' He'd been in this condition for 5 years! I congratulated him and them. 'It only took him 2 hours.' The nurse was genuinely pleased. Everyone was happy, so I controlled my emotions until I got outside. That could have been one of my children.

Meanwhile, the trip to Australia grew its own momentum. And on a coolish day in March 1972 my sons drove me to Heathrow Airport, and I was on my way. This was the first time I had done more than a short, single-engine trip. The jumbo looked huge. It should have bothered me that all the way to Heathrow Paddy and Keith told me horror stories of plane crashes—but it went over my head.

This was in fact an interesting time to be flying round most of the world. Only a few days before a plane had been hijacked and still stood on the tarmac, visible in the distance. Inside the building there was a kind of desperate chaos, everyone trying to be efficient and organised; but in fact every passenger had to have *all* baggage searched, and it took ages. The young woman who was going through my things looked harassed. I said, 'I bet sometimes you wish you could find something to make all this worthwhile'. She practically snorted. 'I certainly don't! If we find anything it all has to be reported in triplicate.'

I was wearing a winter jersey with a metal buckle. Predictably, it rang bells. I was quickly searched and they—and I—were thankful when the belt turned out to be the offending article.

Then we were on board. This was an inaugural flight, going via Rome and Bangkok, and as a result there were several travel writers making their way down-under at QANTAS's expense. I remember having a long conversation with the travel journalist from the Croydon newspaper. At some point I was invited to go up to see the glories available to first class passengers, and in the bar there I was offered a drink. I sat chatting, enjoying the whole thing, and eventually made my way down the stairs to my seat. Unfortunately, no one had told me that a main meal was being served while I was away, and they hadn't thought to keep something for me. I was such a new kid that it didn't dawn on me to make a small fuss; so until the next meal I went hungry.

It didn't matter. The whole experience was too amazing.

Apart from a very nasty headache (the Croydon journo gave me an aspirin) the trip was uneventful. Nobody tried to hijack us, and the plane was very comfortable, mainly because there were many empty seats. I was in the central block, and I had a stretch of five seats all to myself. I don't think that has ever happened to me again. I was able to lie full length and have a proper sleep.

We went via Rome and Bangkok. We could have been anywhere, because I have no recollection of seeing anything much down below. Certainly there were plenty of lights as we approached Rome, and for a first-time flyer that was a pretty sight. But because of the hijacking scares at that time (was that the 'fly me to Cuba!' period?) we were not allowed to leave the plane, either there or at Bangkok. Cleaners came aboard and dabbed around us, and after what seemed quite a long time we took off again for the next stop. Memory tells me that by the time we approached Bangkok it was light—I remember that particularly because as we landed I saw that there were men, presumably airport staff, flying kites alongside the runway. This seemed to me not to be a good idea, though whether it was actually dangerous to have them there I wouldn't know. It just seemed a silly place to do it.

I had a young Thai student sitting next to me for the stretch from Bangkok to Melbourne, our first touch-down in Australia. He was coming back to finish his university career in Melbourne, and he was bemoaning the fact that, in order to pay back to his government the money they had expended on his overseas education he would have to do two years teaching in his homeland. That seemed quite fair to me, but he was really miserable. I asked why. He said, 'Australia is so clean, and Bangkok is so dirty!

We were able to get out of the plane and stretch our legs at Melbourne's Tullamarine airport, and it was a very strange sensation. Not the leg stretching—just the thought that I was now 'down-under', that almost mythical place that I had learnt about in school (without taking much of it in: why were the Darling

Ranges one side of the country and the Darling River on the other? And why 'Darling', anyway?). The air smelt of something new—I found it was eucalyptus. The temperature (it was March) was pleasantly warm. I was still wearing my winter jumper, so I was very conscious of the warmth. But above all I felt that I was at home in this new world, and that surprised me.

I had expected everything to be strange, perhaps even alien. But from the moment my feet touched Australian soil I was home! Even now, after nearly forty years in Australia, I can sometimes find myself wondering why. Why did I find it so comfortable to be in what should feel like a foreign land? I had been to France and Italy, and had found them inescapably 'foreign'. But Australia settled itself around me as if it had been waiting for me.

The last lap! Melbourne to Sydney. We did that wonderful romp down the runway that always makes me think of stampeding elephants (we were in a Jumbo, after all). I know that is a nail-biting moment for some, but I always loved it, and still do.

I was by this time next to a man who pointed out interesting things we were flying over. This included the snowfields, which I hadn't expected—no one in England who hadn't been to Australia would have expected this expanse of snow in a country that had always been thought of as hot and dusty! He told me (and I still don't know if he was correct, or whether I was having my Pommie leg pulled) that these snowfields were more extensive than the ones in the Alps in Europe. Certainly, having just felt the warmth of Melbourne's climate, I didn't expect to look down on miles of snow.

Then it was 'seat belts on', and that downward slide that upsets the ears—and it did—and landing in Sydney. My memories of that are vague. I think there was too much to take in. Through customs, out to the luggage spewing out of the strange creation in the middle of a swirling crowd of people—and through the doors to where Cynthia was waiting for me.

It was quite a moment, slightly bizarre because as I came through the doors a group of Italians swept towards me shouting,

'Mama! Mama!' But it wasn't me they were greeting; it was the little lady in black just behind me.

I'd made it, anyway. I was in Australia for the next five weeks. Much of what I would do was already planned; I had interviews to do and people to meet from the Tourist office who would arrange for photographers to take pictures of my interviewees. But first I needed to find my feet in this new world.

21

Cynthia and Arthur would bring the children, Simon and Fiona, to Dorking for our final English Christmas in 1973; but at this point, early 1972, I had not seen the parents since they had left England—and these two grandchildren were strangers to me. I looked forward to getting to know all of them, children and parents, in their new setting.

Arthur worked in Richmond, some miles out of Sydney, where the air base was; they lived a short distance from there in Windsor. I liked the area; it had what was for me, a newcomer, a very Aussie look about it. This was partly the architecture, so different from what we had in Dorking; and partly the surrounding countryside, which fascinated me. Big eucalypts, seen from a distance, look not unlike the British elms—this was before disease carried most of the latter off some years later. But one of the outstanding visual memories is of the endless miles (or kilometres, I suppose) of overhead wires, supported by what in the UK we would call telegraph poles, and in Australia were power poles.

As I have got to know the country better over the following years I still wonder why it is that in Britain the telephone wires are above ground on poles, while the electricity system is located underground. Yet in Australia, where bush fires are a constant summer hazard, the power lines are above ground and the telephone system is underground. So many fires can be caused by faulty overhead wiring that it seems strange that, since telephone wires are able to be 'buried', the more dangerous power lines are exposed to corrosion and all the damage that can be caused by termites and storm damage. I've never really found out what kind of wood is used for poles here; they have a very rustic look about them, quite unlike the ones in Britain, which almost look manufactured rather than chopped down.

Early photographs of Australian cities demonstrate the constant presence of poles and wires; wherever one looks they are there, drooping across main streets and looping together the little houses in the suburbs. In the new suburbs, of course, such things are discreetly hidden; I suppose in a few more years no one will remember the old days when Australia was sewn together by this endless network of power lines.

I remember a trip to the Hawkesbury River, where I held a fishing line for the first time—and all too soon lost interest in murdering little fish! But the scenery was wonderful. I got ideas for short stories while I was in Windsor, which helped when I got home again and could write them. But one should never try to write about a place on a very short acquaintance: it's too easy to get it wrong. Eventually, I had to live in Australia for several years before I felt able to write about it effectively.

We went up into the Blue Mountains, Sydney's backcloth, but it was a wettish day, and all we really saw was dripping trees and mist. It wasn't until nearly 4 decades later that I finally saw the extraordinary scenery, with its dense valleys and steep cliffs and ancient, ancient rock formations. It is truly awesome, in the proper meaning of the word.

My itinerary for the five weeks I would be in Australia was, first, to Perth on the west coast, where I was to interview several people whose roots were in the part of south-east England covered by the newspaper. This included a very elderly gentleman who had been an architect and was responsible for many buildings in Perth. I remember him saying, 'Of course, England is just one great city all the way from London to the south coast, isn't it?' (He originally came from Horsham in Sussex.) I was really pleased to be able to tell him that there were still miles and miles of green and open countryside, and that he would probably not see such a great difference from when he had lived there.

As I went into the house, greeted by his wife, I was conscious of an interesting smell that I couldn't quite place. She apologised for having the curtains almost closed in their lounge room; 'because of the fruit drying', she said. I wondered what she meant, so she drew the curtains back and showed me bunches of home-grown grapes lying on newspaper on the floor. This was what I had smelt: the warm, sweet aroma of dried fruit. But I had never seen them being dried on the floor of a lounge room before; it certainly wasn't something one would meet in England.

Another interviewee was a member of the editorial staff at the West Australian newspaper. I asked his wife if there was anything she missed about living in WA; she said yes, chocolate biscuits. I was surprised; didn't they make them here? She said it was because the chocolate would melt in the summer. I think the problem was that small shops, delis and so on, were not all air-conditioned at that time; but it was quite interesting to find out as I travelled around the country just what it was that immigrants hankered after.

I recall that when I went back to the UK to stay with my parents in 1978 (their Golden Wedding year) my father asked me if there was anything I couldn't get at home that I would like to have. Even though I was not a passionate sausage lover, I said, 'Yes, pork sausages'. Dad looked at me. 'Don't you have pork sausages?' Well, I don't know if anyone recalls the 'snags-on-the-barbie' things that passed for sausages in those days; the only place I could get a good sausage was in Perth, where there was a food department in a large store, and the sausages were rather better. But it was quite a distance to go for a good banger! Dad took me to his local shop, and we ate the real thing, juicy and crisp and full of tasty meat. Yum! These days, of course, we get so many different kinds of sausages that we are spoilt for choice.

I stayed with a family in Perth, and was shown around some of the city's best spots. I went as far north as Scarborough and Sorrento, very conscious of the heat, though no one else seemed to notice it. The beaches delighted me. We drove through the university campus on the banks of the Swan River, and I was impressed by the beautiful surroundings in which West Australian undergraduates were being taught. I hope they appreciated the splendid gardens and the amazing view over the river. Perhaps one would need to see some of the city universities in the UK, surrounded by buildings and noise and the dust of ages, to understand just how beautiful the UWA campus is.

The father of my host family was a clerk in the fruit and vegetable markets in the city. I was there for a long weekend, and on the Saturday, after work, he came home with a large box full of fruit that hadn't sold: $1.50 the lot. I was beginning to think that I could live in this place quite happily! But it is interesting what things catch one's attention in a new place. At home, tomatoes were always perfectly shaped. I think they came from the Scilly Isles; if they were not perfect they were sold as 'cooking tomatoes'. In Australia the tomatoes all seemed to be misshapen; it was many years before the ones we now buy were in the markets.

I was taken up into the Legacy Lookout—the observation floor of a tall office block opposite the entrance to King's Park. Legacy is the organisation that works for the families of returned servicemen and women, and the Lookout presumably brought in a small amount of money for their funds.

From there the view was striking. One of the things that particularly struck me was how green everything was—parks and trees and road verges. I commented on this, and my host said, 'Yes, we have plenty of water here. Perth is just about built on water—we shall never be short of it'. That was in 1972. Now we know differently.

I had done my interviews. I had got a taste of what Australia was all about. And on the Monday I was off again, back across the endless stretches of nothingness that was how I saw the country from the air. Though that's not quite true—as I looked down I saw a landscape that was virtually empty of people, but was a fascinating blend of earth colours, almost like an abstract painting. It made me think of a huge Italian floor, paved with earth-coloured marble. Now and then there would be straight lines that perhaps indicated the boundaries of someone's land; sometimes something that looked as if it might be an ancient river bed no longer in use. And it went on and on . . . and on. I realised that if I had been flying for that distance over the British Isles, south to north, I would by now be well on the way to the Shetlands, and they are about as far north as anyone wants to be.

But I was on my way to Adelaide in South Australia, and looking forward to another round of interviews.

A government driver had been allocated to me, and he was to take me to the Barossa Valley, a wine-growing area of which I knew nothing. There I was to learn a piece of Australian history which I found quite fascinating. In 1832 a German pastor brought his congregation out to the Barossa Valley to escape religious persecution at home. As a result, the Valley has a strong German personality, with towns and graveyards and a language all imported by people who had presumably not wanted to have to flee their homeland.

I was told that the German language in the Barossa Valley was a little different from the modern German; and that the older German customs and culture had been kept alive and well there. The story was related to me about the first Germans to visit that part of SA after the two wars: because of the upheaval of everything they had known in Germany, some things had been in very short supply, among them (so I was told) the ingredients for the famous German sausage. Sausages again!

So when they arrived in a place where the traditions had been maintained, there in the south of Australia, they found the sausage unchanged from its pre-war cousin. I assume there was much rejoicing. Probably with German beer.

I was taken to a small local museum by my driver. As we drew up outside it he suddenly stopped and said, rather hesitantly, that of course it would be nothing like our great museums in England. Cultural cringe? I said that didn't matter, because I had never seen a museum which was located in a small Aussie cottage with an ox-cart outside, and, once I had had a look around inside, a wooden washing machine (which presumably someone could have brought from the city *on an ox-cart)* and a whole room full of glass bottles of every size and colour that had been used by these early settlers, brought out over many a mile, bouncing over rutted country tracks and finally, apparently, unearthed by energetic history buffs from rubbish dumps. How they would have loved plastic bottles!

I had a vivid picture in my mind of the woman who had owned those bottles, which had carried medicines, soap, and other necessities of life; she was sitting on the ox-cart, looking at the rumps of a couple of oxen (had she ever had to deal with such animals in her former life?). She hadn't wanted to emigrate, perhaps from Britain (not everyone came from Germany), but one day her husband had come home and said, 'My dear, I have sold the house and we are going to Orstralia!' Did she even know where that was? How would she cope with the children on the long voyage out? And, like many a wife, regarding her husband with astonishment and perhaps a touch of horror, did she wonder if he had gone mad? Leave our comfortable home in London/ Bristol/Manchester for—what?

She would soon enough find out. As the oxen swayed their way along dusty tracks, as the heat got to her in her English-style clothes, as the children kept asking 'Are we nearly there?' and as her husband put a brave face on it, she endured the hours, perhaps days of their journey through bush, the unprepared confrontations with snakes and kangaroos and other things of which she had never heard. I wonder if the house was ready for them when they arrived. I hope they didn't have to start to build it there and then, weary with travelling of a kind they had never envisaged. And I wonder, without much hope, whether her husband ever apologised for dragging her away from her friends, family, church, sewing party, visits to people who lived down the road, to land her in this place which she would need every bit of strength of mind and body to survive. Many didn't. For some, I imagine, the shock of what they were expected to be able to do in order to create a home in this alien environment was too much. Perhaps they took to their beds; perhaps they died when the next baby arrived without proper midwife attention; perhaps they simply dwindled and faded like a badly transplanted plant.

Yes, I think I got full value out of that little museum.

I recall being invited by the family of someone I had met in Reigate to go on a barbecue with them. We spread ourselves over a rocky gully, up in the Adelaide hills somewhere, where a small stream trickled, and the men lit a fire. I was told later that was not very clever: the rocks can suddenly split with the heat, and could cause serious injuries. However, nothing untoward happened, and the only thing that bothered me was that I was wearing pantyhose, and it was getting hot! Nobody else had been silly enough to wear stockings; I would have taken them off if I had known my hosts better. As it was, I sat and sweated.

In fact, I was probably more concerned about the fact that the bush was immediately behind us, and I was still very wary of snakes and other wildlife. I took some photographs, and we found a small playground where I think we had a swing. When we were almost back in Adelaide I realised I had left my camera on a seat by the swings. My patient hosts, smothering a sigh of annoyance, left me at the hotel and went back for the camera—which, thankfully, was still there.

Among my various pieces of paper I had a letter from someone influential in QANTAS. I didn't realise how influential he was until I was in SA. Interviews over and packed away in my bags, I made my way to the airport to begin my next leg of the journey: Brisbane. Unfortunately the plane had no room for me—a situation I had not foreseen. I had not yet waved my magic paper at anyone, but I did now. They took me to the airport manager, who sat me down in his office and gave me a whisky, and said they knew how to deal with VIPs. I was a bit taken aback at this. No, I was extremely taken aback! I had not seen myself as a VIP. He said, 'When we get a letter from this man, we know we have to look after you.'

This was very flattering, although slightly puzzling. I wondered for a while if he had got the wrong person; but apparently not. There was no flight available to Brisbane until the next morning, quite early; I would have to stay overnight in an Adelaide hotel.

I didn't mind that. But my baggage had gone on ahead on the plane I thought I was going on, and I would arrive at the hotel with a large brown paper bag and a toothbrush. He didn't seem to think that mattered. He got me into his car and we departed; the hotel was quite possibly 5-star—posh, anyway. And they thought it was OK to arrive with no luggage. What it is to be a celebrity!

The plane took off the next morning with me on board. I had learnt from the airport manager that in the event of a seat not being available for me, I was supposed to be carried first class. I really should have read that letter more closely!

When I reached Brisbane I found that the forwarded luggage had actually been offloaded somewhere else. But it's OK being a celebrity—there's always someone to clear up the messes for you. Somebody went to wherever the bags were and they turned up before long. I was glad of that. I needed clean clothes.

Brisbane in 1972 was not as it is today. I was there not long ago, and how it has changed! I remember that when I got home again after my long trip I said to Derry, 'What is this?' and walked very slowly across the room. He said he had no idea. I said, 'It's a Brisbanian in a hurry!'

The city was like a big country town, the traffic was much less than one would have expected, and the people were relaxed and friendly. But there were odd things about it, too. I was invited to a barbecue run by the local tourist office, and was driven there by the tourism boss—so cautiously that I was intrigued. Was he just a very poor driver, or were there strange rules about driving in Brisbane?

It turned out to be the latter. I had never heard of the road rule that said that a car coming in from the right had priority. It meant that my driver was always on the look-out for something emerging from a right hand entry; so we slowed down in this suburban area of grid patterned streets every time we came to cross-roads. It was actually nerve-racking.

I mentioned my surprise to him, and he said there had been a case in the city where a driver had been correctly crossing on the green light when a car came from the right, where the light was red. It hit the 'green' car—and the green car driver was fined for not allowing the other car through. I found this difficult to believe, since the 'red' driver was crossing against his own light, which I thought would bring severe penalties. Not so! I was very puzzled by this. Some long time later, probably when we were in Australia, that rule was abandoned, and not before time.

On the Saturday night I was invited to the English Club for their weekly dance. I'm glad I went, because it showed me one side of immigration that I hadn't really seen. It was easy enough to see where the Aussie belief in the 'whingeing Pom' came from. The atmosphere was charged—I think that's the word—with a faint resentment that I didn't understand.

What I learnt was that, if you are going to go and live in someone else's country, you *don't* create a Pommie enclave if you want to be happy. I danced with a man who started in, as soon as we took the floor, with his complaints.

'It's a con, you know,' he said, 'this £10 thing to get you out here. You can never raise enough money to get home again.'

'Would you like to go home?' I asked.

"Oh, yes. I'd go like a shot.'

'Why? Don't you like it here?'

'No, I don't! There's no culture here, no culture at all.'

I regarded him (at short range because we were still dancing). He didn't give the impression of someone who valued culture to that level. 'So what do you miss—culturally?'

'Well, everything. There isn't any culture here.'

I decided to follow this through. 'So you went to the theatre a lot in England?'

He stared at me. 'No!'

'The opera?'

'No.'

'Art galleries?' He said no to everything I suggested. So I gave up. If Brisbane was as uncultured as he reckoned it to be, I should have thought it would have suited him nicely. I wonder what he meant by 'culture'.

I vowed to myself that I would never get involved with an 'English Club', or any other gathering that excluded people of another—dare I say?—culture.

Brisbane was as near as I had ever been to a tropical climate. I have no recollection of being beaten by the heat, so I assume I coped with these changes pretty well.

The city surprised me because it doesn't seem to be near the sea. Only a matter of miles, but this makes it very much a river city—a bit like Perth, I suppose. Visits were laid on to various places of interest—the Lone Pine Sanctuary, for example, where I held an albino koala to have my photo taken. It was larger than I had expected, and I was warned by the keeper to hold it firmly, because if it felt insecure it might slide down me, claws out, and rip me! I held it firmly.

The words 'lone pine' meant nothing to me at that time. I still didn't understand the depth of feeling in the country over the Gallipoli campaign in 1915 (incidentally, that began a couple of weeks after Derry was born). Lone Pine was the name of one of the battles for that inhospitable piece of land, remembered through the years for the sacrifices made by the young diggers in that part of the campaign. It would come to mean more to me as the years passed by.

Once my interviews were done I was due to leave for another holiday spot that I was really looking forward to—Great Keppel Island, which lies towards the southern end of the Great Barrier Reef. No interviews here: I was to be the guest of the management of this tiny resort, and it would be a few days of rest and relaxation for me.

I believe the island has gone a bit up-market since 1972, when I saw it. I hope it hasn't been spoilt. It was such an unusual situation for me to be in from first to last.

I was taken to Rockhampton, on the Queensland coast, and was to be flown from there across to the island. At the airport at Rockhampton there were small private planes standing around by the tarmac, and I wondered how we would be going over. They looked too small to be safe.

Well, one of them was ours! Apart from the pilot and myself, there were three other passengers. Two of them were staff from the island, going back after a spot of mainland shopping. The third was a small man with a guitar, who had been engaged to perform in the bar in the evenings. He was noticeably nervous.

As we stood waiting to be taken aboard he turned to one of the airport staff. 'These are nice model planes you've got here.'

The man stared at him. 'You're flying in one.' The guitarist looked as if he'd like to call off the whole booking.

Once in the plane, with me sitting beside the pilot and the other three squashed behind us, we took off. It was no great distance to the island, but I was interested to learn that it was only recently that a landing strip had been constructed. Up till then the planes had to land and take off on the beach. As we drew nearer the pilot said, 'You can see the landing strip in the centre of the island.' I looked down, but I couldn't see anything that looked as if Man had had a hand in its construction.

He assured me it was there, 'just a line down the middle'. We were coming in lower, and suddenly I saw something like a pencil line, not very long, right in the centre of the vegetation. Within moments we were on it, bouncing and thudding along over what had looked smooth from the air, but was about as smooth as a ploughed field in a drought. A wooden archway said, '*Welcome to Great Keppel Island*' in very rustic lettering; we were there!

On the whole I was glad we hadn't had to land on the beach.

I received a real welcome. I'm glad it was a pleasant place, and a good rest, because it was going to make a huge difference to the lives of myself and my whole family.

22

From the island one could see the Queensland mainland across the water. This was especially striking at night. The town immediately opposite to us was Yeppoon, and as the sun sank behind the Great Dividing Range, leaving the hills purple in the twilight, the lights of Yeppoon began to twinkle like stars.

Closer to us were moored yachts, whose riding lights also twinkled. The sky was richly apricot from the sun's last rays. It was an amazing sight, especially for someone who not so long ago had been emerging from a British winter.

At dinner I was the guest of the manager and his wife. While we were eating, I suddenly heard a strange sound, somewhere up above us; it sounded like a stampede of very small buffalo. (I have to admit that I have never actually heard such a thing, but writers are allowed to have flights of fancy).

I must have looked surprised, because the manager said, 'Don't worry. It's only the possums in the roof.' Apparently they woke up for their evening romp about then.

When we were sitting outside later—guests and management and kitchen staff: all very friendly, (except one)—I glanced up at the window behind me that looked out from the bar, which was now closed for the night. Strange, I thought, to put one of those in there. On a top shelf was a small animal, rather like the things people put on the back of their cars, with a nodding head. At that point, the small animal suddenly scampered along the shelf, and I realised I had just seen my first possum. It seems they get in everywhere.

We watched the moon floating high over the ocean. It was idyllic. I was impressed by the kind of people they had working in the kitchen; I learnt that they were mainly university students or graduates who were working through their vacations. The two who had been on the plane were in fact to be married on the island at the weekend—sadly, I would have gone by then.

The only fly in the ointment of my content was one of the guests, an Irishman; he took offence at my Englishness, and laid into me quite unpleasantly. He had it in for the Royal Family, the English church, the English way of life—and me, representing the lot. We could have had quite an interesting discussion, but he was ready to shoot the lot of us 'over there'. I think we managed to avoid an actual row, but it was a salutary reminder that in every Eden there will be a serpent. I remember thinking that the potato famine had not actually been my personal fault.

The guitarist, I'm sorry to say, was not very good. He played in the bar after dinner, but it didn't inspire. Eventually, when he was having a rest, I asked if I could borrow his song book; I found a few songs I knew, and a piano that was reasonable, and sang to the customers. It went down slightly better than the guitarist's efforts. The only one I can remember was *Little boxes*.

I remember eating lunch outside; a wonderful spread on the terrace, the centrepiece being a decorated mackerel, larger than any mackerel I had ever seen in England. It was delicious! I was sorry that I would miss the wedding a few days later—I bet the food was terrific.

We were taken for a boat trip from the island to another nearby. We passed other tiny islands on the way to our picnic site on a sandy beach (with oysters clinging to the rocks); our skipper told us that there were 'virtually no snakes' on these little outcrops. For me, 'virtually' was not enough! My desire never to meet a snake face to face made me very sensitive to such comments. One snake would be ample.

On one evening I went for a walk by myself along the beach. (Nobody warned me about sand flies). It was very beautiful, very peaceful, and I suddenly started asking myself why it was that, because one was a 'professional', one had to stay that way all one's life. I was thinking more of Derry than of myself. He was tired; he was five years down the track after the breakdown, and I didn't think he could take much more of the responsibility and sheer hard work that his job entailed.

I had been pondering on this for some time, probably since I was told by psychiatrists that he would never work again. He'd proved them wrong, but we had to consider the next step. I knew *he* wouldn't. Masculine stubbornness that says, 'I'm all right!' regardless of the facts, gets in the way.

Could we live in Scotland? I've always had a faint hankering to do so, but I couldn't see quite what he would do there. We had enjoyed being in the Dordogne area of France on the holiday in 1968; but that meant he would have to learn a new language, and I didn't see him getting on with the locals. (I could have been wrong. He might have loved it). When I suggested moving he showed little interest.

I knew that if he left the job at school we would have to move. There was no way he could live in Dorking and see someone taking over his beloved music department. Besides that, the house needed so much doing to it, and we were fairly short of the money to do it with. It was a dilemma that I was having to think out for myself. I had always been the one to suggest changes; his concentration was normally on whatever music he was going to produce next; and that suited me, with my never-ending source of new ideas, some good, some bad.

All this went through my mind on that beach. I felt it was the 'professional' tag that was holding us back. Why couldn't *we* work in a kitchen on a small Australian island, and sit out with the guests as the sun went down and the moon came up? It sounded heavenly.

I followed the thought through. Alison and Fiona could come with us. *But what would they do about school?* School of the Air? (I had just heard about it). I didn't think so. By the time I was back in my cabin I had faced up to the fact that paradise would have to wait. But the basic idea stayed with me. We *could* break free and try something new. It was just a question of how and when and where. That's all! Nothing to it!

I left the island that had become so important to my thinking. The pilot said, 'You can control the air conditioning'. I raised my eyebrows. He nodded at the window beside me. 'Keep the window open while we taxi, then shut it when we take off.'

We bounced and bumped down the air strip and soared off into the blue sky. I looked down, and wondered how such a tiny piece of land could seem so secure while one was on it. Islands are strange things. From the air they look as if one good wave would wipe them out; yet, in the middle, there may be quite a hilly place which simply doesn't show from above.

For the rest of that trip my new idea stayed in the back of my mind. I took it out and looked at it from time to time, then put it away for further insight. But at some point I realised what I was actually thinking about: emigration! That was a really big one. It would mean splitting the family, because the older ones had their own lives in the planning stage. It would mean finding some way of financially supporting ourselves. Above all, it meant leaving Dorking and our house. I loved Arundel Lodge. This was partly, I imagine, because we had brought up all our children there, and it was bursting with memories, good and bad.

It would mean going to the other side of the world at a time when my parents were in their seventies and might need support in their old age. Rosemary and Philip were there—and I had, after all, spent quite a lot of time and effort looking after Derry's parents: perhaps it wasn't too much to expect that I shouldn't have to do it again. Philip surprised me by telling me, unasked, that I was not to worry about 'the parents', because he would see that they were OK. This was a big emotional load off my mind.

It would also mean that I would have to organise the sale of our house myself. This was not because Derry was not capable of it. But when he was preparing concerts and carol services and the general teaching schedules of school life, he was not going to be able to spend the time to do the selling. I wouldn't expect him to.

But all this was well into the future. First, I had to get home again and fall into the usual pattern of my days. Then—and this was the big one—I had to put the idea of emigration to him in a way that required the answer 'yes'!

The only thing I had to go on was that several years before I had seen an advertisement for a well-qualified musician to begin and develop a music department at the newly opened James Cook University in Queensland. That seemed to me the ideal job for someone like Derry. When I showed him the advert he stared at it and said, 'Why on earth would I want to go and lived in *Australia*?' And that was that.

So I had some doubts about whether a suggestion that we should emigrate would receive the kind of reception I wanted for it.

I said nothing for several weeks. Then, one day when he was tired and a bit dispirited, I said, 'How would you like to retire to Australia?'

I waited with what might well have been bated breath. He said, 'Well, why not?'

So we did!

23

My trip had been a success. After five weeks I had a file of interviews and plenty of photographs of Australia and my interviewees. I flew home across the Pacific and the Atlantic Oceans, so that I could say I had flown round the world. I managed that again in 2010 when I visited the USA and Canada. I have been so lucky.

From Sydney to Tahiti I sat (in first class, I'm pleased to say) next to a senior management man from one of the oil companies. We crossed the International Date Line, and this led us to discussing the possibility for a writer of constructing a plot which would use the date line as an alibi for the criminal. It must be possible, but the idea has never really inspired me. It's too hard to work out. Perhaps if I had taken the idea up I would have had the backing of international oil to publish it. Or perhaps not.

We touched down at Tahiti and Fiji, and then hit the mainland at Acapulco. Sadly, one airport terminal is much like another, so I wouldn't really claim to know anything about these places I briefly stood in. In Mexico City I tried to carry out a promise I had made to Fiona: that I would buy her a sombrero. I could see them in the windows of the shop, but reconstruction of the airport meant that transit passengers were not allowed in to buy anything. So Fiona didn't get her sombrero until a couple of years later when we were en route for our new home in Australia.

I think our next stop was Bermuda (yes, we did fly through the Bermuda Triangle, and I am here to say it was OK), where the seat next to me was taken by the government psychiatrist (or possibly psychologist) on that island. He spent much of the time ringing for another drink; and I am slightly embarrassed to say that I kept pace with him—without actually being affected. Eventually he was ready to fall off his seat, and I was still stone-cold sober.

It was about then that he made the proposition that I should come back to Bermuda and have a holiday with him. Apparently the work load was very light and he was ready by ten in the morning to wander down to the beach and—presumably—drink himself into a state of euphoria.

Being propositioned is something that hasn't often happened to me. I thought quickly (not wishing to make some coy reply) and said, 'That sounds lovely! Can I bring my husband and the children?' I don't think he actually spoke to me again.

It was cold in England after all that wonderful warmth. As we flew in over the Needles on the SW coast and saw the land laid out beneath us I was struck by how small everything was. I could see the whole of the west country, England's great playground, from the southern coast to the Bristol Channel—a great triangle of land, but so small compared with the immensities I had recently seen. More than that, I could see, mistily in the distance, the southern third of Wales. What a dear little country!

As we came closer to home the pilot announced that we would be flying along the coast to Portsmouth and then 'turning left' to go up towards London. And so we did. When we got close to Heathrow we had to circle and await our turn to land; and, as I looked down, I suddenly realised that we were over Dorking. One of the cabin crew was standing near me. I said, 'Can you get me a parachute?' She looked surprised and asked why. 'Because I've just seen my house down there, and it would be quicker than going to Heathrow.'

And so I returned home, full of exuberance after a busy but rewarding stay on the far side of the world. I was bursting with information and my 'secret idea'—roll on Monday morning when I would be back at work and able to tell my colleagues all about it. Perhaps I was much too 'high'—perhaps for every mountain top there must be a dark valley. I breezed into the reporters' room and was immediately surrounded by my mates, asking all the right questions. But there was a strange atmosphere, and after a few minutes the chief reporter (the man from Bunbury) said, 'The editor wants to see you'.

Well, of course he would! I had so much to tell him. But what he had to tell me was not quite what I had expected. He sacked me!

I couldn't believe I had heard him correctly. I had just done something that no one on the staff had ever achieved before, and I'd lost my job? Why?

He was clearly deeply embarrassed by the situation. 'I'm sorry, Barb. I have to let you go.'

'But why?'

'It's the Chairman. He doesn't like his journalists to get 'freebies'. I'm really sorry.'

I remembered all the journos who had been guests on the flight from Heathrow. Were they all going to be sacked too? I was almost speechless; but I started to argue the toss. The editor was adamant. 'You have to go!'

I'm sorry to say I completely lost my temper and swore at him. 'You *bastard!*'

'Not my doing. He's made it clear that if I don't sack you he will, and me as well. And I have a wife and three children to support.'

I went back to the reporters' room. They had quite obviously known this was going to happen, and they were extremely sympathetic. We consigned all bosses to the nether regions for a few minutes; then it began to sink in. My lovely job, the one I had been allowed to create for myself, the one I had had so many compliments about from readers all over the region—*my job!*—was over. I'm glad to say I didn't start sobbing, though I think I would have liked to. The boys took me out for lunch over the road at the pub—extremely nice ham sandwiches and a half of Double Diamond—and I started to 'clear my desk'.

(Where was the Chairman while I was cavorting—for free—in the Mediterranean?)

I can remember nothing at all about the reactions from my family. The days that followed are a blank. But I do remember a bizarre twist to the tale. I had a call from the reporters to say that they were having a union (NUJ) meeting on my behalf and that I ought to be there. They were going to see if they could get me reinstated.

The room was crowded. I was quite moved; it indicated a depth of caring from the staff that I had not fully realised. Much talking took place, some of it quite angry; but eventually a vote was taken. That was when they discovered that the only fully paid up member of the union was me! This is not a totally surprising result when dealing with a bunch of young men. I'd been a mother of teenagers long enough to know that. But it meant that no vote would be valid—I'd still lost my job. They filed out of the room, a bit shame-faced, and shook hands with me solemnly as if we had just been at a wake. Which in one way, I suppose, we had.

There was a more serious aspect to this sudden dismissal. I had been dealing with QANTAS and the Australian Tourist Commission on a 'gentleman's agreement' basis. No contract had been signed. It was understood that I would be able to provide several pages of enthusiastic commentary about Australia and the delights of flying by QANTAS; now, all at once, I couldn't do it. The paper was not going to take my pieces, and my reputation in certain circles would be badly damaged.

I asked the editor if they would use my articles, and he said no. The only bright glow on the horizon was his comment that the Chairman would be retiring in September, and then 'we might see about something'. We were then in April. Waiting that long would hardly have the immediacy that journalism likes. But it was best I was going to get.

I met the representatives of the two organisations for lunch in London. I was very nervous, not knowing what their reaction would be to my failure to deliver. As it happened, they were very sympathetic; I promised them that *if* the wretched Chairman retired (or perhaps fell off his chair) they might get their pages as agreed. Of course, a promise that *might* be kept is no promise; but it had to do. They fed me on German sausages (sausages seem to have haunted me at that time), and we parted good friends.

In the event, I am thankful to say that when the Chairman did in fact retire in September, I was told that all my Australian articles appeared in the East Surrey Newspapers. I added them up: with nineteen editions over a wide area of Surrey, south London, north Sussex and a bit of Kent this amounted to at least nineteen pages for Australia and QANTAS to absorb. Finally, I felt I had been vindicated.

I sometimes wonder what happened in the long term to the editor.

I did some odd—really odd!—bits of writing over the next few months. My ex-colleagues sent me, from time to time, various snippets of work to keep me happy. I can recall ringing up some quite eminent women and asking them what beauty secrets they had! (I don't think this is really me). But I did have quite a good relationship with some of the major magazines in the UK, and was able to pick up the odd job here and there. A connection with the BBC's Natural History department in Bristol helped; I did a couple of stories for them, pre-publicity for TV documentaries.

That was particularly interesting. I was taken to see an editor at work, painstakingly putting together film clips of penguins in the Antarctic. He explained how the interest of the public had changed over the years. Once it was enough to show a shot of a penguin diving into the water and then reappearing; now the viewer wanted to see the bird go under water, swim around, and emerge on the bank. This meant matching film from above and under the water, and finding a sequence that would blend without showing the joins. I watched him do it.

Another story I was offered was about Iceland. I was doubtful about this, never having been to the country. But I was assured that all the information would be there for me—it was just a question of writing it up. The editor of the quality magazine I was to do it for was very doubtful. She said, 'How can you write about a place you have never seen?'

I assured her that it could be done. She pondered for a bit, then said, even more doubtfully, 'Well, I suppose it will be all right'. I hope she was reassured when she saw the finished article. The magazine published it, anyway.

A team of ornithologists and other scientists had travelled down the length of South America, and the film of their exploits was to be shown shortly. Bristol said, 'Would I come over and do a piece about it?' I would.

I met the man in charge and we looked at some of the film. I was given plenty of information and met the other members of the team. Because of the distance from home I was taken back to the team leader's home for the night. He had the first colour TV I had ever seen; and during the evening as he and his wife and I sat watching it, he turned the colour off with the memorable words, 'Let's see what the *poor* people are seeing tonight!' I went off him a bit.

Their discoveries on that trip were fascinating, though at this distance in time I only remember two properly. One was about a bird that did a complicated little dance each time it found a snail to eat. No one knew why this happened, until the film was run in slow motion. It was not, as they had imagined, some kind of ritual; the bird held the snail in its beak, found a rock with its foot, stepped back and dropped the snail on to the rock, and *hey presto!*—one cracked snail, one good meal!

The other tale was told by a young man who had been bitten by something unidentified during their journeying. The bite healed over after a while and he was able to forget about it. Months later, back in England, he felt an irritation on his side at the place where he had been bitten. To his alarm, a maggoty creature emerged! He had apparently given birth to a South American bug of some kind.

I continued to write and sell short stories, and did the odd interview for one magazine or another. Johnny Morris, much loved zoo man on children's TV, was a delight; Arthur Negus, who had awakened the whole country to the intrinsic beauty of Victoriana (at that time somewhat maligned) was fascinating.

And eventually I travelled to Sydenham in S. London to interview Rolf Harris, who gave me the best advice I could have had as a prospective emigrant: 'Take all your blankets and winter woollies; people think because it's Australia it's always going to be hot. But it can get really cold in Perth during the winter'.

I'm glad I listened to him. That first winter we certainly needed them!

This was all happening during 1972/3, and we were beginning to plan for our emigration.

24

I t's one thing to decide to uproot the family and go to the other side of the world; it's quite another to actually do it. Because Cynthia and Arthur were already there it was perhaps less surreal than it might have been—if they could do it, we could. But the nitty-gritty of emigration takes a fair amount of planning for.

The house had to be put on the market. We needed to have a firm idea of when we wanted to leave England. We had to decide if we wanted a house built for us or whether we would rather rent and have a look around first. Renting was such a rarity at that time in the UK, with rental properties few and far between, that I felt it would be sensible to arrange for a house to be ready for us when we arrived.

This was partly because Derry's state of health still needed watching to an extent, and it was best not to put undue stress on it. Looking for a house to rent, with all the problems involved, seemed much more challenging than building. All the same, if I had known just how easy renting was then in Australia I would probably have opted for that; and if I had, we almost certainly would not have gone to live in Yanchep—and that would have been a pity.

We had to find some way of building at a great distance! Bond Corporation was the only developer that was advertising in the UK, as far as I know. Their adverts regularly appeared in the Sunday Times, and duly caught my eye. The fact that this development was on the west coast, which was one of the places I had been particularly drawn to, was a bonus.

When friends and family knew we were seriously planning this big move we were given all kinds of advice, naturally. Musical friends said we should certainly go to Sydney or Melbourne, the busy centres of music down-under. David Galliver was now Elder Professor of Music in Adelaide: perhaps Adelaide would be a good idea? But I was very attracted to the idea of 'going west'!

Derry and I discussed this. The point was, did we want to be little fish in a big pond (Sydney or Melbourne), or slightly bigger fish in a little pond (Perth)? What could we do if we went there? We were told that 'there's nothing happening in Perth—go to where the action is!' It was all quite confusing. We asked ourselves what we could do, once in Australia. The answer to that was 'quite a lot'. Between us we had valuable abilities, musical and otherwise. We felt sure we could make things happen for us.

There were other issues, too. School for Alison and Fiona. Medical attention for Alison's recurring tonsillitis. What to do about the dogs (2) and cats (2), and above all, where to find the necessary money for down-payments on land and house?

The latter problem was soon solved. My father had no hesitation in lending us the required sums; as always, he was far-sighted and could probably see that this was a very positive move for us.

A deeper emotional problem was raised because we would only be taking the two youngest children with us. If we left in early 1974, as we planned, Alison would be 13 and Fiona 10. Paddy was about to be married; Helen was at London University, and it would be her final year; Keith would be finishing school. Probably it was the most difficult for Keith—he had to go into lodgings until his exams were over.

We made it clear that this was part one of the emigration; part two would be if and when they decided to follow us—and I am thankful and happy to say that eventually they did, and have been able to make good lives for themselves.

Another hazard was the fact that Derry would be retiring from teaching several years early. In 1974 he was 59, with half-a-dozen active years ahead of him if we stayed. I started to look into the matter of his possible pension, and found that he could receive, from his Teachers' Pension scheme, a disability allowance which would be lower than the full-term payment, but still substantial enough, plus his British pension, to keep us going. There was a bit of a tussle over this with the authorities; but at last they agreed that, as long as he never again taught full-time in a secondary school, he would be eligible.

As neither of us wanted him to take on once more the heavy responsibility of full-time teaching, this seemed a good idea.

About this time I met Hazel Adair, who lived in the Surrey countryside just a few miles from us. I was doing a series on famous local women, and she was an obvious choice. Following the war, when she was a young woman, she and her husband, both actors, got into the world of TV. It was pretty primitive at that time, and she made the comment to me that the scripts they got were so bad that the two of them felt they could do better than that. So her new career began. Her credits include a number of well-known TV programmes that emerged at that time, among them *Emergency Ward 10, Compact* and *Champion House*. She was, I believe, writer and producer of these shows, which developed a new style and a much improved quality of production and—above all—writing.

During out first meeting I mentioned that I had just been to Australia. She looked at me rather oddly and said did I know she had been in Australia recently? I didn't. She had gone to find the finance for a feature film she wanted to make about the future lack of water on the planet as the population grew and the climate worsened. This was in the early 1970s. It indicated a real awareness of something that no one else seemed to be thinking about very much; she wanted to set it in South Australia, and had negotiated with Don Dunston, then Premier of SA, for government finance. He had apparently offered her half a million dollars, which meant she needed to find the rest herself. In the end, it proved impossible to raise the necessary funding, and the project collapsed.

But it was an uncanny link between us. We met again, following our interview; she seemed to feel that I could write adequately, because she started telling me about a series of plays she had to provide for one of the new commercial radio stations. She was very busy with other things, and suggested I might like to write one of the 12-minute programmes myself. I was all too ready, despite my total lack of knowledge about writing for radio.

She gave me a script to look at for lay-out, and told me that the series was called '*The King and his Mistresses*', and that it was about the Price Regent, who became George IV; it was intended to be slightly *risqué*. She gave me a book to read and asked me to do a scene from a particular page and bring it back to her.

I romped through it, thoroughly enjoying a change of genre. When I saw her a few days later she walked back and forth in her lounge room, reading my deathless words; I began to think it must be no good when she said, 'How long did it take you to write this?'

I didn't really like to say, but I felt I must be honest. 'About two hours.'

She nodded. 'I thought so.' (*I* thought, 'Oh, dear!')

Then she stopped walking and put the script down and said, 'That's very good. Would you like to do some more?' So I wrote a handful of the scenes; my only regret is that because of the condition of some of these new radio stations (especially the so-called 'off-shore' ones—less politely known as 'pirates') I couldn't hear much more of my work than a distant buzzing and whispering. But it opened a new door for me into the world of script-writing. I discovered I really could write dialogue. And I got paid for it.

Eventually we began to work together on an idea for a feature film, set in Australia and using the Indian Pacific Railway as a central theme. It was to be a full-on dramatic story, and Hazel had wonderful ideas for casting the main roles. I remember that the universally revered Peter Ustinov was one.

Because of her high profile in the world of television these were no empty dreams. She could do it! We agreed that she would do the script and produce the film and I would write the 'book of the film'. I recall one occasion when we had a map of Australia stretched out on the floor and we were crawling round it with

Carmen Silvera, well known as the long-suffering wife in '*Allo! Allo!*'

So this was what I hoped to be doing once I got out to Australia. We went together to the offices in London of the Indian Pacific railway, and they were keen—keen enough to offer us a dormitory train that would leave Kalgoorlie every Monday morning and return at the end of the week—this meant I would be able to get home for the weekend. It all looked very positive.

But no one works with film-making for long without knowing that for every film that gets made there are probably a hundred that never get off the ground. Maybe a hundred is an under-estimate? Who knows? So many dreams go belly-up! For a matter of a few years after we arrived in Australia I would get a letter or a phone call to say, 'It looks as if it's on. Can you still do it?' And I would say yes, and then nothing would happen—again. It has to be one of the most frustrating jobs in the world.

But even though our meeting didn't produce the film of the century, it did create a friendship that has survived for the next four decades. I last saw Hazel when I was in England in 2008, in her apartment in the lovely village of Brockham, just round behind the village green where they play cricket in the proper country style, and the church stands at the edge of the green and watches the scores mounting. I wonder if they still have the gigantic bonfire there on November 5th, and burn poor old Guy Fawkes for the umpteenth time.

So our great family adventure started to become reality. Selling the house, once we had sailing dates, and arrangements made at the other end of the journey, became a priority, and a rather worrying one. There was no way we could afford to 'beautify' the house for possible purchasers—we were up to our ears in selling furniture we would not be putting into store, and trying to live an everyday life with all the usual hazards. The house was put on the market for about £22,000, which seemed to me quite reasonable for a house of its size in the state it was in—not falling about our ears by any means, but certainly in need of more than we could put into it. And it had cost us £4,350 two decades before, which gives some indication of what house prices were already doing in the '60s and early '70s.

On top of that, I was hoping that someone would buy it who would appreciate it as we had done. It was a very easy house to live in; the staircase had none of the bends and twists that make carrying a baby up and down stairs so hazardous; three bedrooms were supposedly single rooms, but perfectly able to take a couple of beds; the garden was enclosed with a high brick wall, Victorian style, and when we arrived to view the place it was quite well arranged and reasonably productive. The kitchen was big enough to accommodate not only the cook (me!) but several children wanting to 'help'. Altogether it had been a good house for bringing up a family.

Its chief problem came with the exterior, rendered white, which needed renovating every few years, and was quite a big job. This was where Derry proved that he was not just a good musician, but also a handyman. While I was in the nursing home following Helen's birth he undertook, it being the summer holidays, to 'Snowcem' the outside of the house for the first time—all the way round!

For anyone who doesn't know about 'Snowcem', it is a cement-based wash (I don't think one could call it paint) that is a bit heavy to apply, but gives a good finish. The house sparkles for a while after it has been 'done'.

I was lying in my bed and getting used to my new daughter while he was climbing round the house on tall ladders; I had a few bad moments, thinking that this would not be a good time for him to damage himself. In fact, he came to see me to report progress, and said the difference between living in my parents' house at the 'good' end of town, and living in the older end as we now did, was that if he had fallen off the ladder in the former place the neighbours would have walked round him and tried to pretend it hadn't happened (they would not have done it themselves: they would have 'got a man in'—presumably a paid handyman would not fall off his ladder), while in our new location the neighbours tended to come round and hold the ladder for him!

The other problem with our new home was that part of the roof was flat, between two gables; and it was sealed with a tarred substance that had probably been there for many years. As a result it tended to leak in wet weather. Not surprising, really, for a house that was built in 1852.

Derry had spent quite a bit of time on the roof, locating the weak spots and presumably tarring them. One day my neighbour Mrs Smith said to me, 'Could you please ask Dr Morgan not to go on the roof while we're having our Sunday dinner? It makes us very nervous.'

The rain still got through, and I think we all knew where the worst leaks were and got the buckets under them before they could damage the floor.

Fast forward to 1974. All these matters were tending to discourage potential buyers. The first of these was a dentist who already had a practice in Dorking. At that time, local regulations said that if the owner of a property currently being used for professional or commercial purposes were to buy another property for the same purpose, the former property must be returned to private use. I think that was the gist of it. This caused some delays in working out how the business could be transferred successfully; as a result we rather gave up on him.

The time scale for us now was that we would leave England on April 9th, 1974, finally arriving in Western Australia—after a short holiday with Cynthia in Canberra—on May 28th. So we were limited in how much time we could allow for the actual transfer of our house to someone else.

Much of what happened to us around that time was so traumatic for me that I think I have deliberately forgotten it. I can remember feeling that I had let some good quality late Victorian/ early Edwardian furniture go far too cheap; and, indeed, I have sometimes wished that we had brought the whole lot with us (borrowing more money from my father if necessary), because the quality of what we found here—within our budget—was so far below what we had previously had. Much of that, of course, came to us through Derry's parents. Bringing and then selling these near-antique tables and so on could very well have paid for our entire removal—but we didn't realise that at the time.

What I do remember, however, is that when everything seemed to have come to a dead stop I suddenly got angry. From the moment when the idea of emigration had come to me I had felt that there was something more than my own wishes behind it; as someone who has always had a belief that there are spiritual influences that can lead us to take the right path, even when we can't see the way ourselves, I felt that I had been started on a huge plan, and suddenly dropped. I was on my way home from the shops, laden with bags and fuming silently in what could only be described as a sort of spiritual rage, silently berating the Lord for letting me down, and saying, in effect, 'You got me into this! Now get me out!'

I have often thought that conventional praying must be very boring to the one who is being prayed to. Perhaps the fact that I was so angry meant that my prayer had greater potency. I got to my front door, and I could hear the phone ringing. I juggled with bags and keys and got the door open before the phone stopped. It was the agent; the dentist had returned, and he was prepared to settle immediately if we would accept a drop of £500. I said, 'Yes— take it.' At that time, well before sending messages on little electronic gadgets that can be answered within moments, this was the fastest answer I had ever had to anything, prayer or not!

So we settled the matter amicably for £18,500 (the price had already dropped to £19,000), and the only real problem was that we had to agree to leave in January. When the news got round that we were temporarily homeless we received an offer from friends, the Plummers, to stay with them until we finally left.

As it turned out, we could have remained in Arundel Lodge for the whole time, though we were not to know that. For reasons that we never discovered, the dentist didn't use the place for several months. It was a bit of a shock for us, months after we had arrived in Australia, to get a cutting from the local Surrey newspaper (the one I had worked for, incidentally) with a photo of *my lounge room* being used as a squatters' temporary residence.

It was something that was happening fairly often in England at that time; accommodation was in very short supply, and an empty house was a real temptation to people who were homeless. One can hardly blame them. It's very much a case of, 'There but for the grace of God go I!'

Later, when we had lived in Australia for four years, I was back in the UK for my parents' Golden Wedding; and I visited Dorking, and went to look at Arundel Lodge. It was looking very spick and span, and I went through my old garden (now a car park) into the reception area (my dining room), and was greeted by the receptionist.

I explained that I had lived in the house until 1974, and just wondered if I could have a quick look round 'for old times' sake'. I was pleased when she said, 'I'm so glad to meet you. It's such a happy house! We've often wondered who lived here before.'

What, I wonder, makes a house 'happy'? I thought briefly of the traumas: Helen's illness, two parents dying in the upstairs bedrooms, Derry's devastating breakdown—just for starters— and was really glad that they had picked up what I had sensed the very first time I went into it: that this was in fact, for some reason, a happy house.

She showed me round: the only moment that almost brought tears, for some reason, was when I walked up the staircase. I suddenly remembered all those babies I had carried up and down; I could almost hear the scraping sound as my father-in-law came down, leaning heavily against the wall for support—the mark his jacket left on it stayed there for ages! But I was glad to see that the dentist had done what I always wanted to do: he had knocked a hole in the wall halfway up the stairs, and there was a window there overlooking the garden. It was one of the odd things about that house: you could actually look into the back garden from only one window.

One of the interesting things, though, was the cellar space. There were four big 'rooms', including the coal cellar, almost enough to create a whole 'downstairs' flat. I don't know what it was used for by the dentist; for us it tended to be a 'glory hole', and anything that went there was more or less lost to human eyes. The receptionist didn't mention cellars.

Up in the two bedrooms (now knocked into one) where the children had slept there were two dental technicians, who were also interested to hear about 'our house'. Part of the upstairs had been converted into a small flat; I gathered this was to satisfy the authorities that the place was also being used residentially.

The only thing about the changes in the house that really annoyed me was that the beautiful oak-panelled doors had been replaced by modern ones—smooth surfaces that had none of the charm of the originals. I couldn't understand why anyone would do this.

Eventually it came to me that perhaps it had been done because now it was a dentist's workplace; for hygienic reasons it is easier to keep flat-surfaced doors properly clean than those with dust-catching panels.

I wished I had known the dentist would do this. I would have offered to buy them. A dozen or so genuine early Victorian panelled doors with original brass finger-plates and knobs would have been worth something in Australia.

Last time I was in Dorking I saw that the house was again up for sale: or, rather, a part of the house, because it had been divided into two residences. I went to the real estate agents and asked if they had any details about it, and came away with a glossy brochure full of pictures, none of which I could recognise as my dear house. I could have gone and looked at it inside, but I didn't want to. I decided I was now over it! The house—and Dorking itself, in fact—had changed, and I had changed, and memories were going to be of more use than wishing that everything was still the same. I loved that house, and I am eternally grateful that when we needed it, it was available. Built in those early Victorian years, it had still been a comfortable and convenient home for a family a hundred years later. One can't ask more than that.

25

And so we came to the end of an era. The journey for Derry and me that had started in 1945 when he entered the school like a gale of energy, and I began to emerge as accompanist and singer; that had continued with our marriage in 1948 and the raising of six children; that had required me to undertake the care to the end of their days of two old people who never quite accepted me; that had seen breakdown and a variety of illnesses; and that had taken me to the far side of the world and presented me with a pattern for the rest of our life together: this was about to change for ever.

A new name came into our conversations: Yanchep. It was strange, exotic; sometimes I wondered if it really existed—there were many times when this seemed very unlikely. It was somewhere that we had decided to live—and we knew next to nothing about it.

Photographs helped, but not much. It was probably easier for me than for the rest of the family to imagine what it might be like; I had at least seen, however briefly, that side of the country. We had chosen our house from an artist's impression; we asked questions of the agents in London, who answered them—though unfortunately not always correctly. The phrase 'fobbing off' comes to mind.

My chief questions were, for instance: *is there a doctor in the town?* (Alison was much given to tonsillitis). Yes, they assured me; there was a doctor's office right in the town centre. And there was; sadly, there was no doctor in it for the next 8 months, and THE major tonsillitis (which happened, naturally, on a public weekend when just about everything, including doctors' surgeries, was closed) meant that we had to make an emergency run to Perth, 50 kms south, to get Alison into hospital.

How far is the nearest main town? Wanneroo, they thought, was the nearest (these two men we dealt with had actually visited Yanchep so that they would know how to answer such curly questions). It was about 13 kms, they estimated—and added: 'Don't blink or you'll miss it'. It is in fact about 27 kms to Wanneroo. Their answers comforted us, and it's just as well we didn't know how inaccurate they were.

Yes, there were good schools in the area, they were pleased to say. But Girrawheen High School, where Alison started in the September, was well past Wanneroo; the primary school at Wanneroo where Fiona was to finish her year was not exactly what we meant by 'in the area'. Both schools required a long, hot journey in a rattletrap old school bus; and that, I'm afraid, is another story for a different chapter.

Still in England, both girls were finding it difficult to come to terms with leaving schools, friends and Dorking itself to go to somewhere they were probably unable to imagine. Eventually, I took refuge in the ploy for the defeated: I asked them what they would like us to give them in exchange for going without a fuss. Bribery!

Alison's eyes lit up, and there was a challenging look in them, too. Without pause for thought she said, 'A horse!' I suspect she thought that would solve the problem; there was surely no way we were going to give her a *horse*?

I said, 'Yes.' I like to think she was slightly shocked. Certainly there was never any more argument about whether or not we should take off for 'down under'. I made one proviso: she couldn't have it until we were properly settled in the house. I really didn't feel I could cope with the whole move, *plus* a horse to be accommodated at the end.

I asked Fiona what she would like. 'A bicycle and a chihuahua!'

Of all the dogs one can have around the house, a chihuahua was probably the last I would have chosen. They are very small, and I wasn't at all sure that Australia was the best place for one. But a promise is a promise. I told her she could have the bicycle straight away, but the dog would have to wait, like the horse, for when we were settled in. I could imagine how difficult it would be to furnish a house while trying to avoid falling over a very small dog.

Alison's horse arrived the following Easter. He was a dear, and much admired by all of us. 'Bluey' was a retired pacer, a style of racing that we didn't know in the UK; and he served his purpose with Alison for many years.

We had been in Yanchep for several months when Fiona came to me one day and said, 'You know I said I would like a chihuahua?' I said I remembered, thinking that the time had now come, and I would have to learn to love that breed of dog. 'Well,' she said, 'I've decided I don't want it.'

'What would you like instead?'

She didn't know. So Derry and I bought her what we hoped would be a good second choice: a baby donkey. She looked stunned (I hope it was delighted surprise and not disappointment) when it arrived in a very small horse-float (a donkey-float, I suppose). This was the first time the owners had sold one of their animals, and they were almost in tears when the time came to say goodbye.

Jerry (or possibly Gerry, because his name was actually Geronimo) was a cute and beautiful little creature, and Fiona looked after him well. Sadly, because the grazing ground for all the local horses was very sandy, colic was a big problem in Yanchep; and one day, a few years later, Jerry became ill and the vet came. He decided the donkey was too far gone and he could do nothing more for him, so poor Jerry was put down, and buried up on the slopes of the Widgee.

It is ironic that the place where the horses grazed has now been turned into part of the great suburban development that has hit the area in recent years. So far, no one has reported that they have found donkey remains in their back yard!

But I am getting ahead of myself. We had booked our passages on the *Australis,* a Greek owned ship with a crew composed of

Greeks and Indians. This was not the £10 job for UK migrants: I don't think we would have qualified, anyway. But we could only really afford a cabin for four well down in the bowels of the ship.

I had what I still feel were good reasons behind the decision to go by sea. This had been a frantic period in our family's history: I hoped that a longish sea voyage would give us all a really good holiday before we had to undertake the business of starting everything up again. I particularly wanted Derry to have this time free; he was very much better from the breakdown 7 years earlier, but he had been working very hard and I felt, rightly or wrongly, that flying to Australia without a real break between the two 'lives' could be very difficult for him. I wanted him to start this new life in a calm frame of mind.

That side of the situation worked well. By the time we were in Australia he was well rested. But the choice of ship was perhaps less fortunate. It was definitely a migrant ship; I was told there were about 600 children on board, and every day at some unspecified time you could hear the thundering of small feet on the deck above as they let off steam.

As a result of its very large number of passengers, the facilities were not as good as they might have been. For example, for mothers trying to keep their children's clothes clean for the four weeks we were all aboard, there was little help with the drying of wet washing. There were some heated cabinets on deck, but far too few; and getting the laundry to wash large numbers of kids' clothes would have been difficult.

Going to the laundry meant working one's way through the broken English of the woman in charge; but first one had to buy soap powder from the shop. I did this, and went to interview the laundress. She took the packet of soap powder and I left our garments with her.

When I returned I was handed my dried clothes—but not the rest of the soap. As only one wash had been done I felt this was not right. I would need that packet next time. But she wasn't going to let me have it! On the shelf above her head there was a long row of soap packets, presumably with only one 'helping' out of each. I argued with her, and she became quite unpleasant.

But I'm glad to be able to say that I won, and walked off with my trophy, triumphantly.

The lack of drying facilities for the occasional things that didn't warrant being taken to the laundry really annoyed me. A tumble dryer was one of the things I had promised myself once we were settled in; and I saw no reason why, if I could buy one for my small family, the ship's owners couldn't do likewise. It needed a commercial size tumble dryer on each deck. Why not?

I went to see the purser. He was Greek, and full of false flattery. This didn't make me feel any better. I started making my complaint—and I was quite reasonable. I simply made the point that, with so many children on board, his bosses should have made allowance for the problems of washing and, above all, drying.

He started explaining how everything was impossible. I said, 'Look, I have six children . . .'

He threw up his hands and opened his eyes wide to express his astonishment. 'Madam, how is this possible!' Meaning, I suppose, 'you are so young, so beautiful, so . . .' whatever else he was prepared to flatter me with.

I said, fairly brusquely, 'The usual way!' I wasn't going to be smoothed down. I completed what I had started to say. 'And if I can manage to buy a tumble dryer, then I'm sure the ship owners can afford to buy a couple!'

He spread his hands again. 'But what can I do . . . ?'

'You can get off the ship at the next port and buy them!' I had had enough. I think I probably stalked out. Of course, I didn't win. The problem remained until we landed.

Of greater concern was the behaviour of some of the Greek crew with the younger, female members on the passenger list. The atmosphere on the ship was not a good one.

But on the positive side, we made friends with our dining room steward, Jarnail Singh.

He was 21, from the Punjab, and he took quite a fancy, in the nicest way, to Fiona, bringing her extra oranges and so on. These young Punjabi members of the crew were, I was told, all from the same area. They would go round the world on this ship for many months, officially not allowed to leave it in port (though in fact we saw him and his mates in Cape Town, so it was possible to break that regulation).

Their time at sea meant that they would have money in their pockets once they were released from whatever contract they had with the shipping company. It may well have been the only way they would ever earn reasonable money—and being forbidden to go ashore meant that they couldn't spend it. I hope this meant that when they got home again they were regarded as rich men.

When we finally left the ship in Sydney we told Jarnail that we would meet him at Fremantle next time he came round the globe. And we did—I think we drove him somewhere in the car and possibly had tea with him in a café.

We did this a couple of times more; on the last one he asked me if I would take him to a bank, because he had some money to start an account with. He showed me a roll of notes, quite a considerable sum; I was impressed that he wanted to bank it, but why in Australia? He said he wanted to come and live here one day, and he thought if he already had money to his credit that would make it easier for him.

We went to St George's Terrace in Perth and took him to a bank. The premises were palatial, and it struck me how odd it was that we, from Britain, should be here with a Punjabi youth who also wanted to leave his homeland in favour of this new country—which clearly he had come to see as his own future, just as we had.

Another fast forward! One day, just as we were setting out for some engagement or other—I forget what—two young Indian men came to the gate. They were well dressed, and both had gold watches and rings. One was Jarnail! We greeted him warmly, not having seen him for a long time. He was looking quite prosperous.

He and his friend had been working in a car factory in Melbourne after leaving the ship.

I was really sorry that we couldn't wait and talk to them—and I have always regretted that I didn't make my invitation to come back the next day more positive. I certainly told them that we would all love to see them; but we really had to go!

I don't think he believed me. It probably felt like a brush-off. They didn't come back the next day, and I am sure in my own mind that he thought we had regretted befriending him. If he is still out there—he would be about 60 now—I hope he forgave us for something that was not in fact our fault, but simply a misunderstanding.

The next day I had a phone call from a company that had interviewed him for a job on the management side; he had left my name and phone number with them as a contact. I tried to explain what had happened. The caller said, 'We were impressed with Mr Singh and would like to ask him to come and see us.' I promised to let him know if he came back to Yanchep. I was grieved to think that my lack of sensitivity might have done him out of a good job.

We never saw him again.

The journey by ship was, in itself, very enjoyable. Because the Suez Canal was still closed to shipping, we visited the Canaries, and both girls got sombreros—Fiona had had to wait since 1972 for the one I should have bought in Mexico City. Better late than never. Then there was the long haul down the west coast of Africa (and I wonder if Derry recalled his time sailing *up* that coastline in the mid-war years after a trip to Karachi when he had that very bad attack of dysentery somewhere off Takoradi).

Eventually the ship docked at Cape Town; and it would have been pleasant to have had a longer stay there. We were able to visit the botanical gardens; that was where we sighted Jarnail and his friends; but we were all a bit concerned at the segregation of races implied in notices around the place. Coming from England, where racial disturbances were not unknown but certainly not supported by government decree, we were uncomfortable with the whole concept.

Derry had celebrated his 59th birthday on the day before we left the UK, and we had decided that we would get him a present on the journey out to Australia. So we went into a shop in Cape Town which had an array of barometers and clocks, and chose him a thermometer/barometer thing to hang in our new hall once we arrived. It's still hanging there.

This shop visit gave rise to a family saying that lasted for a while until we forgot it. Behind the counter was a white South African woman; with her a young black lad who was obviously her assistant. Once we had decided on Derry's present, the woman turned to the boy and said, in that unmistakeable South African accent: 'Boy, tike this pecket and wrep it!' Thank goodness we finally let *that* go!

The sight of Table Mountain behind the city is truly amazing. The cloud that slides endlessly over its steep side is fascinating. It would be nice to see the place again with more leisure.

But we still had a long way to go. I believe it is about 4000 kilometres in a fairly straight line from Cape Town to Fremantle, our next port. I don't know how other people cope with that stretch of the journey; I felt quite ill. Going in a direct line eastwards, losing (I think) an hour a day, plus perhaps the tensions of knowing that one is getting closer to this place that will one day be home: all this affected me quite badly. I felt so absolutely exhausted by losing that hour that I just wanted to sleep all the time. It occurred to me that the ship's crew must have this problem on every trip; always going in an easterly direction simply saps energy. Once they left us (we were leaving the ship in Sydney) they would continue to New Zealand, through the Panama Canal, across the Atlantic, back to Southampton—and then start it all over again for the next round trip. I couldn't have done it.

On the morning of our arrival in WA the ship was full of activity very early. No one wanted to miss the first view of our new home. There was quite a strange atmosphere around as I stood with so many others and watched the sky grow lighter; so many different stresses, so many hopes and, perhaps, fears for the future. But there was, at last, land ahead; I defy anyone not to be moved by that sight after days of ploughing across the ocean with nothing to be seen but water and, at one point, a spectacular storm. The land we saw, which I think most us thought was the mainland, was in fact Rottnest Island; passengers who had done their homework knew this already—the rest of us had to learn what this new place was all about.

We came slowly through the channel between Rottnest and the mainland; there was rain, sweeping in gauzy curtains across the land, and when the rain stopped the sun came out again, and there were rainbows.

It seemed like Paradise! I should say, for those who have not gone through the same experience, that we had rarely seen the sun, in our part of England at least, since the previous October. This combination of sun, rain and rainbows was extremely appealing.

A few days earlier we had cabled Bond Corporation, the developers, to let them know that we would be off the ship for several hours and would like to see our house, if that would be possible. On the dockside, as we came ashore, was a Bond representative—comfortingly, it was one of the men we had dealt with in the UK, so not everything was completely strange. Naturally enough, they had misinterpreted our message and thought we were leaving the ship at Fremantle, which we weren't. But we sorted that out, and he drove us up to Yanchep (which, predictably, was much further from Fremantle than we had been led to believe) to see the house we had been wondering about for months. I recall seeing a notice beside the road that said 'Yanchep National Park' and suddenly realising that this place, Yanchep, did actually exist.

During those months I had been on their backs asking how far the building had developed. They were soothing. Yes, the brickwork was up to window sill level; yes, it was now up to the top of the walls; yes, the rafters were in place—and so on. We had been travelling for a month without asking them anything; but it was a real let-down when we finally got to the street and drove, in the dark, to our block, to see that the rafters were bare of tiles, nothing had been done around the place to clear up the builders' mess, and, once we had peered inside by the light of his headlights, we could see that it was nowhere near being ready yet for plastering.

I had a moment of black panic. This was *my* project, *my* idea—if it all went pear-shaped who was going to be the responsible person? I stared with horror at the tiny space that was to be our bedroom (no windows in yet, but a mighty pool of water where our bed would be), and I remembered the house we had left behind, the comfortably spacious rooms, and a roof—even if it leaked!

But panic never helps anyone. We got back into the car, left behind us what appeared to be a heap of sand and not much else, and bought fish and chips on the way back to the ship. It was May 4th (incidentally, Cynthia's birthday), we would be in Sydney by May 11th for a few days' holiday in an apartment, and then to Cynthia's place in Canberra for another short holiday before leaving for the west—and the rest of our lives!

What did annoy me was that back in about October 1973 I had had a request from Bond Corporation wishing to know when we would be arriving in Perth, *so that they could have the house ready for us!* They even wanted to know, as soon as possible, what colour tiles we wanted in the kitchen, laundry and bathroom. It sounded as if several tradesmen were waiting, tools in hand, for my answer. So I struggled with the concept of colour—what would look best in a north-facing bathroom, yellow or blue (I chose yellow, but how did I know? Would yellow be too bright? Would blue seem cooler?)

Well, I now realised that it was not going to be ready, and I was very thankful that for about the first time in our lives we had been properly cautious: wary enough to ensure that if the house was *not* ready we would have rental accommodation provided—*free!*

So for the first 3 months after we arrived we lived in a small holiday house on Yanchep Beach Road; and slowly we got used to our new way of living, and found that we enjoyed it.

We were able to visit the house every day and see how it was progressing. I was starting to see other houses growing like mushrooms all over Yanchep, and one day said to the foreman on our job, 'This house has taken a long time to build, hasn't it?'

He looked at me a bit oddly and said, 'No, about the usual time.'

'But I see houses going up quickly everywhere. Why has it taken from October to get this one to its present state?'

'October?' He seemed astonished. 'We didn't get the order until January.'

So I began to learn! Everything I had been told in London had been untrue; asking for my tile colour preferences in October had been ridiculous—there were no walls to put them on! When I asked in January about progress they didn't manage to tell me that the land hadn't yet been cleared and there was as yet no concrete laid. No wonder they looked a bit alarmed in the Bond office on that day we landed in Fremantle and wanted to see the house! I'm slightly surprised they didn't take advantage of the dark night with no lights to show us something else and say it was ours. But perhaps that would have been going a bit far, even for them.

Having got that off my chest, I have to say that the house, built by Jaxon's, has been a sturdy, cosy place to live, and I have no complaints with it. We soon realised that we had to keep our eyes very keenly on the ball if we wanted to win this game; and with our daily visits to spur them on the builders did a good job. Watching the plasterer working was a delight—he was an artist in his way, and the plastering has remained in excellent condition for the 39 years it has been in place.

Finally we were able to move in in August, and we have been here in varying numbers ever since.

26

One cannot help missing things after a major move such as emigration. But it's odd what those things are. Living in a holiday house with limited equipment started me wishing I had my own kitchen things with me; but they were down in Fremantle, waiting for the word from us to deliver them to our new address.

We contacted the storage people and agreed to go to the warehouse and pick one of the chests to bring home. I particularly wanted the kitchen things, though there were obviously others that needed a good home to go to. Among these, of course, was the piano.

Moving that from our lounge room in Dorking had been something one would rather forget. Because of the design of the front hall, which I had always felt was quite wide, everything proved to be really difficult when it came to turning a grand piano (on its side and without its legs) and getting it safely through the front door.

Derry was not pleased when the piano movers came to do this tricky job. He had told them that it was a very heavy instrument, and they would need five men in order to get it down the front steps safely. I think in the event there were four of them, and they found it very trying. I can't remember too much about it, so I think I probably took refuge in the kitchen and let the men work it out between them. It was one of those conversations that start, in Australia, 'She'll be right, mate! No sweat! Get her down in a jiffy.' I can't remember what the British equivalent of that is. I imagine Derry gave them a mouthful back! And I assume that they had thought it would be an upright.

The piano, once in the removalists' warehouse, had to have a special crate built for it; and for the next seven months that was its home. Leaving the house in January meant that the piano had had to go with other furniture we were taking with us; most things like chairs and tables are OK in store, but a grand piano, standing on its side for that long, begins to sag. It was so much a part of our lives that we felt quite sad for it.

We left it for a future removal date and took home the kitchen crate. I had been thinking for a while that I really would have to get a tea-pot—clearly we were not yet completely won over by tea-bags. The silly thing was that I couldn't remember whether we had put a tea-pot in the crate when it was being packed. So when it was opened, and the first things I saw were my stainless steel tea-pot (how could I have forgotten that?) and my very favourite kitchen knife, it was like the best kind of Christmas. It indicates just how traumatic a big move away from home and all the things that you know so well can be.

So we were getting acclimatized. I probably broke a law when I didn't send the girls to school until we were settled in the house in August. I felt that settling in was of first importance, and I am still surprised when new families arrive from overseas and the next day, it seems, the children are in class. I think we all need time to sort ourselves out.

Alison and Fiona spent good time on the beach and in and out of the sea. I have to say that 'our' beach, south of the lagoon from which this place takes its name, is spectacular: I have never discovered just how long it is, but anyone at the far end is almost out of sight, and certainly not recognisable. Derry's half-amused comment, standing on the sand, looking north and south, and seeing two or three minuscule people and a dog at the far end, was simply, 'Bloody trippers!'

A man said to me one day, 'You're Poms, aren't you?' I confessed. 'Yeah, thought you were. Those your girls down on the beach every day?' I said they were. 'Middle of winter,' he said.

Clearly it was not done to disport oneself in bathers in June. I knew it was winter, but it was well over any summer temperature we had ever known in the frozen north!

We spent quite a lot of time sitting on that beach; and soon after we arrived I noticed a ship apparently sailing out from the land to the south. Next time we went back to the same spot I saw it again. It didn't appear to have moved, but I thought maybe it was waiting to dock somewhere. At that point I wasn't absolutely sure how far we were from Fremantle; and for all I knew there might have been a small port not far to the south of us.

But the ship stubbornly stayed where it was for days and then weeks; and eventually I heard the tale: it was the *Alkimos,* a ship with a chequered history, and it had run aground some while before when en route to Fremantle for repairs. There were and are many stories written about the *Alkimos,* including a well-documented report of the ship's ghost.

Eventually, many years later, the ship finally broke up, and I understand that divers now go down and swim among the fishes. It was an intriguing part of the coastal scene, and I think its final departure was mourned by a number of people who had taken a warm interest in it since its grounding.

I've never been told if the ghost could swim

As I write, a new 'village' is being developed along Marmion Avenue to the south of Yanchep, named *Alkimos,* and another called *Eglinton,* in recognition of another wreck on this coast that has been a graveyard for so many ships from earliest days.

So here we were, and gradually our new life began to take on a recognisable shape. We had worked out the financial aspects of our new home, and felt we had enough money left from the sale of the Dorking house to keep us going, if necessary (and fairly frugally), for a couple of years. Looking back on it, I am surprised at how unworried we were on that score. It was almost as if, having come to a 'foreign' country—which, thank goodness, spoke recognisable English—we had let the worries and inhibitions of living in our own country disappear somewhere in the Indian Ocean.

But I do recall, very early on, having a sudden attack of panic when I saw the price of something—I know not what, only that it was something quite basic—and it was quite a bit more expensive than it would have been in the UK. I did wonder for a few moments whether after all we would be able to afford this new life. I also remember our daughters running to me in a supermarket, crying out, 'Mum, you can get *English salad cream* here!' Of such small things are our daily lives made meaningful.

All the same, one has to boost the family fortune, and so I wrote to anyone I could think of who might see in the two of us a possibility of employment—preferably something we would be good at, like music for instance.

Derry had met in Dorking Edgar Nottage, a senior member of the WA music education scene, who had shown interest in Derry's past career as a music teacher at secondary level. He was on a short visit to England, and making contact with him was a very positive move for us. He mentioned a forthcoming conference being held in Perth in mid-1974; the director of music at Scotch College, a boys' private school, was involved in this, and Mr Nottage asked Derry if he would teach at Scotch for six weeks to fill the gap. This came within the terms of Derry's disability pension, because it would not be a full-time engagement.

The ISME conference was headed by Sir Frank Callaway, Professor of Music at the University of Western Australia, and getting to know him was another positive. So Derry spent those 6 weeks seeing how the 'private' side lives! He was amused and, I think, rather pleased, that when he had 'played in' the boys for morning assembly, and then 'played them out'—a thing he always did at DGS—they didn't go! They stood and listened to him, then applauded him. I'm afraid the Dorking boys and girls were just too used to being soothed with Rachmaninov and Chopin as additions to the usual hymn singing.

Living in Yanchep posed more than a few questions, some of which were hard to solve. For us in those early days, when there was no bus service closer than the entry to the National Park, and only very occasional even then, there was plenty of driving to do. Derry never drove (when he was learning I felt he was such a menace on the road that I told him I would drive him for the rest of his life—but would he please not drive any more), so I spent a great deal of time on the country road that was then our lifeline between Yanchep and civilisation.

But it was well worth it in this case. Having met several of the people involved in music in Perth, Derry applied for a post at the Claremont Teachers' College (now no more) in the music department. He was interviewed, among others, by Sir Frank, and joined the staff for 1975 as music lecturer. His senior was the organist Michael Dudman; although I daresay Derry would rather have been head of the department I was glad that he would not be in charge. I hoped he wouldn't take on positions that meant he had great responsibilities to carry.

I remember him saying that it was the first time since he had gained his doctorate that he had had to show his Trinity College Dublin certificate to *prove* that he was actually a doctor of music. We both thought it was a bit odd; but over the years I read of several cases of people who had come to Australia with either false qualifications or something definitely not right, and got away with it for quite a while. I suppose there's not a lot of damage one can do by pretending to be a doctor of music when you're not—but pretending to be a brain surgeon on a home-made certificate is something else.

One thing that stayed in my mind for several months was the fact that the salary offered was $11,000 p.a. At the rate of exchange, which was still near enough to the Aus$ = 10 UK shillings, this seemed like riches. By the time he actually started the job it had gone up already—to $16,000. This had obviously been a good move for us. We were feeling very justified in having done something that could so easily have been a disaster.

Meanwhile, I was wondering what else we could do—more particularly, what *I* could do. I had come to WA with the expectation that I would be working with Hazel Adair, but she rang me one day (all that way from England! I hadn't even dared to try and ring my parents yet) to say that the deal was off for now.

I still have notes and bits and pieces that, I suppose, would make it possible for me to write the story in the hopes that someone else would put it on screen. When I have time!

When we had been in Yanchep for a few weeks I wrote some letters to people I had met or heard of while I was so briefly in Perth two years before. One was the editor of The West Australian Newspapers; anyone who had influence in music or writing—the latter could be fiction or journalism, which was helpful—got a letter from me. I told them what we were capable of between us, and suggested that they should not waste us.

But nothing happened, not for several months. Meanwhile, Derry had been asked to do one afternoon a week at UWA, teaching composition. This was Sir Frank's idea. Slowly Derry was getting to know the people who, in the days ahead, would become friends or musical colleagues—or both.

27

With Alison and Fiona at school for the final term in 1974, and Derry getting ready for work at Claremont, life began to settle. Most importantly for all of us, the house had been completed in August—at last! We had to buy new furnishings, put down carpets, look at the heap of sand that would one day be a garden and wonder where to start on it; and we began to make friends locally.

I do remember so well some of the lacks that we were very aware of in our new environment. Having come from Dorking, an old coaching/market town, where everything we needed—schools, hospital, cinemas, shops, churches and so on—was within about 10 minutes of home, it was strange to realise that the only thing that came to the house daily was the milk. Mail was delivered to the resort that would one day be Club Capricorn (Club Cap to the locals), and we collected it from our own pigeon-hole at the little holiday village shop, where one could buy (for a price) the necessities of life—as long as they were not too exotic.

Eventually there was a fuss from the new residents, demanding our own mail boxes; and one day we received notification that we could indeed have individual boxes—but they must all be in the same place, which was not quite what we had wanted. I hope someone has a photo of those boxes once they were put up, all in different styles, all at different heights, some standing proudly, some leaning wearily away from the wind. They were on the side road by Newman Street, off Yanchep Beach Road; and we still had to go and get the mail. But it was a step in the right direction.

There were no street lights, at least in our part of town, and we didn't want them. It was a delight to be able to see the stars unhampered, especially for those who had lived in cities where the lights made star-gazing difficult. We were told that we were to have street lights, and the authorities concerned waited for the applause that should have followed. But we really didn't want them, and we said so.

Well, tough. They knew what was good for us; and so the street lights were installed. One of them was—and still is—right opposite our bedroom window, which makes it difficult to pull the curtains back to go to sleep; the light keeps you awake, and makes the bedroom feel like a lighted stage.

Transport was hazardous. There was a bus, twice a day if my memory is correct, but it only came to the National Park entrance; this meant that anyone using it had to be driven down to the park and collected at the end of the day. It would have been foolhardy to leave the car there all day, even though the petty thieving we now endure was much less then. It was years before a bus ventured into the two locations of Yanchep and Two Rocks; and when it did, it was unfortunately planned so that instead of circling around Yanchep to benefit the largest number of people it went straight along Yanchep Beach Road and turned right into the Two Rocks road. The net result of that was that if you lived on the far side of Yanchep (which we did) you still had to be 'lifted' to the bus if you were not capable of walking that far.

I spent some time on the phone trying to convince the people who had arranged this that it would be more valuable if it offered transport to the maximum number of travellers; and one day the route was changed and we had the makings of a bus service that worked. All it needed now was for someone in authority to realise that a few more each day would be a help; and today the service is very adequate.

So many memories of that time! I recall the day when we 'signed off' for the house. Colin Herbert was then town manager, and he came to our rented cottage to do this final act with us.

I commented that there was no fly screen on the front door. 'No,' he said; 'we don't put them on front doors.' This seemed odd to me, because there was one on the back door.

'Are the flies trained to use the back door?' I asked. He wasn't amused. 'On the specifications of the house it says "fly-screened throughout".'

'But not on the front door.'

'It doesn't say that. It says "throughout".' I was determined. 'If there hadn't been one on the back door I would have assumed that "throughout" meant windows only. But because there's one on the back door . . .'

He gave in eventually. 'All right, all right, you can have your fly-screen!'

I thanked him.

But that wasn't the end of this affair. One day a man arrived with a tape measure. 'I've come to measure for the fly-screen.'

I was really pleased, though it seemed odd to me that it had to be measured. The door was a completely standard product.

The screen didn't arrive, but one day another man came and we went through the same palaver, with the same negative result. When the third man arrived, and then a small Japanese gentleman who explained carefully that he had come to measure door for 'scleen', I began to wonder if this was Wonderland.

I said, 'This door has now been measured four times, but we never get the screen!'

He was unmoved. 'Oh, yes, please, I measure.'

So he did; and one day another man arrived, shouting through the open front door in the manner I was coming to recognise (and not at all like the orderly politeness of Dorking), 'Barb, got your screen!'

Much drilling and banging ensued. Then: 'D'you want the gap at the top or the bottom?'

I was close to losing it. I exploded, 'That screen has been measured for again and again—and now there's a *gap*?'

'I can take it back if you like.'

'No! Don't take it back. We'll never get it again.' I thought deeply for half a minute and said, 'Flies come in at the top, so we'll have the gap at the bottom.'

And that was where the snake came in!

Well, fortunately it was only a small one, and Paddy disposed of it while I was out when it emerged from under the chest freezer we had brought from England—and had presumably been there for the few days we hadn't been able to find it. On the whole, I'm glad I didn't know it was there; though I did wonder where it had gone. There were no pavers outside the front door, so I could see its tracks where it had entered, but there were none to show that it had gone out again.

I had to get used to snakes. We see very few in the garden now, but then, when building had disrupted their habitat, they would meander across the unplanted ground and one couldn't help wondering where they were heading. The funniest sight I ever had, reptilianly speaking, was when the lizards had come out of their hibernation. I happened to be standing by the lounge room window, and saw a bobtail skink making its slow way down towards the house. When it got within a couple of metres it stopped, stared up at the front of the building in obvious puzzlement, had a think about it, then marched on to the house wall, turned right, went round the corner to the left, along the side of the house (me following) to the far corner, turned left until it got to the place it would have been if it hadn't been stopped by the house, then turned right and went on its way to wherever it was going.

They are clearly dedicated to their ancestral tracks!

Let's get the snake stories out of the way. Years later we built a garden room at the back of the house. I was sitting there reading, soon after it was constructed, and saw out of the corner of my eye something at one of the glass doors. It was a snake, sitting itself as upright as a serpent can, and trying to get in through the glass.

I called Derry. 'Can you come and get rid of this snake?' He came, bravely waving a newspaper (through the glass, of course, one doesn't mess with these creatures) and it went away across the garden, seemingly put out about our recent structure.

A week or two later it, or perhaps another identical one, it's so hard to tell with snakes, was at the opposite glass door, waving about and trying to get in. We banged on the window and it, too, went away. But it was a good reminder to keep the screen doors shut.

When, on another occasion, a snake slipped round behind the garage, I called in the local 'snake man'. He came, but said that since these reptiles are not territorial the chances of it still being in the garden were slim. He enlightened me about the habits of snakes. 'They go up into the scrub behind the house to have their offspring,' he said. 'But they go over into the dunes to *cop-u-late*.' He said it like that, quite slowly.

I said that thinking of one snake was as much as I could do; to have to think of two snakes doing *that* was beyond me.

Even later than this, we found a python, the so-called carpet snake, in the back yard. It was a big one, and it had obviously been in a tree, because they told me (I was keeping out of the way) that it had a nestling in its mouth. This had slowed it down, and the snake man came and took it away. He charged me $15 for the pleasure, but at least the thing had gone. The following day I was surprised to see another one wrapped round a branch. This time I could only call the snake man, because we were due somewhere else; so I left the $15 in the meter box, and hoped all would be accomplished by the time we got home. The questions I was asking myself were: is this the same python back for another visit; or did the man only pop it round the back on vacant ground? Do these reptiles hunt in couples, or have we suddenly got a plague of them? We haven't seen any since, so I think it was a one-off!

I was introduced to several very nice elderly ladies in Perth soon after we arrived. They were asking what it was like up in Yanchep, and I think I must have made a joking remark about the wildlife, and said that in England I had been quite paranoid about snakes, but had had to get used to them here.

They were very impressed. They were living in the posh end of the city, so snakes were not really an important part of their daily life. 'How did you come to terms with it?' they wondered.

I said, 'It dawned on me that they had been here probably for millions of years and I had only just arrived. I couldn't really expect to have them all cleared out on my account.' Apparently this wisdom really appealed to them, and I was warmly congratulated.

Sadly—and in this I am on the snakes' side—there is so much building now going on in this area that we see very few native animals these days, apart from kangaroos in the National Park. Habitat has become an important word in the vocabulary of those who care about these things—which I'm afraid doesn't now, and didn't in 1974 when we first arrived, include developers—but if there is one thing human beings are good at it is causing beautiful things and creatures to become extinct. I hope that one day, before it is too late, we or our children on into the future will see sense and make room for these living things to exist alongside us. It's time!

So we gradually got the hang of living in Australia; and in no time Christmas was approaching. This would be the testing time. Our Christmases in England had always been immensely enjoyable, and I wanted to keep it that way.

By now we had had an addition to our household: Paddy joined us from the UK in the November after we arrived, leaving Valerie and Keith to follow in the following year. He found a job, eventually, as a cray-fisherman. Our Aussie family was growing.

Cynthia and Arthur said they and the children were coming over for the Christmas celebrations. I think they were concerned that we might be feeling very homesick; but I don't think we were. It was just different.

My strong point is not in making and baking all the goodies that are traditional at that time of the year. My mother was a wonder with Christmas food; the turkey was beautiful, everything was ready on time, and by the end of the meal she was so exhausted that she had to spend the afternoon lying down. It could be quite dangerous to try to talk to her until she was recovered.

Then it all started again in the late afternoon, and she would provide a spread that must have taken her days to prepare: perfect meringues with cream, a Christmas cake, trifle and fruit salad, and all this after we had had cold turkey, ham, tongue (the latter she very often prepared and cooked herself), and salad. It was all too much, and we were already full from lunch; but it looked and was so good that we ate!

I vowed that when we had our own Christmases we would have the main lunch on Christmas Day, and the Christmas tea on Boxing Day. Anyone who was still hungry at tea time could have toast and jam. As a result, I was never as exhausted as my mother had been, and I think I enjoyed it more than she had done. All the same, the memory of her lunch table covered with the traditional food, and that same table at tea time, with hardly a space between all the goodies—it takes some beating!

So what would our first Christmas down-under be like? It would lack one thing that was irreplaceable: the school Carol Service. For me, Christmas started then, as we ended the service with 'O come, all ye faithful'. How would we match that?

Our other tradition had been a Christmas Eve 'drop-in' party. From about 7 pm people would arrive; parents who wanted to get the children to bed early were the first, and finally there were the ones who wanted to go to the midnight service. So—did we think we could do the same here?

Well, it wouldn't be freezing cold, for one thing; so that meant we could have a *garden* drop-in party. Different, anyway. We had enough local friends by that time to be able to make it interesting. And we would stick by the tried and true pattern—wine and mince pies and as simple as possible.

What I had certainly not expected was that there would be a really chilly wind blowing that evening. We had been warned about hot Christmases. One friend who had already been in WA for 11 years told us of their first Christmas, when she cooked the traditional turkey wearing her bathers, and a packet of butter floated off the kitchen table while she wasn't looking. So what was this chill wind doing, blowing on my party?

We all ended up inside the house; and as we were not equipped for more than a dozen people on chairs, most sat on the floor. Well, as I said, it was different.

It was the next day that we heard the terrible news of the Darwin cyclone Tracy and the devastation it had caused. We listened to the news in horror. Cynthia and Arthur were with us, and she was concerned that he would have to go and fly a Hercules transport plane to save lives or carry in supplies. But that didn't happen; and for the next days—I have no idea how many—people were lifted out of Darwin or made their way south in whatever manner they could, and the whole area was declared a disaster zone. We grew used to seeing heavy duty cars that had come through the red desert sand and were thickly coated in a way that was new to us, fresh from a country where we are free of deserts. And, of course, cyclones.

It was a salutary start to our Australian existence.

But even disasters come to an end. I think it was during that holiday that Cynthia and Arthur went out and left their Labrador dog tied to the car port support for us to keep an eye on. On their way home they saw the dog at the lagoon; it had apparently broken free and escaped. They caught it and brought it home— only to find that their dog was still tied up to the car port. They had inadvertently 'dog-napped' someone else's animal. I imagine they slunk back and released the stolen hound, but I really can't remember. I expect we were all laughing too much.

28

S o our first full year in Australia began. One thing we had not thought of—Alison was a winter baby, her birthday in January; Fiona was a summer baby, born in July. I had not considered the fact that by coming to the ends of the earth they would change places in the calendar.

The school year began and both girls were involved in the longish daily journey by elderly bus that would take them to their respective schools. Derry began at Claremont Teachers' College in February, and life began to take on a more orderly pattern. My life became a series of car drives, morning and evening, because with Derry not driving and the bus service being totally lamentable I was faced with taking him to Claremont and back again, returning home in between trips—I was in that car for about 4 hours a day; eventually we realised that this was not sensible, and he stayed in a hotel near the college for 4 nights each week, and I picked him up on Friday afternoon.

But we hadn't come this far so that we could be separated. It was a difficult situation, especially as he was not very happy with the atmosphere among the staff or the low standards expected from the students. We solved the travel problem by having him come as far as a bus stop north of Wanneroo (he would catch the bus from Perth central bus station), where I would pick him up. This relieved me of much of the driving, only one hour per day instead of the exhausting 4 hours.

I remember him coming home one day, frustrated by a lack of any desire by these students (who hoped one day to be primary teachers) to learn about music. He had been taking a music history class, and was interrupted by one man who said, 'We don't want to learn about all that! We just want to be able to stand in front of a class and teach them a song.'

This attitude was still in evidence when I helped with accompanying the Christmas carol service in one school. With my own knowledge of what a wonderful experience a really good carol service can be, I asked the 'music specialist' if she ever did anything with the children of a more demanding, even interesting kind than I was playing for. There are so many beautiful carols, and they were singing a John Lennon song (fortunately I didn't have to play it: it was on a tape). I have nothing against John Lennon, but it seemed to me a great pity that these children were unknowingly deprived of learning about great music.

The teacher's answer was, 'Oh, you can't do that kind of thing with children today. They won't do it! They only want their own music.' I remembered the delight with which we learned to sing music with depth when Derry came and blew the cobwebs away. I also wondered—at what point in the history of teaching had primary students been allowed to decide for themselves what they were going to learn?

Unfortunately there are all too many teachers who, either because they are themselves badly taught or because they don't have the dynamism in their teaching that is so necessary, let their students leave school without having discovered the pleasures of fine music. I feel strongly about this, because my own experience is that once the better things of life and learning are offered in a palatable manner, young people often lap them up. I am thankful that there are people around now who are making inroads into this desert of ignorance.

As we came towards the end of summer, I realised that things were not going too well with my own children's education. Both had been A grade students in the UK, and it was very alarming to see their grades sliding downhill. There were several reasons for this, as I found when I began to look into the matter seriously. The daily journeys in hot buses were something outside their experience; I pointed out that we had come to live in a place where this was necessary. Fiona told me some time later that she hadn't understood what her very Aussie male teacher was saying. Alison was finding herself in another situation she had never met before: the area where her school was situated was peopled with one-parent families, and she was hearing and learning from her school mates how to play one parent off against the other. This worried her greatly. Thank goodness it did!

Eventually another thing came to light: bullying. As 'Pommie' newcomers they were fair game, I suppose. But even then, in 1975, bullying was not tolerated. The problem, of course, is always that bullies tend to wreak their destructive activities out of sight of authority.

One Friday they came home deeply distressed. There had been bullying on the homeward bus, and they had been seriously frightened. We had a very traumatic weekend, and we talked about it for a long time. This development was creating a real problem: we loved living in Yanchep and we didn't want to move, but the combination of lower grades and fear of bullying was something that had to be solved quickly. We hadn't travelled round the globe to ruin our daughters' education.

There were several choices: we could stay where we were and I could get a job in Perth, perhaps close to a school where there was a good music standard (both girls were musical). Then I could deliver them to the school in the morning and pick them up in the afternoon. This would be more driving for me, but acceptable under the circumstances.

In theory we could put them in somewhere as weekly boarders; but neither of us believed in the boarding school system or wanted to try it.

We could sell up and move to Perth, somewhere like Subiaco or one of the newer suburbs. This had some advantages: it would put Derry close to his work; it would reduce my driving hours; it would give stability to our family life, and it would make it possible for us to choose which school we would like to live near. Only—we didn't want to leave Yanchep.

That weekend, though I didn't know it at the time, would produce another life-changing moment for us. On the Monday Fiona, who was feeling a bit better, went to school. Alison was still upset, so I kept her home. We sat after breakfast and talked about the problem. And during that discussion I was presented with an idea which thoroughly alarmed me. I put it that way—'presented'—because that was how it felt. This was an unexpected development, bearing in mind that I had hoped, once in Australia, to devote myself to writing. It had the same imperative feeling as when I had had the idea of emigrating: and I was equally shaken by it.

There are times in my life when I am very aware of being 'guided'. Who knows where that comes from? As a Christian I sense that it comes from somewhere outside me; but that is difficult to explain to anyone who is not spiritually aware of forces that are in fact inexplicable.

All I can say is that I was 'led' very positively towards a solution that I could not possibly have thought of for myself. I was quite horrified at the thought that was growing in my mind: *start a school.*

I had been in Yanchep for less than a year. I was an 'outsider', I knew nothing about the school system from the inside, I was not a trained teacher, I had never once in my entire life imagined running a school of any kind, nor did I want to. But the idea would not die; it inhabited my mind, sometimes to the exclusion of everything else.

I said nothing to anyone at first. I suppose I hoped that this bit of guidance would go away. But it didn't. As I began to keep my eyes open and talk to other parents in the area, I found that I was not the only one who was deeply concerned about the educational situation in Yanchep. Often this was because their children were not necessarily top grade students, but were steadily becoming top grade truants. It was not unusual, driving down the Wanneroo Road in the mid-morning, to see high school students (mainly boys, I'm afraid) hitching lifts back home to Yanchep and Two

Rocks. Clearly, something would have to be done. But I wasn't sure why I had to be the one to do it.

This would have been in the first term of 1975, probably in March. By April there was quite a band of us, unhappy parents all, looking at the situation and trying to decide what to do. There were rumours that a demountable (transportable) classroom or two might be coming soon to accommodate primary classes; but there was nothing offered for secondary students.

It was the time when there was a considerable amount of government money floating about. People were doing things that had not been thought of until the Whitlam government began to fund them. I had been involved with some writers in Fremantle, with whom I was supposedly writing a film script—cooperating with others who, to be quite honest, didn't seem to know where they were going. I had heard of grants, anything from $3000 to $10000, being paid out to writers and artists who didn't even see the necessity for keeping tabs on what they were spending—and in some cases never intending to complete the work they had been funded for. So much money with so little result seemed to me quite strange.

But there were other things floating about in the seventies; I remember, after a session trying to work out what I was supposed to be writing, being swept off in someone's car to have lunch with some of the group. I can't believe that I was such an innocent: after all, I was 46, long married and with a big family. Where had I been? I suppose the answer to that is *in Dorking, where I didn't know the kind of people I was now mixing with.*

We sat around a large circular table. Practically everyone seemed to be smoking, an addiction I had thankfully given up nearly two decades before. Before long they were all sitting, eyes closed, and taking no notice of me. Nor did there seem to be anything to eat. It was a while before I realised that they were all stoned. I can't remember how I got back to my car—but I do recall being very thankful to be home with people who didn't find *that* kind of smoking desirable.

The film script got finished, don't ask me how; and it went off to Sydney to be appraised, and that was the last I heard of it. I think I've still got a copy of it somewhere. The best part of it was that I got paid quite handsomely for doing it.

But the whole business of starting a school was beginning to hang over me. How could it be done? In fact, *could* it be done? Well, other people had done it. The thing was to find out how, and why. I made a couple of appointments to go to community schools and ask a lot of questions.

What I found was quite intriguing—and not a little bewildering. I grew up with a father who had done well as a Manchester Grammar School boy, won scholarships, 'done his time' at Queens College, Oxford reading Classics, and had a successful career in the British Civil Service. I knew about education! I didn't go to university—my own choice, firstly because I had a place ready at Slade School of Fine Art, secondly because I didn't go there and got married instead. But Rosemary and Philip both went to Cambridge and got their degrees; Rosemary became a teacher of Classics, Philip a mathematician in the area of new nuclear developments. I knew the value of a good education—and I knew that it was a challenge that had to be met by the individual student. It wasn't something that could be applied like a coat of paint from the outside!

So, being married to a teacher who had demonstrated again and again that young people can achieve amazing things—if they put their minds to it—I was quite grieved by what I was seeing around me in Yanchep. These children needed the challenge of a good education, and they weren't getting it.

Were they getting it at these 'new look' community schools? If we went down this road would we be harming them or enhancing their lives? I have to say that I was not overly impressed with what I saw as I visited schools. I was warmly welcomed and given good advice about the difficulties, but, while I liked the freedom that can be given by a small school, I wasn't happy with some of the very slack approaches to teaching that I occasionally found.

I thought very deeply about this. Finally I came up with the decision that, as almost everything that had so far been achieved in the western world had come from men and women who had originally been formally educated, it would be foolish to lose the discipline that a structured programme would supply.

If we started a community school, it would not be a 'go-as-you-please', 'do-as-you-like' place. Our aims would have to include a proper timetable, for the benefit of the students *and* the teachers. But within that structure I hoped we would create a place where the students themselves *wanted* to do well, and could see that if they wished to get the best out of these years in the classroom they would have to put their own efforts into it.

There was also the requirement to produce some kind of result that would impress the government inspector who would come to look at us after a few weeks, and decide whether we were in fact producing an education for our students. On this would depend whether we would qualify for the government grants, State and Federal.

Well—whether this was going to be an educational experience for Yanchep teenagers was something we would have to discover. All I knew at that point was that for me it was by far the biggest and most challenging educational experience in my life. I had to learn how it could be done, what official arrangements there were to assist us, what were the pitfalls, who was the person who would help us most, and how to encourage parents to let us teach their (sometimes rebelliously anti-education) teenagers.

How many teachers would we need? How many students would we have? Should we charge fees or not? In fact, what would it cost, all up, to do this revolutionary thing? And, above all—*where* could we do it?

Well, I've said I felt guided. Once the idea began to be talked about, I started getting approaches from local people who wanted to be included. From memory: a woman who wanted to teach French; another woman who would like to do art work; an elderly man who offered woodwork; and so on.

Yanchep was very new, and I suppose the kind of people who had arrived there *and stayed in spite of the difficulties* were the kind of people who were prepared to take a punt. And for parents whose children seemed to be straying from the straight and narrow it was, just possibly, one answer to their worries. At least they would be close to home, and to an extent under the parental eyes.

Where to put this school was a big question. I had a vague picture in my mind of a row of three small houses, 2-bedroomed would be quite big enough, which we could use for the three levels of high school students: years 8, 9 and 10. I could visualise a kind of 'home teaching' situation with qualified teachers. Having small gardens would mean we could do something with horticulture, possibly have chooks and widen the horizons of teaching. It might also help with the school's financial situation, and even at this early stage I realised that this was going to be the big problem.

Finally, I went to see Colin Herbert, town manager. (He probably had a more high-flying title, but I never found out what it was). At that time his office was in what has since been Martin Dickhart's real estate agency. I sat down and began to put forward my ideas about a school, the problems it might raise, and how I felt we might overcome them.

I don't know what his internal reaction was; he certainly listened very closely, and clearly was evaluating the possibilities. When I suggested that Bond Corporation might have three small houses and explained why, he stopped me.

'You don't want that,' he said, very firmly.

'Actually, yes, I do.'

'No, you don't.'

I often meet this kind of reaction to my cherished ideas. I said, 'What do I want, then?'

He swung round in his chair to point through the wide window behind him, which framed the marina down below. 'You want that bloody great white elephant in the middle of the marina!'

I stared out of the window. I had no idea what the very large building facing the land was for.

'You want the Sail Loft,' he said. 'Go and get the keys from the marina manager and have a look at it, then come back and tell me.'

Keys in hand, I opened the door of the Sail Loft and went inside. Ahead of me was a large foyer with an impressive stairway rising to the right. At the back of the foyer to the right was a small kitchen. Next to that were two rooms which could be closed off.

I went slowly up the stairs. At the top I found a huge open space, with big windows on the land side; and at the back there was a drop to the floor below where—my mind by this time was boggling overtime—two massive and beautiful ocean racing yachts were housed.

I was thinking, 'They would let us use this place? Surely not. Children and vastly expensive yachts do not mix.'

But that would be their problem! It looked as if one of mine was about to be solved. I went back to Colin, and said yes.

He had something else to say. 'It's got to work. If it does, it'll be "Barbara's school successful!" in the papers. If it doesn't it'll be "Bond school fails" and we don't want that.'

That, as they say, was a big ask! But I said we would do our very best to bring credit to Bond Corporation and Yanchep Sun City. I was finding it hard to believe that our accommodation problems were now over. Even more difficult to believe—we were to have the Sail Loft rent free, on the understanding that if they should need it again we would have to move out. In the event, we had that amazing building rent free until 1981, when the America's Cup Challenge created a pressing need in the yachting world to have their building back.

That was a solution no one could have expected, and I was immensely grateful. It was not a totally trouble-free time, all the same. The marina management really didn't want us there, and we had some slightly unpleasant run-ins with the Alan Bond America's Cup team, who were scathing about what we were doing. One of them, I remember, leaned over the banisters leading to the upstairs area (and this was when we had been there for several years) and was very direct, not to say rude, about our presence. 'You shouldn't be here,' he ended. I pointed out that the place had been offered to us by Bond Corporation—I had not asked for it. But he wasn't appeased.

I came back to school after lunch some years down the track to find the entire upper floor covered with a full-sized ocean racing sail being stretched (which of course is what the Sail Loft was actually for). It made teaching quite difficult for the rest of the day, but we didn't complain. It would only have brought forth more rage on our heads. I didn't really mind it being there—it was after all quite instructive for the students, if only the racing brethren could have seen it that way—but it did seem a bit cheeky not to mention it beforehand.

But one way and another it was a happy arrangement, and we were so lucky to have this unique school in the middle of the marina. Despite the dark forebodings of one father with a tsunami phobia (of course, we called them tidal waves then), who was convinced that the entire school and all the precious children would be swept away, it was an excellent solution—and it worked.

As a personal matter, one day I was told that a prize had been offered for the best and most innovative idea in Yanchep/Two Rocks—and that I had won it! $500-worth of landscaping. It was a very welcome outcome, and I still see the benefits of it in the garden after nearly 4 decades.

Now it was full steam ahead to get the rest of the problems ironed out. We held a number of public meetings in the next few months, some of which became very heated.

Trying to explain to people what a community school is poses real difficulties. At just about every meeting one elderly man who was determined not to let us start would stand and say, 'What does community school mean? It means that when it collapses for lack of money the community will have to pick up the bills.' It didn't matter how often I explained, as calmly as possible, that 'community' meant the school itself—that it was a community serving the wider community, and that if it did go broke it would not be the wider community's job to clear up the mess—this man just kept on beating the same drum.

I went to see him at home to try and win him over. He 'interviewed' me over his front gate, and was barely short of abusive. As I gave up and turned to go home he shouted, 'You'll be crucified if you do this!' For once I had the right answer—so often one thinks of the cutting remark later—and I said, 'Well, I shall be in good company!'

I don't know if he understood what I meant. But, sadly, he made things hard for us a number of times, even after we had proved that we were not actually harming anyone, and possibly were doing good in the community. My own feeling is that, because Yanchep/Two Rocks was such a new development, some of the people who had got there earlier had established themselves as kings of the castle, and deeply resented us 'blow-ins' who thought we had a right to be heard and to participate in the growth of the place. It was a pity: his wife was quite a nice person.

So now we could get down to that old nitty-gritty! Teachers, chairs and tables, books, teaching aids—once you start, the list seems impossibly huge. But by the middle of 1975 there were enough parents and friends interested in the project for my load to be lightened a little. And at this point I should make mention of Derry, who supported my endeavours and the preparations for the school unstintingly, and never once said, as he might well have done if he had been another kind of husband, 'You must be mad!'

But there were times when I really wondered if I was. Suddenly I was dealing with the local Shire Council (this was before Wanneroo became a city), and all the members of parliament for the area, Federal and State. It seemed to be an idea that had caught on, and I had a great deal of support from many of the 'authority' figures who had dealings with the Yanchep area. We saw to it that the newspapers heard about it—the West Australian and the Sunday Times took pictures of us—and slowly, slowly the whole business began to take shape.

To put down here the progress over those next few months would take a volume to itself. I had no idea that there would be so many details to work out. Where would we find the basic equipment we would need? Tables, chairs and so on. One community school I visited did away with such things and they sat on cushions on the floor. I didn't feel that was entirely conducive to studying—it's nice to have a table or desk to lean on! Bond Corp had the answer, and we received a number of tables and chairs (presumably extra to their requirements), which we used during the whole of our tenure there. We managed to buy some second-hand desks.

My memory of much of that time is still good, sometimes vivid; but small details have been lost over the 37 years since they seemed so unforgettable. I hope that others who were involved will have anecdotes and memories to fill the gaps. It seems quite strange to me that when all this was happening I was younger than my youngest child now is—and that I am 84 as I write.

By the end of 1975 the whole project seemed balanced on a knife edge. I knew we had the goodwill of the Shire Council, but they wouldn't back the scheme if they thought it wasn't a winner; I knew the MPs were interested enough to do what they could for us. But I wasn't sure about the Education Department. Eventually, an official survey was sent out—I think by the Department—to see if there was enough support in the local area for the school to be supported by them.

I welcomed this. If it seemed that only a few families wanted this to happen we should let the idea go and concentrate of something else (preferably something a bit less traumatic). The surveys arrived by post—just before Christmas! Well, I don't know what other people do when something of that kind arrives while Mum is stuffing the turkey and Dad is getting the fairy lights going; probably most of them were either put in the bin or stuffed into a drawer marked 'to be looked at if we survive Christmas'.

So I was informed in January that there had not been enough positive returns of the survey to warrant starting a community school. How clever of them! I thought. If you don't want people to answer a survey, either send it when everyone is on holiday or ask the wrong questions. 'If you wish to start such a school,' the letter said, 'perhaps it would be better to look at an area to the south of

Yanchep where there is a bigger population'. They hadn't begun to understand what I was talking about.

We were on our own, myself waving the banner and a number of parents following behind. I have no recollection of when we decided to go ahead and take the plunge into these unknown waters; but when we counted heads and looked for the necessary enthusiasm to back the project, we decided there were 46 high school students, covering years 8, 9, and 10, to make it worth taking the risk.

We announced that we would start the school in February (1976), one week after the other schools had begun their term.

Fiona had completed her state primary schooling in the demountables this area had been promised, set up near the caravan park at the holiday village (later Club Cap) and she had done very well. But, as a courtesy to the high school Alison had been at, I went to see the head teacher to explain why I was taking Alison away. I made the point that I had been really concerned about her slow slide from being an advanced student, and the fact that she was emotionally upset by some of the things that were going on around her.

The teacher was sympathetic; but she made the point that if the 'good' students were removed from the school they would be left with only the under-achievers. I could sympathise too, but I made *my* point that I couldn't risk my daughter for the sake of the school. We parted very amicably and she wished me well.

Predictably, February rushed towards me, and I am sure I had many a qualm about what we were undertaking. From this distance it is a blur! We had accepted the challenge, and now we had to prove ourselves.

The day came, the door was opened, the tables and chairs were in place and all we needed were the students. When everyone had arrived and we began the task of recording everyone's name, address, age etc, I counted heads. 45! I felt very let down; we had been sure there would be 46. Who was missing?

I counted again. This time it came right, and I realised I had not counted my own daughter in. With Fiona's name added to the roll it came to where I hoped it would be. Now all we had to do was teach!

From the start, parents were welcome to visit, and a number came to help. While we evaluated the situation, Derry undertook to run a few tests so that we would know what levels of knowledge we were dealing with. Mental arithmetic, spelling: he kept everyone busy as we checked numbers and, more particularly, decided where each student fitted into the three divisions.

The accommodation was clearly going to be a great blessing to us. Plenty of room, and the freedom to use the spaces as they were needed. The kitchen meant that we could do mid-morning Milo or whatever was required; and I believe we began taking lunch orders before long, though my memory of that aspect of schooling is somewhat vague. The room at the back towards the right was the office, where I had a desk (also provided by Bond Corporation) and some cupboards and shelves. The room to the left was useful for a teacher who wanted to do some one-to-one teaching, or for any other purpose where it was useful to be able to close the door.

At the end of that day I should have gone home both exhausted and satisfied with what we had so far achieved; but, alas, I cannot recall anything in any detail. I imagine I would have slept well that night.

Once it seemed that we were really going to do this crazy thing, we had advertised for two teachers. With small numbers— because I could help out if necessary, and there were parents available—we felt that all we required was one teacher to put in place and run the English and Social Studies courses, and one for Maths and Science.

This was quite a challenge for them. I had appointed two men, one with plenty of experience and one very new to teaching. Both did really well to put the courses in motion, not only deciding just what equipment was needed, but sometimes finding it through other schools who had just updated text books and, in particular, science equipment which would save us a good amount of money.

It was sad that the English teacher proved to be unreliable around young boys—in these days we are used to the stories of the distresses caused by men who pursue teenage boys, but at that time in the mid-1970s there were few guidelines for head teachers on how to deal with deviant members of staff. In fact, as far as I could tell, this was not a very serious matter, but I had to deal with it; and that teacher was asked during the holidays, once I had been told about him, not to return for the second term. The only punishments then for such behaviour were the sack, or moving on to another school; without a reference, of course, it became very difficult for the teacher to find another job. I'm afraid I don't know what became of him. He was a family man, and on one occasion I met his wife and daughters. The dilemma for the person responsible for seeing that he was dealt with was to know, as in this case, that reporting him would possibly destroy his family life. I am deeply thankful that I never needed to deal with that particular problem again.

So we started on our great experiment; Alan, the maths and science teacher, was with us for a good length of time, and did a great job, both with his subject teaching and his involvement in the day-to-day running of the school. He was young and energetic, and the students liked him.

But we had to find our English and social studies replacement. I had more or less given up hope of locating someone at such short notice when a woman answered the advertisement and arrived for the interview. I can still see her standing at the office door, wondering what on earth this was all about. There is never any way of telling, before we get to know someone new, how a meeting is going to make a difference in our lives; if I say that Anne and I still exchange Christmas cards and letters, even after three-and-a half decades, it will indicate that she brought to the school, and to her fellow staff members, something of real value.

Anne is English but had lived in Australia long enough to become an Australian citizen. She was an experienced teacher who had become disaffected by the education system in WA, and had just about decided to give it away and go back to England. In the nick of time—for us, at least—she saw my advertisement and decided to come and see what it all meant.

She was very hesitant about making her decision; but finally she took a deep breath and said, 'OK! I'll give it a go.'

So now we had our full complement of teachers; the inspector had been and found us doing a good job; State and Federal funds had arrived; we had two competent teachers and a group of students who seemed to have settled in well; and the Shire President, Charles Searson, had visited us on the first day of the first term with a cheque for a few thousand dollars because, as he said, he 'didn't think we had Buckley's of getting it off the ground!'

On top of everything else, we had a unique situation—who else had a school in the middle of a marina, with cray-boats coming in and unloading, and the operations of the fascinating boat lift to take your mind off the subject in hand?

I began to discover that our hard-line truants had usually come to the marina to spend the day before going home to their trusting parents. So—if your school is where you would from choice spend your day, where can you do your truanting? I mention this because, of all the things we did that I remember with pleasure, the fact that we were probably the only school in the State that didn't have a truant problem is up there in shining letters!

One of the aspects of developing a community school is where the boundaries are. One soon learns that this type of school attracts parents who are at their wits' end about their children—usually, I'm sorry to say, about their sons. It really surprised me, in the early days, that we had more boys than girls. I had assumed that parents of boys would want them in an environment that also included such things as sports grounds, sophisticated science labs, tough male teachers and so on. But it wasn't working out that way. As I got to know them, I realised that many of our boys had developed a real antipathy towards education—a thought that alarmed me. There was a perception among them that the ten years of compulsory school attendance was some kind of obscure punishment for being a child. I found this very sad. We only need to look around the world at countries where children have little or no chance of getting an education to know how much it is appreciated when they do have the opportunity. And I was faced with these lads who couldn't see why they should be in school.

'What would you do if you didn't have to be taught?' I asked.

'Go fishing.' 'Get a motor bike.'

'What is the real alternative to going to school?'

'Well, we wouldn't have to do anything. We could go on the dole.'

'That's not how it works. If you weren't given this opportunity by the whole Australian community to go to school for ten years, you would probably have to go to work when you are nine or ten. That's what happens in countries where the children are not educated.'

They stared at me.

'I was told my grandfather had to start work when he was ten.' I saw that I had their attention. 'And there is another thing. If you were on the dole—who would be paying for it?'

Silence.

'Me!' I said. '*Me*—and all the other people who go to work and are taxed so that you can go to school. If *we* all decided not to work anymore, the dole would come to an end. Where did you think the money came from?'

From the looks on their faces it was game, set and match to me! I found that quick thinking was an essential part of running a school where the students were allowed to express their feelings and beliefs.

29

O ne thing I was quite decided on: our students would not call us by our first names. If we were to deal with a number of children who had 'opted out' of school, I felt that one aspect of our education would be learning respect, not necessarily for authority, but for people in general; and one part of that is addressing people properly.

This is a matter for discussion, I know. The 'first-name' thing is part of the idea that we must be the students' friends, just as many people feel they want to be their children's friends. That's a fine idea—but parents are, after all, parents, and they have the major role to play in the training of their children. I still believe that the child's world is one that the adult should not enter without invitation; their games and that wonderful land where imagination lives for the young child is one that adults have largely left behind, and we cannot break into that world without destroying something of it. I have thought about this a great deal, relating it to my own childhood, of which I have some very vivid memories; and I wouldn't have been pleased if my mother had wanted to join in my play, sitting with us on the floor and, however she tried not to, leading *my* games in the way she wanted them to go. There is something very precious about a child's imaginings, and they should be allowed to develop without outside interference.

I know I was dealing with older children, and sometimes with children who had already been emotionally damaged by their school experiences; but teenagers still live in their own world, and that world should be respected unless we see damage being done. Also, because this was a uniquely different school, unlike anything they would meet elsewhere, it had to be made quite clear that it was also an educational establishment, and not a play group or a drop-in centre. We were there to work in our different ways.

So we started with the formality of Mr, Mrs and Miss! What would come later would no doubt reveal itself as we went along this new path.

Sadly, there was still opposition from some members of the local community. Our students were told that their behaviour must be excellent, especially when they were out in that community, because if there were bad reports about them we might lose the school. Within the first few weeks it had been clear that, given support and the freedom to be themselves, this had been a very good move for the Yanchep and Two Rocks teenage students. In general they were working well, and we had few behaviour problems. It really seemed as if they were enjoying what we were offering.

Odd things happened from time to time, things that made me wonder why some of these young people had been 'sacked' from their previous schools—for some it was as if a tension had been relaxed and they could be their 'better' selves. While the boys and girls who were by nature 'good' students were quietly getting on with the courses laid down for them by the Education Department, the ones who had a reputation for being disruptive, having had a good look around at this new environment, also began to work better.

One of the odd things was the attitude to bad behaviour. It was rare in the times ahead that this got commendation from the rest of the school. I could have expected small riots, instigated by boys who had brought that reputation with them; but it didn't happen.

In spite of this, my reputation was not enhanced for some local people. My friend Vera was helping us set up our financial system; she told me that she had been talking to someone in Two Rocks about the school. This woman said, quite vehemently, 'I wouldn't send a child of mine to that young woman!' (I was 47 at the time).

Vera said, 'Oh, do you know Barbara?'

'No—never met her!'

I decided not to take any notice of that kind of criticism. The school's reputation, and mine, would rest on our achievements.

I believe we offered an interestingly wide range of activities for our students. Up in the Two Rocks town centre was the artistic community—Sid the potter, and craftspeople doing batik, leatherwork, and so on. We arranged with them for the students to go to them during the week and learn various crafts. I think this worked well, barring a few skirmishes with local tradespeople. But I had no reports of bad behaviour among our young people, and that was very pleasing.

Once a week was sports afternoon, and while we obviously couldn't be involved in big team games we could certainly do more individual things. Over the time we were there we were able to give them swimming at the pool in the National Park or at the holiday village; tennis; archery; golf; table tennis; horse riding; and anything else that could be found locally, either short or long term. I don't think they missed much.

I was determined to use the facilities available in Two Rocks, and when I found I had two boys who wanted to do cookery, but hadn't been able to opt for it at their previous schools, I went to see the chef at the Two Rocks Tavern. I don't know how he secretly felt about it, but we arranged for each boy, as the time came for them, to work one afternoon a week in the tavern's kitchen.

It gave me very great satisfaction that both boys became chefs in due course. It was just one more justification for having taken this massive plunge.

Meanwhile, the day by day routine continued. The Sail Loft was quite a hive of activity. Because our system was to awaken the desire to learn in these young people, teachers had a greater freedom than they would have done under the State or private college systems; and they really appreciated that. But I don't want to give the impression that we were simply a kind of reformatory for students who had been thrown out of their previous school. We had several of these; but we had a strong core of youngsters who really wanted to achieve, and these were the backbone of what we were working towards. It was not a play school, and these students were setting the pace and the standards for all of us.

Discipline is a word that is often misused. On one occasion we had a visit from a primary headmaster who was with his students on a school camp at the holiday village. He brought some of these young people with him, and I showed them round.

We had room dividers upstairs in the Sail Loft, just to give a bit of privacy for classes and teachers—not enough to cut out any noise, but at least it stopped them communicating with the class next to them. There was a reasonable hum of sound coming from the groups behind the screens, but everyone was working well.

When we went downstairs and his students went to look at the marina, the headmaster turned to me and said, 'It's fine for you. You can do as you like. You don't have discipline, do you?'

For a moment I didn't know how to answer. He had been around the school; he had seen no bad behaviour, students had been polite to him, teachers welcomed him—what did he mean?

I said, 'Did you see any inappropriate behaviour?'

'No. But what do you do about punishment?'

'We don't usually need it.'

He nodded. 'You don't have discipline.'

'We have *self*-discipline. They know what's expected of them.'

I don't remember what he said, but I know he left behind him a sense of irritation—he didn't understand me, and I didn't understand him! I wondered what sort of report *he* would give if asked.

Years later, on the same subject, I was talking to a primary head at a pre-Christmas get-together arranged by the Wanneroo Shire. By this time we had expanded into the full range from 4 years old to year 12.

'It's all right for you,' he said. 'You can do as you please. *I* have to stay with the regulations.'

I pointed out that in order to get the government grants we had to run a recognisable educational facility. Within those limitations we could certainly do our own thing for much of the time. But I said, 'You could do as we are doing, and it wouldn't cost you a cent more.' He clearly didn't believe me. 'You have the space, the teachers, the books and equipment, everything you need. All you have to do is stop dividing children up according to their ages.'

He was interested but very doubtful. 'It wouldn't work.'

'It's as silly,' I said, 'to make children work in age groups as it would be to make them all wear the same size of shoes because they just happen to be 10 years old.'

Education is not 'one size fits all!' I was glad to have the chance of expounding this particular philosophy.

'All right. So how would it work?'

'Divide the classrooms so that Miss Smith in classroom one has the children for maths who operate best at year one level—regardless of their age. They would soon get used to being in a mixed group, with the chance of going to Mr Black in the second room when they had mastered the first year work. Because what we have found is that the big problem is expecting *all* students of a particular age to work at the same level, meaning that the bright ones can easily get bored, and the ones having difficulty feel frustrated. The same goes for English, Social Studies, Science—if the student cannot keep up there is a sense of failure that begins at the start of the day and goes on until home time. Why put children through such an experience, when it is quite unnecessary? If they can do it in their own best time, they will be happy and productive and it won't have cost you or the government another cent.'

He sounded more interested. A long time after, I read in the paper that a State primary school somewhere to the south of us was doing something very similar to our system. I wondered if my pre-Christmas sherry had borne fruit! I do hope so. It's such a simple solution to a difficult problem.

When a new teacher came to us I would have a chat and say, 'Our job here is to open the children's eyes and minds. Imagine that the child's head you see before you is packed with tightly closed rosebuds. It's your responsibility to help those buds to open and flower.' I hoped that the visual thought would inspire the teacher as well as the child.

I found that the students themselves had peculiar ideas about punishment—as if it was an integral and necessary part of schooling. 'Why don't you cane?' one group of boys asked me.

'I don't believe in it.'

'Caning's nothing!'

'That's one reason why I don't believe in it. If it's nothing, why do it?'

'Well, when you've done something and you get the cane it's all over and done with.'

I had to keep ahead of this. 'I would never cane anyone on the hand.'

'Why not?'

'Because the hand is a very sensitive and wonderful thing, and caning it is wrong.' They were finding this difficult to understand. 'Besides,' I said, trying to look severe, 'if I cane, I cane on the bottom, and once I start I can't stop!' This, for some reason, they did understand.

There are a few outstanding moments that I shall not forget. One involved a boy who had come to us with a very bad record of school attendance and behaviour problems. I took him on with mixed feelings; so when he came to me before school one day and told me 'I kicked the girls' toilet door in, di'n't I?' I was taken aback. This was a boy, I suspected, who had never willingly owned up to anything in his life.

'Why did you do that?'

'They caught me, di'n't they? And carried me in there. An' I was scared and I kicked the door.'

I thought we should go and see this bit of vandalism; sure enough, there was a hole in the plywood door.

'So what do you think we should do about this?' He had no idea. I don't think he had ever needed to think these episodes through; but I was fascinated that he thought it necessary to tell me. 'If we start to damage the building we shall have to move out, you know.' I gave it a some thought. 'I think you and your father should come and mend the door. OK?'

And they did.

On another occasion two boys went up to the town centre to get lunch from the deli, which they were allowed to do; but they failed to return for afternoon school. When they finally arrived, having—so they said—forgotten the time, I asked what they had been doing. 'Playing the games thing at the deli.' This was something that had recently been installed there.

I sat them down and gave them what used to be called 'a good talking to'! I have never found it difficult to talk at length, and on this occasion I managed to keep going for about 15 minutes. At the end of my lecture I asked, as I usually did, what we should do about this.

The smaller boy of the two said he was sorry. The older boy said, 'Well, I'll tell you one thing—I'm not going through this bloody nonsense again!' And I don't think he ever had to.

The third moment involved a boy who had been at a private college, and was well used to formal punishment. He had not been doing well there, and was brought to us. Rather dauntingly, he wore a bush hat in class, which he pulled down over his eyes if he wasn't enjoying the lesson, and pushed to the back of his head when he was. A teacher asked me if we needed to put up with the hat; I said I thought we should—it was his security blanket in a new form.

I managed to snatch a few moments with him one day, and asked if he had been punished a lot at his previous school; he said he had. I said I wouldn't punish him whatever he did. He stared at me. 'If you do something criminal, and that includes drugs, I shall call the police; if you do something to let the school down I shall sack you. Otherwise I shall not punish you.'

A few days later he brought the hat into my office and, without a word, threw it up onto the top of a bookcase and walked out. He never wore it again in class.

A sad moment to conclude. Eventually, the boy who kicked the door in 'did his time' in juvenile detention. I wasn't surprised. His family background almost demanded it. But one day I saw him sitting on the sea wall with a mate, and asked if he was coming to see us. He said no. I told him if he changed his mind he was welcome, and left him.

Half an hour later he came in, with his pal, and I gave them the same tour I gave visiting headmasters. By this time we had a thriving primary, and we sat and watched what was happening. I said nothing for a while, then: 'It's good, isn't it?'

He said, 'Yeah—but it was too late for me.' I think that was truly from the heart.

30

S
o how did it come about that we had a primary class as well as our junior high schoolers?

At the end of our first year two things happened that changed everything. Parents began to come to us and ask if we could do the same for their primary children that we were doing for the high schoolers. This, of course, meant more staff, and making the Sail Loft spaces fit this new need.

At the same time I was approached (perhaps a bit hesitantly) by the students from Year 10. Some of these had never envisaged staying at school after they had completed that officially final year; in fact, they had been praying to leave since they first became high school students! Now they wanted to know if they could stay on and do Year 11.

I was delighted. But this also meant more staff, more money required, more books, more of everything one could think of. It was a very big change to take on; schools of this kind are very vulnerable to financial problems. One soon learns that all too often difficult children have difficult parents—and one of the ways in which they can be difficult is in not paying their way. When they enrolled their children they knew that a regular payment was necessary, and that we were prepared to accommodate them within reason. But it was very tempting, seeing how well the current students were doing, to say 'yes, of course you can stay on'.

And—of course—that was what we said.

So we would start 1977 with children from 6 to 17. We found a gem of a primary teacher, who had been wasting her talents selling vegies in the Two Rocks supermarket. I doubt if we could have done it without her. Janet eventually had about 50 children in one half of the Sail Loft, aged from 4 to about 11 or 12, and there were always several parents there to help—another innovation that we found worked very well indeed. We had our three junior classes nicely filled; and we had a group of seniors who were determined to do well. I felt very thankful. At our peak, in about 1978, there were 80 students in all.

Four teachers divided the top 5 years between them, taking English, Social Studies, Maths and Science at the appropriate levels. I made it clear to the Year 11 students that they themselves were responsible for their own future success. I pointed out that we, the teachers, had already done our studying and exams, and that we were not there to drive them. I put the entire syllabus for the Year 12 exams (then called the Tertiary Admissions Examination: TAE) into their classroom and told them that if they wanted to succeed they must see to it that the teachers kept up with what they needed to know. I advised them to 'pick our brains' while they had the chance.

This unusual approach seemed to work; eventually they did well in their final examinations, a source of tremendous satisfaction to themselves and to the staff. We were even allowed to have our own examination room, with a local clergyman as supervisor, so that they could do the exams with the least disturbance to them. As one of the parents myself, I was thankful that my own girls did well—it had after all been quite a gamble with their education. Our lack of good science facilities was a problem; in spite of it, Alison was able to go to Murdoch University for veterinary studies.

But it wasn't all book work. Anne proved to have skills in putting on pantomimes; and over the years, even after she left, we did several, including Cinderella, Jack and the Beanstalk and Rumpelstiltskin. There were a few students who might well have had parts in such a performance if they had been in a large school; but most of them would never have got to auditions. And what a pity that would have been! Certainly, getting them to learn their lines properly was not easy; but on the night everyone, including a very appreciative audience, had a great time, and the occasional loss of lines didn't seem to matter. When it came to slapstick comedy, the boys especially were in their element.

I have to record the story of the cow in Jack and the Beanstalk. A 15-year old boy came to me and said, 'So what am I going to do?' I said, 'Do you want to be in it?' He said yes. I mentioned that the cow was an important part of the story, and that we hadn't yet got a cow. Would he like to be a cow?

He agreed with some enthusiasm, and got his mate to be the other end of the animal. I told him he would have to make his own costume—and he did. It was a very effective cow, and it had, suspended underneath, the most obscene udder one could imagine.

When the performance came, his part involved walking down the centre aisle from the back of the hall to the low platform we had built. I didn't know that the two boys had devised a dance for the occasion; but when they started, and that udder swung wildly from side to side, they brought the house down! I remember with delight the sight of one father crying with laughter, and similar reactions from the rest of the audience.

Because of my family's musical background we were able to have music and songs to back the production; I seem to recall a flute, trumpet, piano and drums on at least one occasion; and I wrote songs that I felt would be easy to learn. Naturally, a stage production required scenery, and we had a few great evenings when parents, older children and interested friends came and created splendid scenes, slapping on the paint as if they had always been scene painters. The kitchen in Cinderella stands out in my mind.

So we embarked that February with a very full schedule. I think I am entitled to say that it was, like so many unusual ventures, both stimulating and very tiring. My role, apart from keeping this particular boat financially afloat, was to have an eye on how things were going, and all too often deal with emergencies that cropped up. I found myself being cast in another role—family counsellor, for which I was not trained. But when people come with deep problems and ask for help, apart from recommending that they find someone qualified to deal with them, something has to be said.

Often I would suggest marriage counselling; and as often I would be told, 'We'd rather talk to you'. This was perhaps flattering, but it meant that eventually I found myself trying to solve the problems of a dozen families, and feeling that, because we were teaching their children, we had at least to try to find a way out for them.

I was also surprised by the reasons given for why their children, sometimes only 7 or 8 years old, had been expelled from their previous schools. In some cases they were regarded as dangerous, though it was not easy to understand: they didn't seem dangerous to us. It looked like a very severe punishment for a child who had only been going to school for a fairly short time.

The one I particularly remember was a boy of about 8, whose previous school had given up on him. I couldn't see why, and his teachers agreed with me. Then one day he suddenly stabbed a little girl with his pencil point. No great actual harm done, but definitely alarming. We moved him away from the other children, and all was well. Then, later, something else happened that took me by surprise, and I decided to stay at the back of the class for a while and watch.

It just happened that there was a TV documentary about then, called 'The Spike'. It involved a young boy who was 'wired up' for brain scans; and in the upper corner of the screen we saw the scan as it progressed. All at once the even rhythm of his brain patterns was broken, and a sudden 'spike' showed; at the same time the boy's attitude changed and he became restless and aggressive.

A day or two later I was watching our boy when, without warning, his face changed, and he became agitated. It appeared to be identical with what I had seen on TV. The teacher dealt with him, and I went away to think. The 'spike' indicated *petit mal*, the milder form of epilepsy; was this the problem? I had to be very careful; I am not qualified to tell parents that their child is an epileptic. But I couldn't let it go by—this child was going be a little outcast unless someone did something.

I asked the parents to visit me, and told them what I had seen on TV; I made the point that it was not for me to say what should be done, but that if they wished I would write to their doctor and say what I had seen. They agreed. I wrote a letter, the doctor examined him and sent him to a specialist, and the TV programme had been right—he was suffering from *petit mal*. Once he was on medication there were no more problems.

What I found most alarming about this was that this child had been written off in his previous school. Why had no one seen what I had seen? Were those teachers simply too busy, because if so something should be done about staffing and class sizes. No child should be written off without good reason.

The school was well established in its unique 'home' when the developers, Tokyu Corporation and Yanchep Sun City (Bond Corporation) began to plan a marine park for Two Rocks.

This was a formidable challenge, requiring not only a large expenditure (swimming pools large enough for several dolphins to disport themselves in don't come cheap), but also a considerable population to support it. In hindsight, perhaps it was a bit too adventurous for the very small population numbers in the Yanchep/Two Rocks area.

Nevertheless, it was for a few years a real drawcard throughout the northern suburbs, still talked about today with pleasure; and it might have continued for a while longer if new rules for marine parks had not come into force, meaning a further output of around two million dollars—according to what we were told.

It was a great show, though. The leaping dolphins, seals with engaging tricks, showmanship from the young staff who thought nothing of 'riding' on the backs of a trio of dolphins: all very enthralling for the crowds who came, at least for a while.

And it all happened very close to the school. We came back for the new term to find seals in pens just outside our front door. One of our teachers lived on a boat in the marina. He and his wife could hear the wild dolphins swimming close by at night—perhaps searching for their mates, who had been captured and were now awaiting the training that would fit them for the splendid shows that were still in the future.

We were, I suppose, sorry for their loss of freedom; but there was not the sensitivity even in the 1970s towards wildlife that we have today. Nobody protested. Circuses with trained animals were still popular, though most of those have now, I hope, been relegated to the pages of history—in this country, anyway.

So, for a while, Yanchep and Two Rocks were on the map. Dolphins and the Americas Cup—you have to admire the publicity hype!

New regulations for captured animals, making closure of the Atlantis Park inevitable, also meant the loss of the park itself as a centre for Two Rocks. It was a delightful place, and I was very disturbed when I realised that there was to be no maintenance in the future. It was bad enough to lose it as a marine park; but to lose it completely because no one was prepared to keep it in good shape seemed to me to be a shocking waste of all that had gone into creating it.

Some of us tried, through various people with influence, to have the dolphin pool kept, and the children's water playground. But no one was listening. Surely we could have kept that splendid pool, cleaned it out thoroughly, fill it once more with sea water, and let the area have a swimming pool big and deep enough to allow for diving as well as swimming? But someone, somewhere, was determined to reduce everything to rubble, and so the pool was broken up and removed, and the place left to rot.

I wonder sometimes why local people didn't make a bigger fuss about this corporate vandalism.

Not long ago I decided to have a look at the park. I hadn't been in for many years; but I knew that the wire fence that was there to keep us out had a big chunk cut from it, and I ventured in. I found it a very sad experience. Overgrown with weeds and completely neglected, it was almost spooky. I left after five minutes. Whoever is responsible for it should be ashamed. Central to Two Rocks, it could be a delightful spot once more. A good clean up and then a gardener to maintain it as it should be—why not?

31

In the same year that the school opened, Derry was invited to become an examiner for the AMEB (Australian Music Examinations Board), which is located on the campus of UWA. And, as if we were not busy enough, he was also asked to review Perth music for The West Australian newspaper. This involved both of us in quite a bit of evening work—because he was not a driver it was necessary for me to go down to Perth with him, often more than once a week; and that also involved some quick change of clothes and a snack once I got home from school.

At our peak (we added it up), including the Perth Festival—which meant several concerts a week until it was over—in one particular year we did between us 160 concerts. This was after I, too, had been asked to review for The West, so that often we split up for our two concerts, and met again in a mad rush at the newspaper offices in St George's Terrace, where we wrote our reviews in about 50 minutes or less, because if we didn't they wouldn't appear the next day. It was crazy and it was the greatest fun. We heard an amazing amount of music, excellent, good, bad and indifferent, during those years, which came to an end in 1990, when Derry's health began to fail. And we made many very good friends.

Meanwhile, back in school I was beginning to sense that our tenure of the Sail Loft might be coming to an end. The America's Cup race was holding everyone's attention, sailors and land-lubbers alike, and everyone agreed that *we had to win it*. Alan Bond and his sailors were getting serious.

It would have been about 1980 when I started to plan for this next endeavour. There were a few options. One was that we should close the school. By now there was the primary school in Yanchep which would eventually become the District High School. Wanneroo Senior High School was now a fact, and many parents in the Yanchep area preferred to send their children there. We fully understood this.

But we felt there was still room for us to do the job we had started. There were always students of all ages who were not fitted for the 'big school' situation. I discussed with the teachers the possibility of continuing the school in another location, and we agreed that, if we could persuade the Shire Council (this was before Wanneroo became a city) to put up a building suitable for the school during the daytime, we would undertake to provide evening classes for the wider community.

I went to see the Shire President, Charles Searson, at the Wanneroo Council offices. I took with me a rough sketch of the kind of building I felt would serve these two purposes, and also create a meeting place for the local area. Charlie Searson looked at them for a minute, then said, 'You don't want this.'

I said, 'Oh? What do I want?'

He waved his hand vaguely. 'You want one of those Bini shells.'

I had no idea what this was. He explained: it was a kind of concrete shell that was lifted into place by having air blown into it. Once set, it could be used for a number of activities. It sounded very odd; but over the next few years Bini shells mushroomed in the Wanneroo area. It was perhaps unfortunate that they were not very successful, and they have mostly been knocked down and replaced with conventional recreation centres.

Funnily enough, I was in Jamaica visiting my daughter Helen a few years later, and I discovered a Bini shell there, on a school campus. They were invented by an Italian, Dr Bini. I wonder how many he sold.

As a result of this meeting, Mr Searson and I, together with Colin Herbert, as Yanchep Sun City's representative, went walkabout in Two Rocks to look for a suitable site. The Council had plans drawn up for the interior of the shell, which provided for classrooms and good spaces for recreation areas. We finally decided where we thought it should be—and today's Phil Renkin Centre is the long-term result of our wanderings. It was a good location, and we looked forward to making it a hive of activity.

Unfortunately, when the local folk heard that it would house the school as well as giving the wider community a central meeting place, there was uproar. The antagonism to the school had not disappeared, and this roused it again. They were not prepared to share, despite the fact that these were our own children, and that we had a very good record for general behaviour.

It was probably inevitable that, on the day the shell was to be 'blown up' and the school was allowed time to sit around and watch the operation, the power failed, and the semi-inflated shell began to sink. Desperate measures were called for. A generator was brought in to keep things going, and eventually the shell was in place, balanced on its skin that was like a huge balloon, and hopefully 'setting', rather like a jelly! It was very dramatic, and I imagine the youngsters thoroughly enjoyed the possibility that the whole thing would simply collapse.

We looked forward to spending our days in it. But the fuss about the school was so furious that in the end we were not allowed to take up residence as we had hoped. I had to start again.

I still find it odd that there has never been any recognition of the fact that the Bini shell was provided for this community because of the Community School's forward thinking. There had been no intention up to that point for a recreation centre to be provided for Yanchep/Two Rocks.

It looked as if we should look outside Yanchep for our next school site. We negotiated with the Council, and eventually we were offered the temporary use of the recreation centre building in Wanneroo, down by the lake. This was a large open-plan space which we could use well enough for the short term, and we had to look around for something more permanent.

Much of that time has disappeared from my memory; I suspect it was all too traumatic. But I do recall masses of gear having to be transported, and I was deeply thankful for a tolerant and energetic group of teachers who took it upon themselves to make a success of this interim arrangement.

The move took place in 1981. Half a decade of my life had been spent in the Sail Loft, and I was sorry to leave it.

But it was necessary to find somewhere in which to make our new home; and we looked at the fairly new development called Wangara, a trading estate that had been built on what had previously been vineyards. There were empty factory units there; after much negotiation, and wondering if we could afford it and whether it would serve as school premises, we moved into a unit on Baretta Road.

It served us well. It was a large open space, which is what we had been used to, and it took the numbers of children we then had quite easily. One reason for looking towards Wanneroo had been the interesting fact that, slowly over the years, a number of our students were coming from that area. It seemed sensible to be where the numbers were.

It is arguable that, when we knew our tenancy of the Sail Loft was to end, we should perhaps have closed the school down. After all, there was now adequate schooling available for every age group in Yanchep/Two Rocks. But there still wasn't anywhere that would deal, as we felt it should be done, with the students who simply didn't fit in to the 'normal' pattern. This included Aboriginal children, and during our tenure in Two Rocks we had had several of these students.

I feel very privileged that, within a couple of years of arriving in Australia, I began to work with Aboriginal families. I had no previous knowledge of what problems or benefits this might bring to the school; but they were children who were not doing well at the larger schools, and we were prepared to see how we could help.

It proved to be stimulating and sometimes difficult. But it was very worthwhile; and I have some delightful memories of the ups and downs of dealing with the kind of children I had never met before. We had a family of perhaps eight youngsters when we were at Baretta Road; they were all in the care of their grandmother because their parents were unable to look after them. She did a great job. My job, of course, was to see how we could educate them without offending their aboriginality; and I think we did, to a large extent.

It was a learning curve for all of us. One Monday none of them were in school. They hadn't returned by Wednesday, so I asked if anyone knew where they were. Yes, they had gone to a funeral. Well, in our culture this doesn't take 3 days! When they had been gone three weeks, suddenly arriving back one morning, I said, 'So where were you?'

'Had to go to a funeral, miss.'

'It took a long time.'

'Down to Harvey, miss.'

'Does that take three weeks?'

'Had to go to another one, down south.'

I realised this was a cultural thing I had not known about, and let it go.

An Aboriginal pastor who sometimes came to talk to the children said to me one day, 'Be patient with us. We're only 200 years out of the jungle!'

I hope I was always patient with them. They were lovely children. And I've often wondered what happened to them finally. Did we make a difference in their lives?

Ken Colbung, the Nyoongah elder, had started the Aboriginal school in Gnangara, and I suggested once that perhaps their grandma might prefer to send the children there. She was quite definite in her refusal. 'They've got to grow up in a white world—they've got to know how it works!' It was a good argument; and it was a salutary experience for me.

So we settled into our new home; and we made the most of it. Room dividers worked well there, and we were able to provide a fairly varied educational diet for our students. It had been an ongoing shock to me, coming from a school situation in England where behavioural problems were few and expulsion was rare, to see so many young people who had been in some way damaged by the time they were senior primary students; and I was often surprised by the numbers of early teenage boys who had been given up by their parents and former teachers. The cry of 'What can you do with him—he's fourteen!' began to annoy me. Some of these boys reacted badly when they first came to us; but I think I can claim that most of them eventually calmed down and began to see the benefits of living a more orderly life, one that might hold within itself some promise for the future.

We tried not to be 'preachy', but we did talk quite a lot about love, and the need for love in these young people's lives. Too many parents and teachers seemed to me to feel that the bringing up of a child was a matter of battling for supremacy; when we talked of love, we were not being soft—it's quite hard to love a child of any age who had just thrown books at you, which did happen to me occasionally. But there is great value in sitting down and talking with young people who have sometimes never actually held a conversation with an adult that didn't include anger or frustration. I often found their insight into what life is all about extremely fascinating—and sometimes very sad.

Looking back on my own childhood, I fully realised how fortunate I had been. Nothing really compensates if parents are not loving, or show no sign of understanding the needs of their children. Nothing much is going to help in the future if he or she has been made to feel useless. And—from the teacher's point of view—nothing is going to be easy if the child has never been taught about behaviour and decent manners and how to appreciate the needs of other children. It's unfair to expect the teacher to do all these things in the time allocated for learning.

I have sometimes wondered how many mothers (and possibly fathers) have started a child off on the wrong foot for school at the tender age of, perhaps, five, by saying 'I'll be glad when you go to school!' From day one the school is seen to be a threat in operation—and it takes a remarkable teacher to offset that first impression.

We did well enough at Wangara to be able to rent a further unit when we needed it. Every day was full on, but it was also stimulating, and in general the adults in the equation were satisfied with the situation. Judging by their attitudes, the students were enjoying it too.

We were highly regarded by the educational authorities whose job it was to place needy children. The 'need' could be anything from a broken home which resulted in putting the child in care, to behavioural problems that the department concerned felt we could handle better than a more 'normal' school. By this time we knew we had a high rate of success with children in crisis; and it was also comforting for our budget to be paid 'full fare' without having to chase an unwilling parent.

One case that I remember with satisfaction concerned an Aboriginal girl of about 14, who had been brought south from an Aboriginal settlement in the far north of the state. She had done so well in her primary schooling that they felt she would benefit from going to a state school in Perth.

Whose idea this was I cannot imagine; but once she had been brought to Perth, settled into a hostel for school children away from home, and registered in the nearest high school, it was presumably imagined that she would flourish.

It took very little time, once she arrived in the hostel where she was clearly out of her depth and unhappy, to discover that her trip to the metropolis was not going to work as they had hoped. She was brought to us in desperation, and I agreed to do what we could to help her.

I cannot even imagine what it must have been like for her. Here she was, straight off a reserve where she was with people she knew well, plonked down in a large hostel with white girls she couldn't relate to, and being expected to 'fit in'. It was never going to happen.

Our teachers kept an eye on her; and it became clear that she wasn't going to open up to us. She did no school work, spoke to no one, and was obviously miserable.

At last one of the primary teachers said that the only time she saw her joining in anything was at recess, when she would go into the primary department and enjoy playing with the small children. We decided to let her go and help the primary teachers, and see what might come of it.

We were able to call on an Aboriginal social worker; when she came I asked her to take the girl out for a walk, talk to her, try to find out what *she* wanted—something that no one in the department had asked. Then she was to write down for me what the girl had said, and we would take it from there.

Later I was handed a sheet of paper on which there was half a page of neat writing—done by the girl herself. There was nothing stupid about this child! She knew exactly what she wanted to do— go home, and work in her auntie's primary group. This seemed a very good idea to me.

I rang the department. I was asked what they could do for me. I said they could buy an airline ticket for the north of the state, take the child to the airport and see she got on the plane safely—*and never do such a dreadful thing to a child again!*

I am happy to relate that they apologised for what had happened, and as far as I know the girl was restored to her family, and went on to help auntie in the primary class.

But in spite of our combined energy and enthusiasm for what we were doing, this was becoming quite a heavy chore for me. I recall that when I first ventured into the scheme I was warned by a man who had started and run a community school that I should not do it for more than three years. After that, he said, you'll burn out.

Well, I had done about seven years, counting the nine months it had taken in 1975 to get the school up and running. For me, it was changing from a highly stimulating activity that I knew was proving successful and valuable in many ways; because the one area in which it was not successful was finance. It was becoming ever more difficult to find the money to keep going; I think we had explored every channel that might hold an unexpected glitter of gold. I was getting much too tired.

The opening of school for the beginning of 1983 proved to be too much for me. It is an object lesson for those who have pushed themselves too far—you think you can do it for another month, another week, another day. But something breaks you, and in my case it happened on the way to Wanneroo one morning. I was concerned about the financial situation, but I was expecting to carry on and solve it. Then, just before I reached Wanneroo, I suddenly exploded at the wheel of my car. I roared with anger, and burst into tears. When I got to school I was still crying; I stood helplessly, wondering what was wrong with me. Sensibly, our secretary and one of the staff sent me home.

I have no idea what Derry thought when he saw me; but I give him full credit for the next fortnight, when I alternately slept and wept and he let me, producing meals when I needed them, and making no demands that I should tell him what was the matter (one of the most irritating questions possible, when you don't know yourself what ails you.)

I never went back, except on one occasion as a visitor. The school was wound up by one of the parents who had been very much involved with us from the start; and after several weeks I began to feel almost human again.

I don't call it a breakdown, though perhaps it was. I call it a burn-out, because that was how it felt. Everything I had put into the school since the first mad idea came to me had eventually burnt away energy and imagination and the desire to keep the school going. Among the effects of this collapse was my memory for names. I'm afraid I sometimes offended people whose names I had known perfectly well while they were parents or friends of the school. It was as if the whiteboard in my brain had been cleaned with a sponge.

Slowly I got these pieces of memory back. I could look at the Sail Loft without feeling grief. And I had the reassurance that what we had done had been of value, both to individuals and the wider community. We had seen children and teenagers who had been unable to cope with school turning around and making something of themselves, and that was what it had all been about.

Three decades later I still, from time to time, meet or hear about some of the students who passed through our hands. I have been thanked, because I am still here in the district; but they have much to thank those others for, who spent time—sometimes only a few months, sometimes much longer—creating a space in which young people could feel that they really mattered. As always, underpaid and overworked; but there was an aura of goodwill that could only be healthy for children who had seen school as a threat and penance.

My sincere thanks and gratitude to all of them who, for eight years, helped to create a situation that was probably unique, not only in its location, but also in its vision for youth.

32

At this point, the conclusion of the great experiment, I am going to backtrack again.

My 'English' years had involved a considerable amount of time in church activities. Not surprising, really, with a sister who became an ordained Methodist minister, and a father who achieved the highest honour for a lay person in the world of Methodism—he was for a year the Vice-President of the Methodist Conference. I transferred to the Church of England when I was married.

When we had settled down in Yanchep I realised that there was no provision for Protestant residents. Catholic mass was celebrated on a regular basis, but that was all. I put a notice in the little local newsletter asking if there were others who would like to participate in the simplest form of worship—house meetings.

I had one answer—Vera, who became a long-time friend. Because there were no others we decided to wait, and then try again.

Our second attempt brought a small number of people together, and we began regular meetings. Vera proved to be excellent at finding speakers from many different denominations.

When the school opened a little while later, and we bought a piano, we moved our group into the Sail Loft on a Sunday morning. Over many months we progressed to a congregation of around thirty—and, more surprisingly, we also had a Sunday School of 30, which Vera ran.

Then, when we were well established and totally non-denominational, a blow fell. Vera and I were summoned to meet the Bishop and the Vicar of Wanneroo—to explain ourselves! Part of the problem seemed to be that we had not sent them any proportion of our collections. We made the point that we were not an Anglican group, nor did we take a collection unless for a special reason.

This they could not comprehend. We were then accused of being 'dangerous and schismatic women'. I felt this was going a bit far. I said we had felt a real compulsion to start this group. The Bishop said that surely, if this was a *divine* compulsion, it would have come to the clergy? I said that perhaps the clergy weren't listening. I was stunned. Anyone remember Joan of Arc? We had done no harm, and we had brought local Christians together. If we were to *ignore* sincerely held compulsions, where did that leave us?

Finally, I was given a choice: be a good, obedient Anglican woman—or I could do the other thing!

So I did. I am no longer a regular church-goer. But having had the time to think for myself, away from the rules and regulations of the church, I believe I have found a deeper spiritual faith.

Perhaps I should thank the Bishop.

33

S o it was back to what I suppose you could call 'normal'. No more rushing out in the morning to meet everyone's problems; it was probably heaven, but I have to say I don't remember much about it. What I do remember, from then on, was music! Concerts every week, sometimes more than once; Derry and I both reviewing, and it didn't matter any longer that we didn't get home until after midnight. I could lie in!

We would do this for another nine years; the system we developed was fairly sensible—Derry would send in to the West Australian a list of all the concerts in the month ahead, from student recitals at university level to major concerts with international orchestras and performers. It was stimulating and sometimes really exciting, and neither of us would have missed it for anything.

Once the list had gone in, the editorial staff would decide which ones should be reviewed: Derry did the 'biggies', generally, and I did family concerts, and on one occasion I even reviewed the reverently received Ravi Shankar playing Indian music—about which I knew absolutely nothing. I said so to the sub-editor. He said they hadn't anyone else, and I'd have to do it.

There is nothing quite like sitting and listening to something you know little about, and thinking that tomorrow morning all the Perth music-lovers who *do* know something about it will be reading what you have written.

I listened carefully; and for 50 minutes I was thoroughly intrigued as this improvisational music slowly developed from low and slow to dramatically insistent. By the interval I felt I could write something fairly worth reading—I didn't try to pretend I knew much about this style of music, but I was enthusiastic. Sadly, the second half, which I was now awaiting with interest, did not have the same effect on me. But I could appreciate music played with superb skill even if I didn't quite know what it was saying.

The other genre that had me flummoxed for a while was the contemporary music created at the university. Derry wouldn't review it! So I would go to the Callaway Auditorium wondering what I would be expected to write about this time. Much of what I heard didn't seem to make much sense, musically or otherwise; and one evening I sat and had a silent argument with myself. I was here, I had a job to do, and it was time I worked out what was blocking me.

It was the use of the word 'music', I decided. To me, 'music' implies a certain beauty and a meaning, however much one may have to search for it, and I couldn't hear it in these creations. I was trained to hear melody, harmony, rhythm and development, and I wasn't hearing them. So what did these students comprehend that I couldn't? If those four qualities were absent, what was present?

I decided that what I was listening to was in fact simply 'experimental sound'. Using electronic means as well as the tried and true instruments of the orchestra, the young musicians were simply experimenting. And once I had understood this I was able to listen, if not with great pleasure, at least with a modicum of understanding of what they were searching for.

Some of it was ridiculous. Some appealed to me. But nothing in this world of creative talent ever happens without someone breaking the mould and looking for something new.

In the more traditional world of music, we heard some wonderful concerts. Among the visitors were the Israeli, Chicago, Halle, BBC, and Japanese orchestras; and we heard chamber music names with a world resonance. We had found that Perth was not a musical desert; though it didn't at that time have a thriving youth orchestra, as some of the other states did, and we missed choral music for quite a while. The busy time was during the Perth Festival, early in the year. We could be going up and down the Wanneroo Road three or four times a week while that was on. The manager of the Concert Hall said one evening, 'We should put a double bed on the roof for you two! You seem to be here all the time'.

We heard wonderful music, and met some extremely interesting performers. At Leeuwin, down south for the open-air concert, we shared a moment, together with several others, with Sir Georg Solti; and met Michael Tilson Thomas during his brief visit. We enjoyed the concerts with WA's fine West Australia Symphony Orchestra (WASO), and became good friends with its then conductor, David Measham.

Smaller-scale music took us to York, WA's oldest inland town, for the music festival that was held every second year on Foundation weekend. The foundation of WA as a colony took place in 1829, and is now a public holiday in June. The festival was run by UWA, and once we knew what the programme included I would make a plan that would help us to cover as many of the recitals as possible.

The newspaper allowed us half a page—pretty generous, really, but only just enough to mention as many of the performers as we could get into the space. The recitals took place all over York: in private homesteads, small local halls, hotels, churches and the Town Hall, an impressive building for such a small place.

Because Derry didn't drive, I did all the outlying concerts, tearing from one to another because each lasted one hour, and I didn't want to miss too much of the next one. Meanwhile, he would be pounding the pavements of York in order not to miss the performance at a church, or hotel, or anywhere one could reach on foot. One memorable place was the converted church at Tipperary, where the recitalists sat in what had once been the tiny chancel. More recently I spent a couple of nights there and had my breakfast in it.

We had a hectic and delightful time; I recall driving down the main street and seeing him going in the opposite direction on his way to the next venue—we waved! Altogether a really fun experience, and the music was good, too! Getting all that into one review was not easy, but I think we did it creditably.

As this was happening, I was also beginning to write again. Eight years of schooling had put it in the 'too hard' basket. But it seemed that the enforced break had begun to bear fruit—I discovered once again that writing is really important to me. A flyer from a Melbourne educational publisher was asking for submissions in the genre of juvenile fiction. I decided this was for me, and began to write. The result was *The Boy from the Hulks*, aimed at early teens, a historical novel about young Lemuel, transported for a crime he didn't commit, and how he made good.

Rather to my surprise (but very much to my delight) the publishers accepted it. I felt that at last my foot was in the door, and immediately started writing a sequel: Lemuel as a young man. I was annoyed when this, *The Colonial Boys,* was not accepted. I spoke to them and asked why. They were not very forthcoming, and I was disappointed, because I had had in mind that I could write a series, following Lemuel and his family through the years, in which any young person who read them would gradually get to know the history of Australia since settlement. It was not to be.

A year or so before the 200th anniversary of that settlement, in 1988, I heard that there was a prize available for a novel that was appropriate for the celebration. I had already begun a story about an English orphanage, and a group of children in the late 1800s setting out for Australia; I thought it might make a good novel. I combined it with another idea I had had, and began writing *Dutch Point*. This was a book that required quite a lot of background of the early settlement days; but fortunately there is plenty of information available—even without the benefit of Google. I had bought a very fat book of Australian history, and I used it constantly.

My entry was, of course, rejected for the prize. I don't know who won it. But I knew I had written something readable, and I was determined.

At that time I had an agent in Sydney and she really did what she could for me, sending it around the mainstream publishers, and inevitably getting it back with their regrets. Often enough I got a letter, rather than a rejection slip, and this began to annoy me, because it tended to say, 'we liked your book, but it is not for us at this time'. I got to a situation where I wished they would simply say 'please don't send us any more rubbish!' I thought it would be more honest.

I used to take a UK writers' magazine. I must have seen a particular advertisement several times before, but on one occasion it leapt out at me. In my frustration I wrote to this private company in London, and asked what it would cost to publish my book. I had recently received a bequest from my father's estate; and I was determined to spend some of it on getting the book into print. It cost me $16000 for 1000 copies; and I still (15 years later) have copies available. 'Don't pay to have your book published,' the doomsayers repeat endlessly. But I have no regrets; they printed a very handsome book, and, based largely as it is on the Yanchep area, it continues to sell here. We should remember that many books in 'the old days' were self-published. By Dickens, for example.

Having now two books to my credit I felt justified in writing more. *The Boy from the Hulks* was published in 1994; *Dutch Point* arrived from London in 1998; over the next few years I wrote three more novels: *Coulter Valley, Klara* and *Ripple in the Reeds.*

But I was less than enchanted with the publishing systems, here and world-wide. New writers have often been told, 'If your book is worth publishing it will eventually be taken up by a publisher'. Well, let me tell you, new writers—that is not so. There are thousands (probably millions) of books being written every year that are readable and would please the reading public. It is simply not possible for the existing publishers to present them all. Look in any bookshop—the shelves are full of new books, mainly by well-known writers whose work will always bring in the dollars; and they will not be on the shelves very long before they have to go to make room for yet another batch. I know; mine were on a few bookshop shelves and did not sell.

Because I am often complimented about my books (this is the ultimate applause the writer wants) I could presumably imagine that a mainstream publisher would have taken them up and done reasonably well with them. But we all have to face the facts: commissioning editors may like our work, but if the accounting department cannot see a million dollars in it you can forget it. The creative spirit can wilt under these limitations.

All my novels went through this mill, and got nowhere. I saw another advertisement, this time for a Print-on-Demand publisher. I had no idea what this meant; but I emailed them (again in the UK) and received a reply that seemed to hold out some hope. POD is no longer new in the publishing world; but then, ten years or so ago, it was. People were as nervous of it as they had been of the old-time 'vanity publishers'. But I really liked the whole idea. Basically, it did away with the expensive business of warehousing thousands of books that might or might not be sold (thereby not cutting down trees wastefully). The author had total control of the book, which doesn't necessarily happen in the standard publishing world. And it was quick! One's precious book would be ready to sell in a couple of months; the old-time system can take two years.

Yes, the author pays to have it set up; but at much less cost than before. My last book, out in 2012, cost me about a tenth of what *Dutch* Point had cost. The benefits were that it immediately became available on Amazon or could be purchased as an e-book; and there were world-wide book fairs and all kinds of other tempting things to whet the literary appetite. Also, because the book exists on a disc, and is also capable of being sent by email, it will never go out of print. As the author, I can order my books and get a good discount; and the books are printed at the time and in the quantities that the buyer wishes. One copy or 500—it's no problem. Self-publishing has come of age and is now respectable!

The publishers are Trafford, and I now deal with the American company that at some point bought out the original set-up. It has contacts with Pearson, the giant publishing concern, and with Penguin e-books. I can order a new batch of books, and they will usually be with me in WA in two or three weeks. It's a great system, and I'm thankful I took the plunge several years ago.

It is a bonus that the product itself—the book, paper and print—is a pleasure to hold in the hand. It never looks like a cheap paperback, and it is available in soft or hard cover.

Since Derry died I have done three collections of my short stories, written over about 4 decades, and they have been well received. As long as one knows when to say 'no' if a 'special offer' comes up that one doesn't want, this is, for me at least, the way to go. Major publishers are not really interested in new writers, unless their books demonstrate the 'cutting edge'—all editors are looking for something that has never been done before and will make millions, while the average reader is looking for something recognisable at an affordable price. I feel quite delighted that I came in at the beginning of this 'new' publishing method.

Unusual for me! I normally wait until things have grown old and can be proved to be totally reliable. Something told me that POD was the publishing ideal for the future.

As I write, I have another novel in the wings, waiting for me to finish these memoirs. I started it several years ago, just before it became necessary to devote more time to Derry in his struggle with Alzheimer's Disease. In order to write effective fiction it is important to be able to get back into the mood and atmosphere one had created for the previous chapters; this is very difficult when one is looking after an invalid. So the story went on the 'back burner' until I could devote proper time to it.

I hope I shall have finished it and got it into print some time in 2014.

The most recent collection of short stories, *An Empty Bottle*, has on its cover a water colour painting of just that—an empty wine bottle. It came about because I went to San Francisco in 2010 to stay with an old friend. In his retirement Peter has created a small music publishing business, and has published two of Derry's short works, sonatas for violin and bassoon respectively. While I was in SF he took me to his watercolour class one evening. I resisted, unsuccessfully, because it was about 60 years since I had painted anything other than doors and window frames. But he remembered that I had been accepted in my last year at school for Slade School of Fine Art in London.

So I went to the class, certain that I was about to make a fool of myself. I took an empty wine bottle with me, recalling that I had once done a painting of some laboratory glassware that my art teacher was very complimentary about. Glass is notoriously tricky to put on the paper; but I was determined to go down with flags flying!

The result was the bottle on the cover of that recent book. It has been favourably commented on, and perhaps, one day when I can think of nothing else to do, I will pick up a brush again and remind myself that once *I could do it!*

The silly thing about this episode is that I had no story about an empty bottle to put in the book. So I had to sit down and create one. It seemed a bit back to front, to do the cover and then write the story, but I think it worked.

34

In early 2013 I was invited to attend the 30th anniversary celebrations of the Wanneroo Civic Choir. This is a flourishing choral group that has made strides since its inception in 1983.

It is a matter of pride to me that this excellent choir was my baby! How delightfully the baby has grown.

In those days, as the Wanneroo district was beginning to develop from a small settlement to its ultimate role as a city, many societies were coming into being. What I missed, with my musical background, was choral music. I was at a meeting where ideas were being floated, and I said I would be prepared to start a choir if anyone was interested. The idea caught on.

I was still at the school in Wangara, and this meant that we had somewhere to hold rehearsals. We called ourselves 'The Baretta Singers' after the road the school was in.

Over the years, when the school was no longer operating, the rehearsal venues changed; and after I retired as choir-mistress there were several able musicians who led the choir onward and upward. Carols at Christmas, light-hearted programmes given in many a hall—slowly the choir developed its style and competence, and in now a well-respected addition to the Wanneroo cultural scene.

I wonder if I ever expected, thirty years ago, that this group, under its later name—the Wanneroo Civic Choir—would still be a thriving body capable of presenting a fine concert to celebrate those three decades of music making. And what fun that concert was! Delightful music and moments of pure humour.

Who remembers, as I do, the evening we were having our coffee break, and there was plenty of chatter going on? Many of us were from England; suddenly a small voice piped up: 'Are there any other Australians here?' We acknowledge these days the contribution to multi-culturalism made by incoming people from many lands, but often forget that many of the attributes of modern social living have come about—music, drama, sports and (never forget the fish and chips!) food—because the immigrant British missed what they had known at home. On another occasion, when I was involved with the Limelight Theatre in Wanneroo, I became very aware of this. Practically everyone associated with that theatre at that time was British. When you come to a new homeland and there are things you deeply miss, you get on and create them for yourself.

Well, the choir that filled a gap in the Wanneroo culture is a mature body now. I am proud to be its Patron, and hope to be around for its 40th anniversary. May it continue to give pleasure to Western Australia's music-lovers for many years to come.

35

All these activities, emerging out of the demise of the school, were an indication of the kind of intensity of thinking I had needed during those administrative years. It was a flowering that I welcomed, having wondered from time to time whether I would ever be able to think like a writer again.

As a small child, sometimes allowed to use my father's typewriter, I was a real scribbler. One of the things I clearly recall writing was a play—inspired by a play I had read in one of my Christmas present books when I was about 7. My knowledge or understanding of drama was nil; but that doesn't stop a determined scribbler. I decided that I could do it.

The play I had read was about a king and queen and their daughters. The only bit I remember from it is the ending: the king is rejoicing because his daughter is to be married.

'That's one gone off; my heart is like a feather.
Come, Queen and daughters, let us sing and dance
together!'

I realised that one had to have names of the people in the play: they were there at the top of the page. So I invented several girls' names and carefully wrote them down. Then I had a sudden alarming thought: where would I find people with those names to be in my play? Obviously I had not understood the first thing about this new activity. It was enough to stop me, and the play never got written.

I dimly recall writing a Christmas play for performance in the church; my main memory is of trying to persuade the 'actors' to learn their parts. I was much later to realise that this is probably par for the course in amateur dramatics.

So we come back to the decade following the closure of Yanchep Community School. In the mid-1980s I suddenly decided that what I really wanted to do was write a play and see it on stage. But what?

By the early 1980s I had written the school's pantomime script and enjoyed doing it. But writing for children, where people are prepared to make allowances, is not quite the same as creating a work which will stand up under the critical eyes of adults.

I knew I was able to write convincing dialogue. As a short story writer in those earlier days I had discovered how important it is to develop a story through dialogue, which does two things—it opens up the character to the reader, and it should lead inevitably towards the climax of the tale. So perhaps I *could* create a drama which would make use of what I had learnt in fiction writing.

I had a lurking feeling that I would write a comedy, and I had always been told that comedy was hard to write. I agree—but if that's the way one's mind works there's not much one can do about it. So it would be a comedy. About . . . ?

Suddenly I had what I still think was an audacious and possibly idiotic idea. I could almost see Shakespeare, Hamlet completed, at its first reading. I imagined the frustration he would feel when some of the less gifted actors trampled their way through his creation, his explanations to his wife, Anne, of why he had to keep scribbling when there was so much to be done around the house. I thought it had possibilities.

As usually happens at these 'light bulb' moments, I couldn't get it out of my mind. I went to bed, and it was being played out on the dark ceiling. After a while I knew I had to get up and start writing. I think Derry grunted as I got out of bed.

After about 90 minutes I climbed back into bed and fell soundly asleep. I had written the first scene. When I awoke in the morning I hardly dared look at what I had written in the midnight hours. But I liked it; I could see it happening; I thought, yes, this was worth going on with.

The play was 'Bard', and it was read on one momentous day by the community theatre in Wanneroo, which would later become the Limelight Theatre once they had their own purpose-built building. They had agreed to put it on—at that time in the community hall at Wanneroo—and, with surprising courage, allowed me to direct it.

I had made it clear that I wanted all participants to know their lines by a certain date. I still think this is a reasonable request. But I never found a way of enforcing it—I was lucky if a few of them were reliable in this way. But in spite of all the hiccups that are lying in wait for the director, we had a ball! I thoroughly enjoyed it, and I was told by one experienced member of the cast that it had been the happiest production he had been in.

Anecdotes abound in theatre stories! I asked the cast to invent their own 'business' on stage when they were not actually speaking. One young man in a minor role decided to wander around 'Shakespeare's house' looking at the pictures on the walls. He ended up at a 'mock' mirror, staring at himself rather pompously. Then he carefully 'popped' an imaginary pimple before returning to the script! It went down well.

The men found it difficult to get used to wearing tights, but it was necessary. One of them, playing an elderly actor, turned his back at rehearsal, and revealed strands of thick knitting wool running down inside his wrinkly tights—perfect, and very amusing, varicose veins.

It was performed on several nights in 1988, and it had an interesting result. One member of the reading group, taking the part of Shakespeare, was a valuable 'back-stage' worker. But he was permanently in a wheelchair, and so could not be cast in plays. I was very taken by his voice, which was so appealing, and made so much sense of 'my' words, that it seemed a great pity that he could never use that ability on stage.

Once 'Bard' was behind us, I began to wonder if he would even want to be on stage. When it was put to him he was delighted.

And fortunately I had had an idea—the wheelchair would be a part of the character. And I wrote another comedy, *'Ultimo'*, in which he was a puppet-maker. This gave us the opportunity to create a 'magical' scene, with puppets kindly loaned to us by the Fremantle puppet theatre. It was fun to do, and it was put on stage in the new Limelight Theatre in 1989.

In that same decade or so I also wrote a few one-act plays; and one of these, *'That's Showbiz'*, was performed at a community theatre awards night in Perth. Ray Omodei, the adjudicator, awarded it a certificate as 'the best new pure comedy', which was deeply gratifying.

A while later I received a call from a community theatre company in New South Wales, suggesting that a short story of mine that appeared in Australian Women's Weekly would make a good one-act play. I couldn't see it myself, but told them I had a few one-act plays which might be useful to them.

Eventually they did a run of my plays, including *'That's Showbiz!'*, and I gather they went down quite well with their audiences.

Another one-act comedy that won an award was written for teenagers: *I want my mummy*. This was performed by a youth drama group in Bunbury. It is set in Ancient Egypt, and the title refers to the mummy of Tutankamun. Since those days I have written several more full-length comedies; but the opportunity for staging them has not been there. One day, perhaps! The important thing is always that one should 'have a go'. If there is an idea burning in the brain, get it out on paper.

We were coming into the time when Derry would require a lot of attention. So it was encouraging to have a rather odd and totally unexpected phone call one day. I had been selling short stories to a South African magazine; this caller had a very foreign voice, and asked if I was 'Miss Rotwell'. I said I was.

The lady told me she had read my stories in the South African magazine, and that she was from Dubai. I asked her to repeat that: it didn't sound likely. But it was so, she was calling from a magazine in Dubai which would like to buy my short stories. She hastened to say they couldn't buy any with alcohol or adultery in them! I said I didn't write that kind of story. But I read through a few of the available ones, and was surprised how many times people raised glasses of wine to each other; and, more surprisingly, how many very delicate indications of naughty goings-on I had included. I was very careful which tales I sent to them.

So for a while I was selling internationally.

36

Books are written about diseases, and Alzheimer's Disease has, I'm sure, more than its fair share of book space. We are told that if we keep our brains active we may be able to avoid this tormenting illness. I think this is wishful thinking. I shall never know what triggered it off in Derry's brain, which had been active—examining music students for the AMEB; writing Perth music reviews for, first, the *West Australian Newspaper* and then, for two years, *The Australian*—until he was about 77. Who can tell? Perhaps his breakdown in 1967 had something to do with it; perhaps it was wrapped up in his personality; or maybe his war service and the stress of losing his first wife, Nancy, so soon was partly responsible.

The thing creeps up on one slowly. Every carer for this disease will have a slightly different story to tell. I noticed, around 1988, that he was beginning to behave like an old man—as he sat writing his reviews at the newspaper his head would be shaking slightly. I can remember saying, 'Don't do that! It makes you look old.' But since he didn't know he was doing it my remarks had no effect. To me, it looked as if he was doing it on purpose.

Then, occasionally, he would get stuck with what he wanted to say. I would be typing my review, if I had been to another concert, while he was writing his in longhand so that I could type it on to the copy paper. Obviously, if I hadn't heard what had gone on at his concert I couldn't help him; but increasingly, if we had both been to the same venue, I would find myself suggesting what he might write. After all, we were under pressure, and he wasn't getting any younger—but if the reviews were not delivered to the sub-editors by 11 pm they wouldn't get into the paper the next day.

I was also disturbed about how he was coping with his other reports, for the AMEB. He was a highly valuable and respected examiner, and I didn't want him to go out under a cloud because he had messed up someone's marks. I suggested that it was time to pack it all in and have a bit of rest for both of us.

Added to this was the fact that the newspaper was beginning to cut down our 'bookings'. They felt, perhaps, that a change was necessary—I don't believe we had fallen down on the job. But it was certainly becoming more difficult to cope with the constant driving to Perth, and I was concerned about him; though there was nothing to say at that stage that his problems were anything more than advancing years.

Then two things happened—not suddenly, this is an insidious disease that creeps up on you. The first was one that perhaps only I could have noticed. We played piano music quite often— arrangements for two pianos of concertos (he played the solo part, I was the 'orchestra'), and other music that had been arranged for our two instruments. It was one of our retirement pleasures. We were playing some Bach or Handel—I haven't checked which composer, but it was either a Brandenburg Concerto or a Concerto Grosso—and we came to what I called 'a twiddly bit'. It was slightly complicated to count, consisting of semi- and demi-semi-quavers— something that I might have had to look at fairly carefully first time round, but which Derry, with his great ability for reading and counting twiddly bits, should have been able to play almost in his sleep. But he couldn't get it right at first, and later was again unable to remember how it was supposed to go.

We stopped, and I said, 'No, it goes like this,' and played it to him. He got it after a couple of false starts; but I was really surprised. I could not recall a single instance in all the time I had known him when a rhythm had fazed him. Again, I told myself it was part of ageing.

The second surprise was when he was doing our tax returns. He had always done these, and since there had been no complaints

321

from the tax office I assumed that he got them right. But when tax time came again, this time, I saw him struggling with the figures. Like so many musicians, he was good at mathematics. Now, it seemed as if he couldn't understand what happened to the totals when he subtracted one from the other.

I think it was around that time that I began to wonder if there something more than age affecting him. It was 1990, and I decided that it was now past the time for retiring. He was 75, I was 61. I put my foot down fairly firmly and said that we were not doing any more reviewing, he was not doing any more examining, and we were going to take thing easy for a change. To my slight surprise he agreed.

Then he was rung by a friend who had been reviewing for *The Australian* and was now returning to do the job we had been doing at *The West*. Would Derek like to take over reviewing for *The Australian*. I said I didn't think so; but being a good wife I went and asked him. To my alarm he said yes, he would like to do that. And so we started again, against my wishes, on the musical merry-go-round. I suggested that he and I should share a by-line, so that I could also do concerts; my motive was really because I could see that he might not be able to write effectively, after the experience at *The West*. But the editor we spoke to said no, just Derek.

There wasn't quite the same pressure this time. After a Saturday concert we could go straight home and write the review up the next day and ring it through to Sydney. But it was soon clear that this was going to be very difficult. We would sit down, Derry with notes he had made, I at the keyboard waiting for him to dictate, and he would sit there, unable to think how to start. I waited; after a while I would say, 'How do you want to begin this?' and he would hum and hah, and in the end I would suggest an opening sentence. He would say 'Yes, that's right! Good! Put it down.'

Then another sentence; and another. In the two years he sent reviews in to the newspaper neither he nor the editor ever realised that I was writing them. I must have used female low cunning, because Derry seemed quite happy in the belief that he was doing it. I was simply concerned that he would not be able to cope if he lost the job through inability. Finally, I told him it was over and that he was to let the newspaper know that he was now retiring—properly! It was 1992, and he was 77. Enough was enough.

From then on it was downhill, though so slowly that it was difficult to notice it unless one looked back to how he had been 6 months or a year ago. Two decades later I really don't remember exactly what his progress was like. It was simply something that we had to get through somehow or other; and I began to discover the associations and people that could help us.

Perhaps one of the most surprising things about this time was that, unlike many Alzheimer's sufferers, he became very quiet; it seemed to me that I had lost the tiger—I always described him as 'volatile', a polite way of saying he could be explosive—and gained a pussycat. It was a great help in a difficult situation that he was so, and also that he did not become a wanderer. The opposite, in fact. He just wanted to be here at home, with me. So many victims of this cruel disease have to be put into nursing home care because their families cannot cope with their outbursts and their tendency to find any unlocked door and go through it. So, even though it was a long and emotionally testing time for both of us, we were able for several years to enjoy doing things together. We became known in the cafés of Yanchep and Two Rocks. I believe in one we were known as 'orange juice and flat white', because that was our regular order. (Derry was 'orange juice'!)

It sounds strange to say that, in the midst of such traumas, we were quite happy. His sense of humour remained with him for a long time, which was a tremendous blessing. There was no way to tell how long this was going to last, and it simply became our way of life. I was, from time to time, thankful that I was 14 years younger than he was—if we had been the same age it would have been doubly difficult to cope with.

The doctor diagnosed Alzheimer's at some point in all this and we were sent to a specialist. He told me what was usual in such cases, demonstrating it on a whiteboard on the wall while

Derry was elsewhere being tested. The board was divided into three sections. 'From what you tell me,' said the specialist, 'and what I have observed, it is clearly Alzheimer's. The normal progress is about nine years, and we see it as three and three and three.' He gestured to the board. 'I think your husband is probably just about here,' and touched the bottom third. Then he turned to me and said, 'How long do you think he has been like this?'

It was then about 2003. I said, 'About fifteen years.'

'Ah,' he said. 'Five—and five—and five.' That was the point at which I lost faith in diagnoses. It seemed so unscientific. And we didn't go back.

Derry was never told what the problem was. By the time he might have seriously wanted to know he would not have been able to remember what he was told. Whether he ever suspected, I have no idea. It never seemed important that he should be able to say 'I have Alzheimer's Disease.' And since there was no cure, and I didn't want him constantly bothered by people, because this would only have worried him, we got on without anything beyond some medications from our own doctor, and regular carers.

He had had a heart problem a few years before, which was nicely under control by now. Ventricular tachycardia first, and then, a couple of years later, atrial fibrillation. He had the necessary tests in hospital, and was so well medicated that they never needed to change it right up to the end. He was basically a very healthy man physically, and had always had little time for illness.

So we embarked on a journey for which no one can be really prepared. It is difficult to recall details of a period like that, because one doesn't want to dwell on the negative aspects at the time. But now and then I would make notes about his condition and how it was affecting us. The Alzheimer's Association were very helpful, as were the Silver Chain nurses, who made it possible for me to keep him at home. I promised him that I would do this, although I was constantly urged to 'get him into a nursing home—you can't manage him in this condition'. But I knew I could; I stuck to it that nursing homes were out of the question. It was all very well-meaning, but it wasn't what I wanted. Constant praise for the fact that I was looking after him was all very well, but it was misplaced. As far as I was concerned, 'in sickness and in health' really meant what it said; I assured all the well-wishers that I would know when the time came to make a change—and it wasn't now!

Gradually he began to forget the names of people he knew well, and then he began to forget the people themselves. He was always very courteous when we had visitors—because I was very much tied to the house I liked to have friends in when possible. He would say, 'How are you? How nice to see you!' and then, when they left, he would say, 'Do we know them?' This is quite distressing when they are friends of long standing; I was grateful that so many of these nice people were able to cope with him so gracefully.

He became noisy at night, groaning in his sleep. I would wake him up and ask him to be quiet, and he usually apologised, went to sleep and started again. Then he began kicking the base of the bed with one foot; this made it impossible for me to get to sleep, and eventually I bought a single bed which I managed to fit in at the end of our double bed. Nights became more disturbed, and it was not unusual for me to have only a very few hours of sleep. I found that one can survive this!

I kept a note of one day six months before he died. When I read it now I can hardly believe it happened. It has a surreal quality.

Friday evening: D very concerned about break-ins—wanted bedroom door closed, light on, woke me 6 times to check on door etc.

Saturday: all day trying to plan trip back to 'Yorkshire', not England, to see parents and Forest Hall. I explained that parents are gone, sold up to go to Dorking, died. No good! D determined to go.

Saturday night: about 4 hours sleep. 5 am up. Forgotten more or less about trip, not sure who I am or where our home is, v. polite and cheerful—surprised to see my car is just like 'theirs', my handbag just like his wife's. Went for drive, home for lunch. Complete flop in afternoon, deep depression overwhelmed by awareness that he had to get something unspecified to people whose address, name, phone no. he didn't know—would I find it?

Endless discussion. Non-stop talk for hours. Couldn't convince him that I couldn't help without info. Dreadful day.

Evening: agreed that 'they' were causing great hurt to both of us—would forget about them. Thought he had been going to see his parents.

Was 'seeing' people everywhere—garden during day, in lounge in evening. 6 at one point including small children. This continued on and off.

Still unsure of where his home is. But seems to know who I am.

Went to bed in two bad moods at 11 pm. 11.30 he got up to go 'downstairs', so I had to go too. 12.45 am and we are still sitting in the lounge and he shows no sign of going to bed! Not going to be a good night, I fear. But quite cheerful.

Bed suggested by me at 1.45 am. D said he would ask his mother what she thought about it, and went off to look for her!! But does say he hasn't seen her for a couple of days. Woke me at 4 am by trying to open front door—was going to get ready for 'them'. Finally, after some drama, got him to bed—we slept until 8.40.

During Sunday he twice said he would kill himself.

It's strange to say that this became normal for us.

Now and then he was quite sensible. One evening, at bedtime, about 4 months before he died, he suddenly said, 'Once I was a clever fellow in my way, and now I'm nothing'. Those are the moments that break your heart.

Because I am blessed with a quirky sense of humour, these dark moments would sometimes appeal to whatever it is that makes us laugh.

Wanted to paint 6 'things'. Didn't know what they were. Got quite peevish. I pointed out 'no paint, no brushes, and we haven't painted anything for years'. Said he had done quite a lot of painting in the past year. Wanted a second cup of hot choc, but let it get too cold. I warmed it, suggested he should drink it. He said, 'no, it's for painting'. I said no one paints with hot choc. He said yes they do.

326

Wanted to go to bed. Immediately in bed wanted to do his painting. I gave up and played Free Cell!

It wasn't all grim. Nine months before his death, Derry wanted to play the piano. This happened occasionally, and I was finding it very hard to listen to the fumblings and mistakes of this man whose piano playing had once been so excellent. Because his eyes were so bad by now that he couldn't read music (and of course his memory for it had almost gone) I had suggested that he should improvise. I remember saying, 'Bach was a great improviser—why don't you do the same?'

On this occasion, it was fortuitous that I had a good microphone set-up in the studio. I had been recording some of my short stories. As he sat down I switched the mike on. I am so thankful I did. Without the limitations of printed music he began to play, big, strong chords that made real sense at a time when his conversation often did not. He modulated without any difficulty; he developed the theme, and his hands were as strong on the keys as they had been long before. I was deeply moved.

Twice more this happened. Once was about 6 weeks before he died, when I had two visitors over for lunch. I asked him if he would like to play for them, and he said he would, in that slightly vacant but always courteous way he then had. We helped him to the piano; and once again he played with a power one would not have suspected he still had. My visitors were, as they said, gob-smacked! So was I.

A couple of weeks before Derry's death, Keith and his family were with us. I asked if he wanted to play for Keith, and he said 'all right'. By now he was extremely frail, but we got him to the piano and he sat down. To our surprise he played very quick music that required good finger-work, and there was no hesitation. It was not like the big chords of the previous occasions; and it lasted for a very short time, though we asked him to play a bit more, and he did so. It was astonishing that such memories of the act of piano playing should still be somewhere there in that confused, failing brain.

Later that day, we were all together in the lounge. Derry was sitting in his chair, but mentally far from us; hard to tell whether he knew we were there or not. Carl, Keith's son, a fine jazz guitarist, was standing beside me, watching his grandfather; he said something that he would not expect to be so memorable for me: 'He was the man, wasn't he? He gave us the music'.

And indeed he was: and indeed he did! His legacy of music is still there, running through the family in diverse ways. I think he would be pleased about that. *I* was very pleased and thankful for myself that Keith saw him in that final stage—the support that comes with shared memories is so important in a family.

Once I knew there was only one way out of this problem I started to make plans. I didn't want to have to do everything in a rush at the last minute. He was going to die—the doctor thought it would be about two to four months—and there would be plenty to arrange once it happened. I put on the computer a list of the departments and so on that I would have to notify, complete with addresses; and the people who would want to know.

I planned his funeral. I knew he would not want it to be a badly arranged affair—his planning for concerts had always been meticulously carried out, and I wanted to do the same for him on this very special occasion. I thought it through carefully, and came to the decision that he would not have wanted eulogies. These, to my mind, fall into three classes: someone trying to tell funny stories about the departed; or family members choking back tears; or someone who hardly knew the deceased giving out incorrect information about their lives. We didn't need any of those.

In the end I decided the best way to do it was to write his biography to fill an A4 page, and give it to people as they arrived for the service, together with the service sheet. During the opening music they would have time to read about him; and as most of them would not know anything about his early days it seemed a sensible way to let them find out. On the other side of the page I put a facsimile of the first page of his violin sonata. It was printed out on slightly thicker paper than usual, pale beige rather than white, and I felt it looked dignified and yet interesting.

So I was prepared for the inevitable. My lists of names proved invaluable. We had discussed the question of burial versus cremation, and were both quite certain we wanted the latter. I was as ready as I could be.

It was important to me that I should not have anything to regret afterwards. I have seen the effects on families when they look back and say 'if only'. Because I would keep him at home, if possible, until the end, there would not be the lasting regret that so many feel. And in spite of what everyone seemed to be telling me, I *was* coping, and I knew I could go on coping as long as his condition didn't make it impossible.

In the days after Keith and his family left we returned to our peaceful existence; Christmas was coming, and as it would certainly be his last I wanted it to be as pleasant as possible for him. We had our 59th wedding anniversary on December 18th, and he was just about conscious of the fact, even if only briefly. A few days before, he was sitting in his recliner chair as I sat beside him. After a while he slowly turned and looked at me and said something that made me think he didn't know me.

I said, 'Do you know who I am?' He regarded me for a moment then said, 'I don't think I've ever seen you before in my life.' I smiled at him and said, 'That's odd, because I am your wife.'

'Well,' he said, 'that's strange. That's exactly what a woman said to me a few weeks ago.'

'That was me.' This seemed to upset him. I asked him, 'Do you know how long we've been married?'

He shook his head, very confused. 'About—two years?'

'Fifty-nine years,' I said; and he looked down at the ground, clearly distressed.

'Oh—that's a long time.' I agreed. It certainly was!

But it was coming to an end. That weekend things changed radically. One evening I was about to get him to bed when something happened to him; perhaps a slight stroke, or something in that much-damaged brain seizing up. I would normally get him out of his chair into the wheelchair, take him to the bathroom, then to the bedroom and get him to bed.

This time wasn't like that. It was as if suddenly his arms and legs were made of wood, and it became impossible to lift him upright. He grew frightened, and flailed out at me. I couldn't think what to do. I was very lucky that my friend Rosemary, who lived next door, was a nurse. I rang her and asked her if she could help me to get him to bed. But even with two women who were used to lifting ailing bodies, we couldn't do it at first. He became really abusive in his fear, unable to stand, and it was impossible for quite a while to move him into the wheelchair. He was rigid. What normally took me about half an hour from chair to bed took us an hour and a half. But finally he was in bed, and we thankfully went back into the lounge room, sat down, exhausted, looked at each other—and laughed! It's the best thing to do at moments of despair. I thoroughly recommend it.

I had always said that I would know when the time had come for serious help; and this was it. It was fortuitous, and wonderful for me, that a nursing home had opened in Yanchep only six weeks earlier; I thank God that I had resisted putting him in elsewhere for so long, because Bethanie Beachside was only a 4-minute drive away. All the alternatives would have had me travelling up and down the Wanneroo Road day after day. I felt blessed.

Fiona came; and we arranged with the nursing home that I would bring him in on the following Wednesday, December 19th. I asked the Silver Chain nurse to come with us, and so we set off for the last time from home.

It is either a failing or a blessing that my family seems to see bizarre humour in the most trying situations. Thank goodness for it! That 4-minute ride, once we had managed to get him and his rigid legs into the car (I don't remember why we didn't arrange for an ambulance) was all too soon over, and we were trying to get him out at the other end. The nurse went to find a wheelchair, and I started to lift his legs so that he could turn enough to get out of the car. Fiona went into the driver's seat, and started to push him from behind. When we finally got home, not a little distraught at the way events had gone, she said, 'While we were trying to get him out I could only think of the time Pooh got stuck in the rabbit hole, and everyone was trying to push him through'.

Once inside, we took him to the lounge room, where there were several elderly people staring rather blankly at a TV screen. I suddenly wondered if I was doing the right thing for him. Surely he wasn't like them? Then he started banging his fist, quite deliberately, on the table in front of him. It had a formica top with little black marks in the pattern, and he seemed to be trying to hit them. I couldn't think what he was doing. Fiona thought he was trying to kill flies! So—yes, he probably was in the right place. But it was very hard to leave him there.

I can remember almost nothing about that Christmas. I think Fiona must have done most of it. I spent a lot of time at the home, and was distressed that he was very noisy and that there seemed to be nothing anyone could do about it. I doubt if he knew he was doing it. Until his doctor prescribed something to calm him he was going to be a noisy patient. At last, once I had seen the doctor, they were able to give him morphine, and he became more peaceful.

Once Christmas was over I fell into a sort of rhythm; but it was to be short-lived. I invited two friends to come for coffee on the morning of the 28th, but asked them to be there by 10 am because I had to be at the home before 11, when they would hopefully have completed the morning chores. As the car drove into the front yard the phone rang; it was what I didn't want to hear. My visitors were greeted at the door with 'He's gone!'

It was good to have them there. They took me to Bethanie and stayed with me, made cups of tea, and generally supported me. Derry looked to me like an Egyptian mummy, and I reminded myself that he was, after all, 92. The end of an era for him, and for me.

My only real regrets over all this are that I wasn't with him that last night, and that if I had known he would only be there for 9 days I would have kept him at home and brought in two full-time nurses to look after him. I could have stayed, if I had known that the end was so close. There was another bed in his room, and I wished that I had used it and been with him for the final moments. But I knew that I had done as much as anyone could for him, and put up with difficulties that most people seemed to think were insuperable. I don't know who it was that said 'love will find a way', but I think it's true. After 59 years of a marriage that was not always easy, we still loved each other deeply, even though his love was sometimes obscured by clouds as his brain deteriorated. And that love is always a blessing.

During those final months he would sometimes say, 'Oh, darling, I do love you'. And I would say, 'Thank you, that's lovely. I love you too.' The fact that he would say the same thing in exactly the same tone of voice about ten times in the next hour didn't change the fact that he really meant it. I used to think of the millions of women around the world whose husbands never tell them that they are loved. I knew I was!

What do you do in the afternoon of the day your husband dies? I had rung Valerie, and she came round as soon as she could. It seemed to me that one should do something very meaningful on such a meaningful day, but I couldn't think what. I was feeling quite high, knowing that I had been released from an impossible situation, just as he had; but there were hours of the day left, and I didn't know how to fill them. I would be very busy in that inevitable 'clean-up' mode very soon; but Valerie asked what I would like to do, and I suddenly knew that I wanted to be in the National Park. It was a place we had both loved, and I felt almost as if I would be near Derry there.

So we went to the park; and we bought two bottles of lemonade and sat and drank them on a bench in front of the Yanchep Inn. How many coffees had Derry and I drunk there, sitting on the front terrace and watching the kangaroos on the lawn?

Fiona came back from their family holiday in Dongara, and my new life began.

37

Considering that we had been married so long, and that Derry had been a part of my life since he arrived in Dorking in 1945, I am sometimes surprised at how easily I moved into that new life. My decision that the mourning time had been while he was slowly leaving me had been a good one. I have never felt deep grief following his death, though I miss him daily, and feel especially near to him when I am listening to music—more particularly when I play the CDs of his performances in England or his compositions in the UK and in Perth. I have wept, sometimes daily, because he was no longer with me; but I felt so very thankful that he had lived a long, active and productive life in spite of his 1967 breakdown and the later Alzheimer's. I was always grateful for having our large family—though I think it sometimes surprised him to think that he, an only child with few relatives, had six offspring!

I regretted the fact that his personality, upbringing and the hidden trauma of his war service had led him all too often into temper outbursts that were distressing, but also puzzling. I have often wished that it had been more obvious to me that his anger was usually based on fear—as if he felt things getting out of his control, and didn't know how to stop it.

But our latter days had been loving and friendly, and that is a blessing. My memories of him are warm and happy; he was a very unusual man, with wonderful gifts, especially in the way he was able to give to one generation after another of school students a love of choral music that would live with them for a lifetime.

Death brings all kinds of responsibility with it, and I was going to be busy for a while sorting out the paperwork. The first item, of course, was the funeral. On the day following his death there was a knock at the door. A young woman stood there— the representative of the funeral directors I had chosen. She was wearing an appropriate expression for the occasion—but I wasn't! I was still very high. She said the usual 'sorry for your loss', and I brought her into the garden room, where Fiona and I prepared to plan this final service for Derry.

It's odd to have to be so practical over something that can be both distressing and mystical. We went through a book full of glossy pictures of flowers and coffins; I really felt I wasn't actually there for much of it, and the young woman probably thought I was being difficult on purpose. It just seemed so strange to be asked what kind of coffin I wanted for the dear departed. (Though thankfully she never referred to him in those words).

As I was looking through these ornate creations for disguising the reality of the aftermath of death, I caught sight of the fact that they were all made of jarrah. All at once I had the thought that all over Australia people were being cremated in coffins made of a wood that we know is under threat; and the idea made me suddenly angry.

I said, 'Is the coffin burnt as well as the body?'

She said, 'Oh, yes.'

I said, 'Well, that's dreadful! All that lovely wood being burnt!'

She stared at me. 'Well—we do have environmentally friendly ones.' So we turned the page, and there were what looked to me to be identical coffins, equally polished, equally impressive—but about half the price, and made of replaceable timber. I knew he would be pleased about the price, even if he wasn't too worried about the destruction of jarrah forests.

After the funeral one guest came to me and said, 'That was a beautiful coffin.' I said, 'Yes—and it was environmentally friendly!'

So, coffin and flowers chosen, young woman off with all the necessary pieces of paper signed, what next? Because my family members were spread around the country and needed time to arrange their journeys west, I decided to have the ceremony on January 10th. It was to be at Pinnaroo crematorium, and I had ordered a double session—one in the chapel, and one in the lounge next door so that people could meet over a cuppa, and either talk about Derry or not as they wished. The Rev Jeremy James, with whom we had become good friends during his time as rector in Yanchep, was to officiate, and I had chosen the music with great care. The Wanneroo Civic Choir—my baby from a quarter of a century ago—attended to help with the singing of a hymn; and we arrived for a 2 pm service in this beautifully kept place, where the kangaroos still roam in the bush.

But about ten minutes before we left home I was rung by my young lady who was in charge of the occasion. The crematorium's computer had 'gone down', and when it came up again I had lost the second booking. No lounge for our cuppas! They were deeply apologetic, but said that we could have our get-together in the café, and they wouldn't charge us for the refreshments. As these turned out to be cups of tea and coffee plus a few plates of biscuits I didn't feel this was ultimately a great concession. But with ten minutes to go there wasn't much I could do.

We were welcomed by quite a crowd of people, many of whom I hadn't seen for a long while. I was very touched by their good wishes and condolences. The outpouring of affection at such occasions is very strengthening. At 2 pm my young lady said it was time to go into the chapel: The Family first (she spoke in capitals), and the hoi-poloi presumably afterwards. I had arranged for the coffin to be in place before we entered—watching a coffin being carried in always makes me nervous in case anyone trips up. Unfortunately, the coffin wasn't there. I turned to my escort and said, 'Where is it?' At that moment a white hearse drew up (I had asked for white; in the mood I was in I would probably have accepted a safari vehicle with zebra stripes), and three very distracted people lifted the coffin on to a trestle and hurried it into the chapel. It wasn't how I had expected it to be. My young lady looked distraught and was stammering apologies.

Once the coffin was in place we followed it in and sat in our appointed places. I was very pleased with the service; the music sounded excellent and I knew that Derry would have been pleased, too. Only one more slight hiccup occurred during the service: at that very solemn moment when the coffin leaves and you begin to realise that it is indeed over, he's gone, the mechanism that conveys it within the catafalque, down and out of sight, suddenly got up speed, and several people mentioned that he seemed to have left us very swiftly. I don't know why it happened; but it was suggested Derry had got a bit bored with the final moments and managed it himself. Certainly he wasn't one to enjoy standing around.

On the subject of that word *catafalque*: while we were planning everything with my young woman I was puzzled by a word she kept using. It sounded like *catapult*, but I knew it couldn't be. I had always thought of the place where a coffin rested as a bier. All at once I realised that the word was *catafalque*. I was thankful. The idea of Derry being catapulted out of the chapel was too bizarre even for me.

We had a very pleasant tea party, in spite of being in the wrong place. The scenery there is delightful. And there are only two things more that are worth recording. One was the phone call some days later to ask if everything had been satisfactory for me. I said no, and told them about the few things that had gone wrong. They apologised and asked if there was some way they could make it up to me. I said, yes, they could reduce the cost! After a while they rang back and offered me 10% off. Derry would have appreciated that.

The second was when I went, some weeks later, to collect his ashes. We were going to have a small ceremony of our own, and scatter them. At the crematorium I had to sign papers, and eventually the ashes were brought to me. I had never seen an urn, but had expected something of the kind. But they were presented to me in a rather up-market carrier bag with a rectangular cardboard box inside. I gazed at it for a moment. It's hard to get emotional about a carrier bag, even an up-market one. The woman who gave it to me wore that 'funeral director's' expression. I felt quite light-headed.

'How bizarre,' I said, 'to take one's husband home in a carrier bag!' It was a moment I felt would have been appropriate delivered in a Dame Edith Evans voice. The woman stared at me and said nothing. I don't know if she was shocked, or whether she was used to dealing with demented widows.

We scattered him, not far from home, sometime in April. It was over, and I was preparing to go on a memorable journey. Members of the old students' association at Dorking Grammar School (as it was when we were there: now it's The Ashcombe) wanted to have a memorial service for Derry; and I wanted to be there. In the years during which I looked after Derry I seldom went anywhere further than the nearest shopping centres; now I was going to travel the world! I was looking forward to it, but I was a bit apprehensive. I thought I could manage myself so far from home, but there were moments when I doubted.

Still, once the tickets have been bought and reservations made one can only go forward. I planned it carefully so that I could stay with as many old friends as possible in the time; and I knew that there were several people in the UK who were looking forward to seeing me again after so many years away.

I would leave home at the beginning of June, and planned to come home in November. It was my new life about to begin.

38

T his was the first time (and may well be the only time) I have travelled in business class on a plane. I recommend it: comfortable seats with leg room, and personal attention from the cabin staff.

But it's still a long flight.

My five months in the UK were well worked out. I would be going the length and breadth of the country, something that one rarely does when one lives there. I stayed at first near Chichester with Annabelle and Richard—for several days we were able to have breakfast in their garden because it was so warm. I had booked in at the White Horse Hotel in Dorking (another thing one doesn't often do when living there; if you've got a home to go to you don't stay in local hotels), just for the weekend when the memorial service was arranged. My room was up a winding stair, I seem to recall; and Rosemary joined me on her arrival.

My memories of that service are recorded on a DVD. But I would hardly need it to remind me of what a wonderful occasion it was. St Martin's Church is large, and it is where we had our very special carol services each Christmas. Then, the church would be full to the doors, and I have to admit that Christmas has never been quite the same since those days. On this occasion it was less full; but as I looked down the nave I saw people I had never thought to see again, certainly not once I had emigrated.

We left England in April 1974. From that day I don't believe Derry ever gave that part of his life much thought. He'd done it, and it was over. He only looked ahead. Once we were established in

Yanchep, and living a new life, he hardly ever mentioned anything about Dorking or the school or anything else worth recalling.

Yet here were perhaps a hundred or more people from his past, most of them students from his teaching life, and they had come because they wanted to acknowledge what he had given them all those years ago: an abiding love of choral music, and the ability to sing it. The youngest of them had to be at least nearing fifty; and there were some of my own contemporaries there, which made them anything from 70 to 80+. He had never kept in touch with anyone—I did that. He didn't talk about them; and by the time he was deeply into Alzheimer's he simply didn't remember anything about them.

Rosemary led the service, with assistance from The Venerable Tom Walker. The title doesn't sum up the man! I recall him, when I was a prefect, as a mischievous small boy; but he created prayers for that service that I hope I shall never forget. It was all beautifully designed as a very personal act of thanks to Derry for his influence on their lives. I felt very proud of him, and immensely pleased that these old friends had wanted to do him such honour in a place where he had been very happy.

The reception at the White Horse afterwards was quite a remarkable gathering of people whose only point of contact was that they, and I, had all been students at the same school. It convinced me that Dorking Grammar School, over the years, had done us all proud. Countless past students have had distinguished careers in all kinds of situations and in many parts of the world.

I was to be guest of honour at the AGM lunch later in the year, and I hoped that somewhere Derry was able to know that he had been well remembered and excellently farewelled by the people to whom he had given so much.

It was time to begin my travels.

Rosemary and I began the journey to her home in Derbyshire. We went via Northolt so that we could see the church we had been brought up in. It had special meaning for me: at the age of four, in 1933, I was present at the opening ceremony, where I 'helped' to lay one of the foundation stones. I can just remember walking forward, holding someone's hand (I think it was my father's), and tapping the stone.

It was fortuitous in the extreme that we went on that day in mid-June. The place had changed radically; where I remembered fields were now suburban dwellings and shops; but the church was still recognisable. There was a man doing some renovation round the side of the building and we told him what our interest in the place was; he immediately sent us to a nearby house to meet his wife, who would, he said, be very pleased to see us.

Indeed she was! We had managed to arrive during the week when they were celebrating their 75th anniversary. That certainly emphasised the fact that I was now 79. I thought how amazing it was that we should be here just at that moment. We were given an excellent meal and invited to stay until the weekend, when they would have the main celebrations; but sadly we had to be on our way. They would have liked us to talk about the early days that we both remembered; but we said goodbye and continued north.

Wirksworth, Rosemary's home, is a very hilly town, and is therefore not an easy place to visit for someone whose legs dislike slopes. But it is surrounded by wonderful countryside; the dales are spectacularly beautiful. We fell into the local Methodist routine: coffee or lunch at whichever church was providing them, and services which were sometimes led by Rosemary and sometimes by other preachers. It was restful, and very different from both Dorking and Yanchep.

I was looking forward to going even further north, to the Orkneys, where I was to stay with friends. This was quite a trip, and I did it by train. It took about as long as the flight from Singapore to UK. But it gave me what I wanted—the chance to see as much of my native country as I could fit in to the time.

People at home had warned me that I might not like what I saw of England: too crowded, too dirty, the roads grid-locked and no one ever talks to you! I was really glad to see that none of this was accurate. There are still long miles and acres of land where very few live, either farmland or in the open countryside; the towns and villages looked to me to be clean and well-kept, except in the worst areas of the cities where there were closed shops and neglected places that heralded the coming financial crisis. This was 2008. Within towns and cities there were often traffic problems, as there are anywhere in the world today; but once one was out of those areas there were miles and miles of country roads where there was little traffic—and I was surprised and delighted by the wild flowers that grew along the roadsides and in the hedges. I never remember seeing so many wild rose bushes while I was living in England.

As for people not talking to you—I had some really interesting conversations with men and women who were my fellow travellers. So I decided that my gloomy friends in Australia, with their depressing forecasts, had spent their time staying with equally gloomy relatives. *My* overall impression of England, Scotland and Wales was of a huge and magnificent park, well-maintained and cared for. In every town and city there were huge baskets of flowers, mainly petunias (whoever had cornered the market in petunias must have made a packet), in the main streets, on the roundabouts, in the parks, outside the ancient pubs, and hanging by the front doors on many private houses. It was spectacular in its use of colour; I was deeply impressed.

One conversation stands out in my mind. I was staying in Canterbury—a sentimental journey for me, because Derry and I had stayed there when we had been married less than a year. I had booked on the internet a room at the Falstaff Hotel, where we had stayed; it stands just outside the West Gate, and is dated around 1403. Our bedroom on that first occasion had a sloping floor that went down in the middle and up the other side: intriguing. I went to the reception desk and was met by a very smart young man, possibly Jamaican—I imagined how odd it would have seemed in 1949 to have been dealt with by a black receptionist. Unfortunately, the really odd thing was that I found I hadn't booked—at least, not for the date I was expecting. He was charming but definite—there was no booking in my name.

As I was beginning to wonder what on earth I had done wrong, he found my reservation—for September, and this was still June. I don't know what I had done; but he did eventually manage to fit me into the modern annexe. For a moment I was disappointed, because I had wanted to be in the old part of the hotel. Then I found that the 'modern' extension was actually Georgian, which would be old enough for most people. I accepted it with great relief.

I recalled having a meal at the Weavers House with Derry, just down the road, and walked to it now through the old town. The outside dining area, covered with a great canopy of vines, is right by the river that flows through Canterbury. The tables are close together—and this is where I had a very interesting conversation. Because I was alone, I was at a table for two; next to me was another table for two, and there was a rather heavily-built man sitting at it, also alone. We sat in close proximity to each other; but of course we were being very well-bred, and didn't speak to each other. We hadn't been introduced!

After about ten minutes I began to feel that this was ridiculous. We were almost touching—but we mustn't speak. I mustn't because I was an unattached lady, and he mustn't because I might take offence. So I said, 'I know we haven't been introduced, but I am from Australia, and if I was at home I would have said 'hi!' and we could have chatted.'

He turned to me with what I think was relief. 'I'm from America, and at home I would have done exactly the same thing!'

We had a most intriguing chat. I discovered that he was the United Nations delegate to the Bishops' Conference, which was meeting in Canterbury at that time. I learnt that the bishops, from all over the world, were staying at the Falstaff—one reason why the receptionist had had trouble finding me a room. He told me that when the arrangements were made they found that the bishops were all to be there, but their wives had to stay somewhere else! It seems there was an outcry, and quite right too. What on earth did they think all those bishops were going to get up to?

Finally, the too-sensitive authorities gave way, and the wives were accommodated with their husbands.

The following morning I saw him again at breakfast, and was introduced to a few of the senior clergy—though not, as far as I recall, to a bishop.

My cousin Dorothy lives in South Wales, and I hired a car to drive there. The UK is a bit short on small cars that have automatic gears, and since I broke my left leg in 2001 I have needed an automatic. I was offered a large, family car, and set off on my travels.

Travelling on my own did not bother me by this time. In fact, I think I prefer it. Perhaps this is the result of having been part of a big family; now I can go where I like, when I like. Dorothy lives in an area of great scenic beauty, in a delightful house surrounded by garden; it stands at the foot of the Brecon Beacons.

We spent a few days together exploring the South Wales scenery. We went to look at the memorial park that has been built on the site of the Aberfan disaster in the late 60s, when many children and some teachers died under a tide of slurry from the mines. There is a sign telling the story in English and Welsh; and I remembered well the day it happened—I was glued to the TV all day as the news came in, and much of the time I was in tears, as I suspect many other parents were around the country.

At that time I had started writing for the local paper, and I felt strongly that I wanted to say something about this tragedy. I wrote a piece and sent it to the editor, and it appeared in the next edition. A few days later a neighbour, a Welsh woman, stopped me in the street and thanked me for what I had written. It had meant a lot to her, she said, because as a child she had gone to that school. In the following week I met another woman, who I had not known had contacts with Wales; and she thanked me too, and said she had friends in Aberfan; she had sent the cutting to them, and it was now on the notice board in Aberfan's local hall.

It was perhaps the first time I had really comprehended that, once something is printed, there is no way of knowing where it will end up. I was thankful that I had made the effort.

While I was with Dorothy I kept thinking that I could easily get the ferry over to Ireland and have a look round; perhaps go to the north, where Derry's family came from. But I kept putting it off, and in the end I faced the fact that I couldn't be bothered. Not the best way to visit anywhere. So I put it off, and at the time of writing I still haven't been to the Emerald Isle.

I stayed with friends in so many places during that time. I went to Cornwall to see my cousin Alex, and we ate Cornish pasties in a light drizzle, and then a cream tea before my stomach had quite got over the lunch. We went to Polperro and Looe, both places I had been to years before with the family; and I located the Crumplehorn Farm, where we had stayed. What an evocative name! It sounds as if it is straight out of a children's book, but quite normal in those southern counties of England. The UK has so many gloriously crazy place names.

It was good to see Alex after a very long time during which we had never met. I began to realise just how many relatives I had, spread around the world, and when I added the numbers of good friends who were also ready to accommodate me, I felt rich! Cousins Pat, Peter and Brian in the north; Ken and Cathy on the south coast: the Rothwell genes are well spread across the country.

There were two places I had wanted to visit, but preferably with someone who knew the way about. One was Cambridge, the other Oxford. My father went to Oxford; my siblings went to Cambridge. I arranged to stay with another Old Dorkinian, Karen, in Oxford, and found her stories of her career in academia very interesting. Before that, I spent a few days in Bedford with her sister, Fiona, Cynthia's long-time friend. It was while I was there that I had the news that no mother would want—*my* Fiona was suffering from breast cancer, and was due to have a double mastectomy the next week.

This was devastating, so far away from home, and upsetting for my hostess. I needed to get home as quickly as possible; but I was going to Oxford in a day or so, and I decided that I would cope with the change of plans while I was there. Bedford is a bit of a blur as a result. I saw much less of Oxford than I had expected, but Karen was very positive and helpful, and eventually I was able to book a flight home on the following Monday (the operation was, I think, Thursday), though with some difficulty. There were no economy flights, and my business class seat couldn't be transferred—it was all very frustrating.

Then I discovered that my Visa and savings bank cards were not able to cough up the required amount of money because of the day limit on these cards. I really didn't know what to do; Karen said, 'Well, you'll have to take it off my card!' I protested. How could I take the equivalent of $8000 from someone who really didn't know me that well? But she insisted; with that direct thinking that comes from being an academic she saw it as the only solution, and she was right; I thanked her and agreed. I would transfer the money as soon as I was back in Australia—which, of course, I did, and with the greatest thankfulness.

What came next is Fiona's story. All I will say is that she came through the ordeal magnificently, and that we are all very proud of her. Any mother will know how I felt. I am just so thankful that she had such innate strength that she was able to deal with all the aftermath of the operation so successfully. Thank God she had that strength.

I went to Cambridge while I was waiting to get that weekend over, and stayed with niece Caroline, and Martyn. Rosemary came, and we did manage to see some of the colleges, and get a feel of the place. Perhaps one day I shall see it more thoroughly, and in a less stressful state of mind.

I lost the final month of my holiday; but I had had a wonderful time, met many delightful old friends and made new ones, caught up with relatives, and realised that I still had the warmest feelings for my birthplace. It is a beautiful country. Recent TV films have shown the rugged side of the British Isles, and it is indeed a place of contrasts. The programme *Time Team* makes one realise how thick on the ground and under it is the ancient history of the place—something that passes one by when living there. I remember with fascination the 5000 years old village, Skara Brae, set on the shoreline in the Orkneys; and the more recent Italian chapel, built by prisoners-of-war during World War II out of scraps in a Nisson hut, and the beautiful art work in it. Britain is full of surprises, and doesn't deserve the reputation of being only a fog-ridden, cold, wet island. I love it!

39

With my travels over—for the time being—I needed to get back into some kind of new routine. Fiona seemed to be coping well with her health problems; the rest of the family also appeared to be doing OK; it was time for me to look at my own life and see what I could make of it.

I had a novel I wanted to finish. It was a story of adoption; the idea was inspired in me by my grandchildren, Josh and Ambini, who joined our family as babies and brought great joy with them. Cynthia had become a grandmother again (strangely, on the day of Derry's funeral), Jackson, son of Simon and Jodie; as time went on there would be three more great-grandchildren for me—Leighton and Ruby, and Abby, grandchildren of Val and Paddy. So far the total was 14 grandchildren and eight great-grandchildren—I was beginning to feel very matriarchal!

It struck me as interesting that, although I never knew *my* great-grandparents, who died long before I was born, these new 'tinies' would know me if I managed to live long enough. I suspect it was fairly unusual for my generation to know their forebears that far back; perhaps now that we old ones are keeping healthy and active this will be the pattern for the future.

But the novel still languished in the computer. What kept me from it was, in part, writing this book of memories. There was also the holiday in 2009, when Valerie and Fiona and I went to Lombok and, at last, saw Helen and Gaz's lovely restaurant. What an undertaking! And how well they had brought this dream of theirs to fruition.

I misbehaved myself there by having a bad attack of stomach problems; but I recovered in time to have a good holiday, and Lombok is certainly a beautiful spot. We stayed at the Novotel, which is built right on the beach; among my recollections is the man who smoothed the sand every morning with two water buffaloes which dragged a plank across to make it acceptable to us, the visitors!

The view from Helen's restaurant is as stunning as it had looked in photographs; I could understand how they had come to love the place when they first went there—but it wouldn't be for me. The amount of poverty around them I found disturbing. I'm afraid I am no longer the pioneering type. But I can appreciate to the full what Helen and Gaz achieved over the years they have lived there.

As I write (mid-2013) they have just sold the restaurant, and gone their separate ways; Helen is establishing herself in Bali. I wonder if this means we shall all start holidaying there?

My next escapade was in 2010. I had a round-the-world trip, flying to San Francisco to stay with the Ballingers as my first stop. I hadn't seen Peter for about 40 years, so this was really a time for catching up. I accompanied his viol group one day on his attractive chamber organ, and the next went with him to his watercolour class, where I did that painting of an empty bottle.

Next stop was Vancouver, prior to getting on the train that would take me through the Rockies. I had been told so many times that it would be a memorable experience; and it was. My mother had been to Canada in about 1925 on the way to her cousin Anne's wedding; and we had grown up with tales of Banff, Lake Louise and Calgary; the latter is close to where my cousin Pat was born. I doubt if anyone who was there in the 1920s would recognise it now. There was still some snow on the mountain tops, and it was truly a spectacular scene, with a rushing river appearing from time to time, complete at one point with white-water dare-devils on rafts. We crossed the river on bridges that made us hold our breath until we were over; and everyone was on the look-out for bears.

Sadly, the bears were not playing. But at the very last part of the trip someone suddenly called out, 'Bear!' and we all rushed to the windows to look. Too late; it had gone. The person who had seen it said it was a small cub.

From Calgary by air to Toronto, and a visit to my cousin Frances—another person I hadn't seen for more than 40 years. A good stay, and I was pleased to meet her husband (she said I had already met him when they went to the UK on their honeymoon, but I really didn't remember). They took me to Niagara—probably the high spot of that part of the trip. It is an amazing sight! It's difficult to comprehend the amount of water that flows over from the Canadian side, especially when you consider how long it has been doing it. Standing facing the falls the effect is stunning; turn around and see the garishness of hotels and a casino and it's impossible to ignore the fact that humanity all too often loses the plot when it comes to enhancing beauty in nature.

Within sight is a bridge that leads to the American side of the river and the American Falls, which flow into the river at a different angle. To cross the bridge requires a passport—another peculiarity of human nature. Strange to realise that the other bank of the river is off limits if you haven't got that little book with you!

It was truly a holiday for meeting up with old buddies. In an attractive heritage-style town near Toronto I stayed with Gerald and his wife Gayle. Gerald is now confined to a wheelchair—though once I met him I realised that 'confined' is not a good description of his situation. He and the Venerable Tom were a lively couple of boys in my distant memory; and Gerald has not lost that ability to have fun. Staying with him was a joyous experience.

They live in a house built in 1831. It has all the charm of that period of architecture, including steps and stairs everywhere—not easy to navigate in a wheelchair, but they have conquered the problems with lifts and ramps in a way that has not interfered with the overall character of the place.

In spite of his difficulties, Gerald can still sing! I accompanied him once, and at about 75 his voice was still strong. We swapped stories about 'the old days', as one does, and especially the pleasures of choral singing under Derry's baton. Good to hear how valuable those experiences have been for so many.

I had decided to go by train from Toronto to Montreal, so that I could get to see Canada from ground level. It's a long journey, but I found it interesting. I think I had expected a landscape rather like the prairies, so I was quite surprised at how much smaller everything seemed—paddocks and houses along the railway line looked much as they would in Australia. What I shall chiefly remember about my arrival in Montreal is the length of the station platform. Because I was doing a 'round-the-world' trip I was allowed two suitcases; and even though they were 'wheelies' it was quite difficult to steer them along a platform cluttered with off-loaded baggage and freight. I knew my final Canadian host would be waiting for me somewhere, and I began to wonder if he would give up and go home, I was so slow getting to the exit.

But thank goodness he was there! Gordon and I were classmates in the VIth form in 1947, and I had hardly seen him since. We had exchanged emails, and he had come to Derry's memorial service; and in 2009 he had visited me in Yanchep for a few days. Now was the return visit.

He has had a distinguished professorial career in many universities in a subject I know absolutely nothing about: econometrics. And he is still active in the field at the age of—dare I say it?—85. There really must have been something in the air around war-time DGS to have produced so many long-living and hard-working professionals in such a variety of subjects.

Of all the cities I saw during that holiday, I liked Montreal best. It has maintained its own character better than many others—in some of them you could be anywhere in the world, but Montreal has a distinctive French flavour. This is not simply because the street signs are in French; the architecture has that continental flair.

We drove around the city in the next few days; I tried to avoid going up a mountain in a cable car, but was persuaded that I would enjoy it—which I did. We saw the Botanical Gardens, which were excellent, especially some of the plants under glass; and I saw a raccoon for the first time, as we stood at a viewing spot, looking over the city to the St Lawrence River in the far distance. The raccoon came out of some bushes and waited to be fed by the visitors—who, of course, obliged. It would take the tit-bit and disappear back into its bush; but it was completely unafraid of the people standing around it. It reminded me of the Rottnest quokkas.

I took quite a nice picture of it; unfortunately, the next year when I went to Tasmania to see Paddy I lost the disc of my Canadian pictures, so can only rely on my memory. In a double whammy, I lost the camera, too, while I was in Hobart in 2012. Very odd; I've always been so careful!

Then it was off to Heathrow and Manchester. Looking down from the plane as we travelled north over the landscape that, when we were small, took about 7 or 8 hours to cover (the plane takes about three-quarters of an hour), it struck me again how very green and pleasant this land is, with a town here and there, then a city; but so much countryside, far more of it, and far more surprising than I had expected. I think it would amaze anyone with a preconceived idea of what the British Isles really are like. Perhaps someone should run tours for sceptics and watch them change their minds.

40

B y this time, Yanchep as I knew it was being rapidly changed by developers. This is never a happy situation for people who have grown to love a place for its natural beauty and laid-back life-style, and Yanchep and Two Rocks folks were beginning to realise that things were going to change, like it or not.

This is a delightful rural area. On one side we have the Indian Ocean; on the other, endless miles of bush. Those of us who have been here for decades have always known that there would be development one day; when we arrived in 1974 the intention was to create a city within the next 30 years. 39 years down the track this is finally happening.

The problem is that all the promises made by the developers who have come and gone like the winter rain have been forgotten. What an opportunity lost! This could have been a truly rural city, full of natural parks, and with the proper respect being shown for the beauties we have all around us. Sadly, today's developers can only see dollar signs where we, who love the place, can see creative opportunities. So the bulldozers roll in, and the bush disappears within hours.

What happens to the wildlife that has lived there for untold centuries is anyone's guess. Because we now have Marmion Avenue as a second exit road from Yanchep (necessary if there is a major bushfire) we also have a scattering of developments, all of which look identical, all of which are white or light-coloured— and all of which are virtually roof-to-roof. Where I live is now called 'Old Yanchep'! *We* have space; we have gardens where one can actually grow trees; and we have roads which curve gently around the contours of the land, just as our homes are built to accommodate what has been there for ever and a day!

So what does one do—apart from voicing one's complaints? Sometimes it is necessary to bite the bullet and accept that once developers and councils get together it is very difficult to stop things happening. Several of us decided that if we were to be changed into a new suburb it was essential that we should at least make it a good place to live. Sport always gets the first bite of the apple; but there were enough of us, believing that the cultural side of a community is also vitally important, to inspire the formation of a group of like-minded people to develop this side of community life.

So TRYCAN was established. *TWO ROCKS/YANCHEP CULTURE AND ARTS NETWORK.* And here I must express thanks to the developers, who made it very easy for us to do so. It was, after all, in their interests too.

At the same time, another project was going ahead in Two Rocks: *The Little Mermaid Theatre.* This is the brain-child and 'baby' of Ted, who has fought his way through the years with little encouragement from outside, until now, when the theatre, occupying an empty shop in the town centre at Two Rocks, is beginning to make its mark with the local population.

I was very pleased to be invited to be Patron of this endeavour; I hope it will continue to prosper, and especially that it will attract more young people to take part in its activities. Ted and I are well beyond our 'use-by' dates! But there are good signs that the needed participation will be there when the time comes.

There is one more wish on my list: to get the Two Rocks Town Centre heritage rated at a higher level than it now occupies. Its Italian/Mediterranean design is unique on this coastline, and it would be a crying shame for it to be reduced to rubble so that we can have a brick-and-tile shopping centre in its place. Even worse, a builders' delight—a block of high-priced flats! This place should be kept—and yes, there is a certain amount of up-grading needed of an area now 40 years old; sea and wind are merciless when it comes to the destruction of buildings, but surely something more positive can be done than simply knocking it down? Who else has anything like it? Those of us who were here when the Atlantis Marine Park was open have long regretted that the authorities, who could have done something there once it had to close down, did nothing; we are left with a desolate, overgrown mess that was once an attractive focus for Two Rocks. Shouldn't someone in authority be putting that nice little park back into circulation for more than drop-outs and druggies? And can we not do something better for the town centre than neglect it until it falls down? The wider Yanchep area has been sadly neglected by two decades of so-called developers who prefer to leave things until they become forgotten, when they can bulldoze them and build yet more money-raising apartments.

People power is a reality these days—and so is ageing! If I were forty years younger I would be making a big noise about this deliberate neglect, which we see in so many places. I tried fairly hard when Atlantis closed to have the park kept, including the dolphin pool, which would have been a big asset to the local community, once it was cleaned out and any necessary repairs done on it. But for a busy person there comes a limit to the time available for knocking one's head on a brick wall. A classic case is the homestead once belonging to the Hon. Mrs Lindsay, who in the 1920s lived in a cottage in the dunes which has now become a kind of local icon. Shall we knock it down, let it collapse of its own volition, or develop into something better? The arguments and discussions have gone on and on, and I am thankful that my day for marching with a metaphorical banner is over. But I am pleased that we were told recently that a proper plan has been agreed for its future, and we shall wait to see how it is implemented.

My occupation now is writing, and keeping up with more friends than I would have thought possible at my age. I suppose we all think that as time goes on and our contemporaries die we shall become more isolated. I have found that this is not what happens, to me, at least. I know there are elderly people all over the place who have little going for them, either in occupation or in companionship; but I find that I only need to hold out a hand and someone will clasp it, physically or emotionally. I know there will be cases where misfortune has created a dark hole that has to be negotiated; but it is so necessary to be prepared to meet people, even people we do not know, and to understand that *we* may have something to offer that will help *them* through the bad times.

If I were to be brave enough to offer a small solution to the problems that assail us in old age it would be to urge my fellow-wrinklies to keep laughing—and keep praying.

At its lowest level, prayer helps us to bring our thoughts into order, so that we can see what the priorities are. At its highest level—who knows? Those of us who pray know from our own experiences what things can be wrought by prayer.

41

This seems to bring us up to the present day. It has been a wonderful experiment, delving back into my past, seeing where it has all come from, and evaluating my experiences from the earliest days. I have found that there are memories that stick out in our lives like spikes; once those memories are evoked a whole sprouting of other, forgotten incidents come to mind; whether this is good or bad probably depends on the circumstances, but I found it to be a bit like clearing out a room that had been allowed to get clogged with old furniture, tattered clothes, books without half the pages—things that seemed worth keeping once but have gone past their use-by dates with a vengeance. In these pages are some of these bits of broken memorabilia. I hope they will intrigue a reader as they have fascinated me.

I have often been told often that I should write this book: 'you've had such an interesting life'. At first I was surprised; then I began to think that, yes, it had been interesting; it had been full of interesting people, challenging episodes, near-disasters (I doubt if any life is free of those), and successes.

It also contained difficulties to be overcome, relationships to develop, minor problems to solve, new things to learn, illnesses to work through—all the day-by-day things that are sent to try us.

But at the end of it, with the memoirs safely collected and analysed, I know that I have been extremely fortunate. This is not a vague feeling: it is based on much thinking and pondering on what *could* have been my lot in life.

My blessings have included a family of lovely people who care about me and show me their love in many ways. I hear too many sad tales of elderly people whose families are either neglectful or simply impatient with the things that come with old age: physical slowness, sometimes confusion, a propensity for telling the same stories over and over again, problems with eating, forgetting who people are—the failures of the elderly are frustrating to the young. I am well aware of this. Looking after Derry's parents during their final illnesses, and then, much later, looking after him, has taught me all I need or want to know about old age.

But we can't help it, folks. And guess what! One day you may find yourself in the same situation. Though I most sincerely hope not. It's not a happy way to end one's stay on this lovely planet.

I have always been thankful for having married a man who, in the sixty-two years I knew him (first as teacher, then as family friend, then as husband for 59 of those years) never made me feel there was anything I couldn't do if I set my mind to it. This is a rare gift from a husband, I find. I have met so many women who feel demeaned simply because they know that whatever they do will be met by a lack of interest from their partner. I was encouraged to work for my ARCM singing diploma when I had only just had my second baby; to take up writing once we had completed our family (1963); to assume a second identity with my pen name of Barbara Yates Rothwell; to sing for him in oratorios and concert operas and never comment that perhaps I wasn't up to it (because there were times when I might not have been); to have the six children I so much wanted (though he did point out that we couldn't really afford them); to have dogs even though he himself was not a 'dog' person (he preferred cats); and to take my advice without an apparent qualm when I suggested we should emigrate to Australia, though we had no jobs to go to and would have to split the family to do so.

For all that our marriage was not a sea of serenity at all times, it was the right one for us, and now that he has been gone for nearly six years I can see the value of our time together very clearly. I cannot imagine ever wanting to be married to anyone else, and for all these things I thank him. It was a truly equal partnership.

I have also been blessed from my earliest days with parents who, even though there were times when I kicked against them, always let me know that they were proud of me. I knew very well when I had fallen from grace, but these momentary slips were not held against me. Money was quite short in the early days, so we soon learnt that we couldn't have everything we wanted. But we always had what was necessary. All three of us, Rosemary, Philip and myself, were born in the Depression years, so it may well have been more difficult than we understood for Mum and Dad to keep the standards high. But I doubt if we ever suffered real financial hardship. Dad was a first-rate organiser of whatever he took on, and I think he had the household economy fairly under control! Perhaps the greatest lesson we learnt from them was that the family was important, that letting the family down was the one thing we mustn't do, and that we each had a responsibility to do our best, not only for 'the family', but for ourselves too.

I am grateful to them for setting our feet on a path worth following.

Since coming to Australia I have lived in a delightful situation, within sound and sight of the sea (something I always wanted when I was very young), and with a real country aspect. In Dorking I came very close to this: an old market town with the Surrey hills all around, it could hardly be bettered for beauty and sheer convenience of living. Yanchep, when we arrived, was more of a settlement than a town, without any of the facilities we had had in England. The challenge was clear, and we accepted it and, in fact, thoroughly enjoyed the problems it posed.

But, looking back, I realise that I have always lived in good places. Eastcote in north-west London, where we were for my first 9 years, was brashly new, a village suddenly becoming a town; but it was clean and not too far from country scenery. Dorking's scenery is well known, and I grew up with the constant presence of Box Hill, which itself has an amazing history. Living in an area where Roman legions once marched, where the remains of Roman roads have been swallowed up into the highways that today's traffic demands, where, only a few miles away, there was once a major battle between the local people and the invading Danes—reports said the streams 'ran with blood', and a Danish helmet was unearthed just a short while before the war—all this can give one a feeling for history, if one has the sensitivity. It can also deaden that sensitivity! Norman castles? Fifteenth century hotels? Ruined pilgrim chapels? So what? Perhaps our understanding of such things is now being awakened by TV programmes. How many undulating pieces of land have I, as a child, run up and down, not knowing what might lie beneath?

It was a pleasant change from all that to be part of a north country family. My childhood was enhanced by the times we went up to Salford to stay with Grandma Rothwell. My cousin Pat was there, and her two brothers, Norman and Brian, who scared the living daylights out of me when I was six or seven. Not having bigger brothers, I held these strange creatures in awe.

In those pre-war days that whole area was grimy with the dust of coal and factories; it seemed normal to me at the time, but looking back I wonder at the fact that people managed to live normal-span lives while inhaling the invisible specks that must have been there perpetually. It was impossible to touch anything out of doors without getting dirty fingers. If it rained while the washing was on the line there was a cry to bring it in—before it could be speckled with black marks from the raindrops.

The skies were seldom blue; normally there seemed to be a light overcast that nobody noticed. (Beijing has apparently inherited that atmosphere; let's hope they find some way to clear it before too long). Going to that same area today is an eye-opener. City buildings are no longer black with soot. A mighty clean-up even made the water in the Salford dock area clean enough for them to hold the Commonwealth Games water events on it. Fifty years ago no one would have thought it possible. Of the River Irwell, flowing through the city, it was said that, if a dog fell in, it would die of poisoning before it could drown! It seemed to us, as teenagers, simply a part of the environment, and I doubt if we ever questioned its real possibilities.

Yet that part of the country is very beautiful. When I flew over it from Heathrow I was amazed by the greenness of it, all the way north; and I remember my school friends, who would pull faces if I said I had been to Manchester for my holidays. Never mind! It added colour to my young life—even if the colour was black!

Perhaps, finally, I am grateful for having been given strength—physical, emotional, mental, spiritual—when it was needed to deal with the storms and difficulties of life. We all hope for a life free of extreme worry, but that is not really what it's all about. I am well aware that each life-determining problem that has arisen has brought with it the ability to cope. This really is a gift; it seems to come from outside—family, friends—but also from somewhere mysterious inside. It is a time when one can be thoroughly thankful for having been given a consciousness of spiritual values in one's formative years. This is nothing to do with one's religious leanings. It is an acknowledgement that there are indeed, in Shakespeare's words, 'more things in heaven and earth than are dreamt of in our philosophy'. It is a wonderful world, and I have no doubt that somehow, in spite of our mismanagement of it, this Earth will survive and continue to provide for our needs.

All the same, we have much to learn, not only as individuals, but as a great body of frail creatures who once thought we were invincible, and now know better.

42

C oming to the end of this kind of highly personal research into one's own life feels quite strange. When I began I warned people that it would probably be a 10-volume saga! Well, it isn't quite that. But it is *my* story; my children's own stories are up to them to write. Sometimes—which pleases me— we are surprised by our children: I still find it odd that Helen, Keith and Fiona all became builders, creating their own homes. That's something I could never have done. Helen in Lombok, Indonesia, Keith in southern New South Wales and Fiona in Myalup have all left their mark on the landscape. Perhaps one day we shall read those stories?

And, fairly hot off the press, Cynthia achieved her ambition last year and got the degree she had been studying for. Paddy, after a working life first, in the Merchant Navy, and later in northern W. Australia skippering tugs and other harbour boats, is living happily in Tasmania with second wife Lee. Alison has established herself in Sydney as a soprano specialising in contemporary music, and co-director of Halcyon, and has recently remarried. I have every reason to be proud of all of them.

What to put in and what to leave out is a problem; but as I ploughed on through these 85 years of mine I found it all fell into place quite happily. I hope it will help my family to know a bit more of where they have come from, and other readers to understand what at last led me towards this final chapter.

I have remembered things that I thought were quite forgotten (and probably forgotten things that I ought to have remembered). But I doubt if there will be a sequel!

And having remembered so much, I can now say confidently with long-ago author Laurence Stern that 'mirth, smiles and laughter' are indeed vital commodities that help to create the lubrication that keeps us moving on Life's Highway.

That, and Love.

THE END